LIFE MEANS LIFE

NICK APPLEYARD

LIFE MEANS LIFE

JAILED FOREVER:
TRUE STORIES OF BRITAIN'S
MOST EVIL KILLERS

JOHN BLAKE

Published by John Blake Publishing Ltd,
3 Bramber Court, 2 Bramber Road,
London W14 9PB, England
www.johnblakepublishing.co.uk

First published in paperback in 2009

ISBN: 978-1-84454-668-8

British Library Cataloguing-in-Publication Data:

A catalogue record for this book is available from the British Library.

Design by www.envydesign.co.uk

Printed and bound by CPI Group (UK) Ltd, Croydon, CR0 4YY

7 9 10 8

Papers used by John Blake Publishing are natural, recyclable products
made from wood grown in sustainable forests. The manufacturing processes
conform to the environmental regulations of the country of origin.
Every attempt has been made to contact the relevant copyright-holders,
but some were unobtainable. We would be grateful if the appropriate
people could contact us.

ACKNOWLEDGEMENTS

Special thanks to my girlfriend Emily Lyons for all her help reading, writing and researching this book. It could not have been published without her. Cheers also to Deano and Mark Harris for their advice.

CONTENTS

INTRODUCTION

While anyone convicted of murder in the UK is automatically handed a life sentence, for only a tiny fraction does life really mean life. This grisly elite includes Dennis Nilsen, who butchered a string of young men in London, Rose West who – with her husband Fred – raped, tortured and murdered girls and women in the Gloucester area, and Ian Brady, one half of the Moors Murderers.

The crimes involved are of unparalleled savagery, perversion or scale. For these killers there is no hope of rehabilitation for society has ruled they must never walk the streets again. They are the men – and one woman – who committed the crimes that shocked and outraged Britain, and the courts have ruled they must end their days behind prison bars. In their wake, they leave a trail of death and devastation that both fascinates and revolts the world. Their trials have uncovered stories that horror writers would discard as outlandish; fascination for them is so enduring that every scrap of gossip about their life behind bars is devoured by the public, even decades after they were caged.

Crimes of this magnitude inevitably spark debate over the restoration of the death penalty. Within living memory every killer featured in this book would have gone to the gallows. In 1861 the Offences Against the Person Act dictated that anyone who murdered a fellow human must be executed, and so it was that all convicted murderers died, by hanging, for almost a century.

After many years, campaigners for the abolition of the death penalty secured a partial victory with the 1957 Homicide Act, which restricted capital punishment to cases of the five worst types of murder. They were, in the words of the Act: 'Murder in the course or furtherance of theft, murder by shooting or causing an explosion, murder while resisting arrest or during an escape, murder of a police officer or prison officer and two or more murders – of any type – committed on different occasions'. Killers who did not meet the new criteria for hanging were given mandatory life prison sentences. This substitute sentence did not mean a lifelong period of imprisonment. Rather, it meant the prisoner would spend a finite period in jail before being released when he or she was no longer deemed a danger to others.

The 1957 Act received as much criticism as it did support. After all, why should someone who shoots a man dead be eligible for execution, while another who intentionally kills by strangulation or with a knife is not? Also, murder in the course of theft was punishable by hanging, while murder in the course of rape merely carried a jail sentence. In many ways, the new death penalty guidelines were as unfair as before.

Eight years later, the 1965 Murder (Abolition of the Death Penalty) Act replaced capital punishment with a mandatory sentence of life imprisonment. The last executions in Britain were Anthony Allen, 21, and Gwynne Owen Evans, 24, who were hanged respectively in Walton Prison, Liverpool, and Strangeways Prison, Manchester, on 13 August 1964. They had murdered a man while robbing him in his home on 7 April of the same year.

For almost two decades the basic rules of sentencing for murder in Britain went unchanged until 1983 when the 'tariff system' was introduced. The new rules allowed Home Secretaries to set the minimum terms that convicted killers would serve before being eligible for parole on life licence. The arrival of the new system brought with it the 'whole life tariff', a sentence reserved for those who commit the most heinous of crimes. Successive Home Secretaries used this power to increase the sentences of several high-profile murderers, many of whom feature in this book.

In November 2002, new human rights legislation and a Law Lords ruling stripped Labour Home Secretary David Blunkett of the power to set tariffs. Lord Bingham said the power exercised by the Home Secretary to decide the length of sentences was 'incompatible' with Article 6 of the European Convention on Human Rights – the right of a convicted person to have a sentence imposed by an independent and impartial tribunal. The minimum length of a life sentence is now set by the trial judge although the Attorney General can still appeal to the High Court if he considers a sentence unduly lenient and the Lord Chief Justice then has the power to increase that sentence.

In response to being stripped of the power to keep killers behind bars, Blunkett outlined new minimum terms to be used by sentencing judges. All convicted murderers are now sentenced to 'life' in prison but judges set their tariffs. 'Starting points' of 15 and 30 years are available to trial judges, depending on the severity of the crime. These tariffs can be lowered by 'mitigating' factors like provocation and increased by 'aggravating' factors, such as the macabre disposal of a body. Whole life orders are the starting point in any case where two or more murders are committed that involve a substantial degree of premeditation, or sexual or sadistic conduct. This also includes the killing of a child involving any of the above factors.

Schedule 21 of the Criminal Justice Act 2003 operates as a guide to all sentencing judges in Britain. Section 4 (2) of Schedule 21 states that a whole life order applies in the cases of:

(a) the murder of two or more persons, where each murder involves any of the following –

    (i) a substantial degree of premeditation or planning,

      (ii) the abduction of the victim, or

      (iii) sexual or sadistic conduct,

(b) the murder of a child if involving the abduction of the child or sexual or sadistic motivation,

(c) a murder done for the purpose of advancing a political, religious or ideological cause, or

(d) a murder by an offender previously convicted of murder.

Schedule 21 also states that to qualify for a whole life tariff the offender must have been aged 21 or over at the time of the offence.

Soham murderer Ian Huntley, who killed 10-year-olds Holly Wells and Jessica Chapman in his home in August 2002, did not have his minimum prison term set at his 2003 trial because the system on serving life sentences was being altered at the time. Instead sentencing was postponed until 29 September 2005 when the trial judge, Mr Justice Moses, had to consider the new principles set out under the Criminal Justice Act.

In deciding whether to issue Huntley with a whole life tariff, the judge had to consider the principles set out in Schedule 21. Explaining his decision not to issue such a sentence, Mr Justice Moses said the Huntley case lacked a proven element of abduction because the meeting between the girls and Huntley, while his then girlfriend Maxine Carr was away, had been by chance.

The judge explained: 'It is likely that the defendant took advantage of the girls' acquaintance with Carr to entice them into the house, but that could not be proved.' He added: 'Their presence in the house thus remains unexplained. There is a likelihood of sexual motivation, but there was no evidence of sexual activity, and it remains no more than a likelihood. In those circumstances, the starting point should not be a whole life order.' Instead, the judge chose a starting point of 30 years and added an extra 10 years because the murders were 'aggravated' by

Huntley's abuse of the girls' trust and his deceitfulness afterwards. He said: 'The two children were vulnerable and obviously trusted the defendant because of his position in the school as caretaker and relationship with Carr.'

Sentencing Huntley, Mr Justice Moses emphasised: 'I have not ordered that this defendant will not spend the rest of his life in prison. The order I make offers little or no hope of the defendant's eventual release.' Huntley will be eligible for release in 2042, by which time he will be 68 years old. Even then, he will have to convince the parole board that it is safe to release one of the most publicly despised killers in recent history.

The latest case to call into question the rules governing whole life tariffs came in August 2008, when cop killer David Bieber won an appeal against his sentence to die behind bars. Bieber, a former US marine, shot dead PC Ian Broadhurst during a routine check on a stolen vehicle he was driving in Leeds on Boxing Day, 2003. The gunman shot the policeman point-blank in the head as he lay injured on the ground pleading for his life. Bieber was also convicted of the attempted murder of two of Broadhurst's colleagues as they attempted to flee the shooting. Three Court of Appeal judges held that the facts of the case, 'horrifying though they were', did not justify a whole-life term because the 'substantial degree of premeditation or planning' detailed in Schedule 21 was not involved. Instead, Bieber was given a minimum term of 37 years.

Among the murderers featured in this book are a number of notable omissions, the most obvious being Britain's most notorious serial killer, Yorkshire Ripper Peter Sutcliffe, who was convicted in 1981 – before the inception of whole-life tariffs – of murdering 13 women. At his trial at the Old Bailey, Mr Justice Boreham 'recommended' Sutcliffe should serve at least 30 years before being considered for parole.

The Ministry of Justice says Sutcliffe is not on its official list of 36 whole-life sentence prisoners because his tariff has never been 'formally' set. As detailed earlier, from their inception in 1983 until

November 2002, the tariffs for mandatory life sentence prisoners were set by Home Office ministers. As part of this process, prisoners were entitled to submit written representations to the Secretary of State before their recommended tariff was officially set. The representations gave the prisoner the opportunity to say what he or she thought the tariff should be and were typically prepared by a solicitor.

The Secretary of State would not set a prisoner's tariff until the written representations had been made. Solicitors acting on Sutcliffe's behalf did not submit these representations, presumably because they were well aware that his sentence would inevitably be increased from the judge's recommended 30 years.

By virtue of Schedule 22 of the Criminal Justice Act 2003, the High Court is responsible for setting minimum terms for all those prisoners who, like Sutcliffe, were sentenced before the Act came into force but did not receive a tariff from the Secretary of State under the previous arrangements. There were almost 720 such prisoners when the Act came into force. The majority of these cases have now had a minimum term set by a High Court judge and several of them feature in later chapters of this book. Decisions on some cases have yet to be made. According to the Ministry of Justice, it is impossible to predict when individual tariffs on these prisoners are likely to be set.

Many of the killers on the official list of whole-life prisoners have appealed, without success, against their sentences. Others have accepted from day one that their crimes warrant the ultimate penalty available to British courts. Some are murderers who have killed again while out of prison on life licence, others are psychopathic serial killers who hunted strangers to satisfy an uncontrollable bloodlust. Several men featured within these pages are sexual perverts who killed to indulge their sick desires; other sexual killers snuffed out the lives of their victims simply to avoid identification. A few murdered purely out of greed.

Some of the killers you will have heard of, others you will not. What they all have in common is the fact that they will die behind bars.

1

'THE LITTLE DOCTOR'

*'I know where you live. I murdered a young girl in
Iffley Road four years ago.'*

Andrezej Kunowski (to a stranger in the street)

Name: Andrezej Kunowski
Crime: Multiple rape and murder
Date of Conviction: 31 March 2004
Age at Conviction: 47

L ike many thousands of Poles before him, Andrezej Kunowski
arrived on a coach at London's Victoria Station in October 1996.
He'd endured a bus journey of more than 30 hours from Warsaw
and carried with him a tourist visa. But he intended to work in the
UK illegally.

Kunowski had £500 in his pocket – a fortune in his homeland but a
pittance in one of Europe's most expensive cities. A tiny man at a
diminutive 5ft 3in tall, the former cosmetics salesman would have been
rather smarter than his fellow down-at-heel passengers. He tried to
dress well and smell sweet, with a fondness for cheap cologne. When
his neatly combed brown hair began to thin, he took to wearing a
hairpiece. In his homeland, this dapper, shiny-shoed man was dubbed
the 'Little Doctor'.

But there was another difference between Kunowski and the other

Poles who arrived at Victoria that unusually-warm morning: he was a psychopathic sexual predator, later described by one senior Metropolitan Police detective as: 'The most dangerous, and certainly most prolific sex offender I've ever met.'

On Thursday, 22 May 1997, foreign student Trajce Konev was delayed while sitting an English exam at college. For the first time ever, he had left his 12-year-old daughter Katerina home alone. 'I raced home fast on my bicycle,' recalled Trajce, who two years earlier had moved to the UK with his family from the war-torn Balkans. He was already worried because his daughter hadn't answered the phone when he called to check she was OK before setting off. He arrived at his first-floor flat in Iffley Road, Hammersmith, West London, at 4.30pm to find the front door open and the living room door jammed shut.

Trajce continued: 'I knocked on the door in case Katerina was changing and said, "It's Daddy, open up!" There was no answer. I thought she was playing games with me. I shouted through the door, "Katerina, Katerina, open the door!" Nobody answered.'

And so he knocked again, harder this time, but still no answer. Trajce knew his daughter was in there and he panicked more. 'I could hear noises from inside the sitting room,' he recalled. He tried shoulder-barging the door but it was barricaded from the inside. Then he looked through the keyhole and saw his daughter's schoolbag on the floor. He knelt down and peered under the door, only to find Katerina was not alone. 'I saw two men's black shoes,' he said. 'I just froze. I knew something was wrong; I was so scared. I thought that maybe if someone is inside and she cannot get to the door, he must get to the window and jump.'

The frantic father ran out of the flat, where he saw a strange man climbing out of his living room window, clutching a bag. 'We came face to face,' he said. 'I noticed one small drop of blood on the left of his face. He was staring at me. I asked him, "What are you doing in my house?" He was just so calm; he didn't say anything: he just looked at me. He had a knife and I thought he was going to kill me. I turned a little and he managed to escape. He ran off down the street and I followed him.'

Trajce sprinted after the intruder through a few streets and across a building site but just as he caught up with him, the stranger yelled for help, claiming he was about to be assaulted. Two workmen intervened and told Trajce to leave the man alone and so he escaped his grasp.

The assailant ran into the road and tried to hijack the car of a 42-year-old woman whose son, aged four, was sat in the passenger seat. 'I saw two men, one on either side of my car,' she said. 'One had blood on the side of his face as if he had been punched. He tried to get into the car through the open window. I wound it up and sped away; I was terrified for my son. One of the men was shouting, "Call the police!"'

The stranger then tried to commandeer a lorry in Hammersmith Grove but was forced out by the driver. Next, he jumped in front of a Fiat Uno. The driver, Christina Kearney, later said that he shouted, 'Help me, help me – call the police!' But his act was short-lived and, once the car was stationary, he brandished a knife and ordered her out. He sped off in the car to Hammersmith Bus Station, where he disappeared aboard the number 220 bus to Hammersmith Broadway.

Meanwhile, Trajce decided against explaining himself in broken English to the duped workmen and sprinted back home. He was back inside the house at 4.50pm and managed to kick open the living room door that had been propped shut from the inside with a chair. Lying on the floor was his daughter, barefoot and unconscious, wearing a cardigan, white T-shirt and elasticated tracksuit bottoms. She had been garrotted with a piece of cord cut from a Virgin Atlantic flight bag that she used to carry her schoolbooks. The garrotte, which had been tightened round her neck with a pen, was so taut he couldn't release it with his hands and so he used a knife to cut it off. He said: 'I started to cry and shout her name – Katerina! Katerina!'

Moments later, the police burst in. 'I was bending over her, crying, when they arrived. I remember one of the officers telling me to help him to resuscitate her,' he said. 'He showed me where to push her chest, but I just couldn't do it – I was just so shocked. I felt weak and hopeless. I didn't want to touch her in case I hurt her.' Katerina was dead.

In the absence of an assailant, Katerina's father became the initial suspect in her murder. Police doubted his story of finding a stranger at the flat and he was taken to a nearby police station. Trajce recalled: 'My wife and son were brought to the station to see me. I was wearing a white forensic suit. My wife Zakalina just started shouting, "What have you done?" She was kicking me and screaming at me. All I wanted to do was hug my wife and cry with my family. I had lost my little girl, but my wife was attacking me and my six-year-old son was looking up at me with hate in his eyes. I remember just banging my head from wall to wall in my cell; they must have thought I was a madman. They thought I had killed my Katerina.' However, within hours Trajce was released when eyewitness accounts and CCTV footage backed up his story. Police also found fingerprints throughout the flat that did not match those of any member of the family.

At a press conference held days later, Trajce said: 'I put Katerina on a bus to school on the morning of her murder. It was just a usual morning; she just smiled. When you saw her face, you didn't need to listen to words from an angel. She was the best. At everything, she was the best – maths, music, sport, she was perfect. She worked so hard. All her friends loved her. For her, the world was there to love.'
Of her killer, he said: 'This is not a man; it's a monster without feelings. Animals don't kill like that, without reason. At the first chance, tell the police. We don't know how many more children he could kill.'

Katerina's murder was linked to two earlier incidents in Hammersmith involving a man fitting the suspect's description. The previous February, a balding man of Mediterranean or Arabic appearance followed a girl home from school, tried the door and rang the bell before running off. And just 30 minutes before Katerina was killed, a similar-looking man had tailed another 12-year-old to her home near Iffley Road and watched the property for several minutes before leaving.

'Although he did not attempt sex, we believe that Katerina's murder was sexually motivated,' said Detective Chief Inspector Hamish Campbell as he appealed for information about the crime. 'We suspect that strangling her gave him a kick. He is a sexual predator who stalks young girls because they are less likely to put up a struggle. It is very rare, thankfully, that a stranger kills a girl in her own home, but he obviously spent some time targeting Katerina.'

Despite CCTV footage and forensic evidence placing a stranger at the scene of Katerina's death, it was to be six years before her killer was finally caught.

In September 2002, Kunowski tied up and repeatedly raped a foreign student after tricking her into viewing his bedsit. He approached the girl at London's Ealing Broadway tube station while she waited for a friend. Noticing that she was looking at adverts for rooms to rent, he claimed there was a vacant bedsit at his nearby flat.

He led her into his grubby ground-floor bedroom and locked the door behind him. The girl, who had only weeks earlier arrived from her native Korea, said she wanted to go back to meet her friend, but he ignored her pleas and pushed her onto the bed. She tried to fight him with a ballpoint pen, but he overpowered her and then tied her hands together with rope and repeatedly raped her for three hours. She was only allowed to leave the flat after promising to phone him the next day.

When he was tried at the Old Bailey the following May, Kunowski claimed the young woman had consented to sex, that it was a 'thank you' for helping her find somewhere to stay. But the jury didn't believe him and he was jailed for nine years.

While he was in prison, detectives checked his DNA and found it was a match with a hair on Katerina Konev's cardigan. His fingerprints also matched those found on a window at her home. Kunowski denied the murder and in March 2004, once again he underwent trial at the

Old Bailey. The overwhelming evidence against him, coupled with his weak defence of mistaken identity, meant the jury took just two-and-a-half hours to find him guilty of murder. Kunowski showed no emotion as Judge Peter Beaumont told him: 'I would be failing in my duty if I did not ensure you spend the rest of your life in prison. You took the life of a child who was just beginning to enjoy what this country had to offer her and her family as refugees from hardship abroad. It was a life of great promise. You ended it in circumstances of great violence and terror.' As he was led to the cells, Kunowski applauded himself.

Afterwards, Katerina's mother wept: 'I hope her evil killer burns in hell. I hope he suffers every minute of the rest of his life.'

Following his trial it emerged that Kunowski fled to Britain as prosecutors in his native country prepared to charge him for the latest in a string of sex attacks that stretched back three decades. Born Andrezej Kembert into a working-class family in 1957 he was sent to an orphanage at the age of two because his mother, father and grandmother had been jailed for theft. His grandfather was locked up in a state psychiatric hospital for unspecified sex offences. When his mother Elzbieta was released, she reclaimed her son and married a bricklayer called Stephan Kunowski and her son took his stepfather's name. They moved to Mlava, a bleak rural town 80 miles from Warsaw. The young Andrezej was not an easy child and he was prone to violent fits which he rarely remembered afterwards. He also had a habit of staring at pretty girls in a trance-like way that scared his mother.

By the age of 13 he was drinking heavily. He rarely attended school and when he did so, he was troublesome, often groping and trying to kiss his fellow pupils, regardless of their gender. After one particularly violent assault outside class, the police were called and he was packed away to a facility for delinquent juveniles where his aggressive sexual urges were allowed to fester.

Three years later he tried to rape his 16-year-old neighbour and was jailed for three years. He was released in the summer of 1976, but the following year he was jailed for two years for the attempted rape and murder of another young woman as she walked home. However, he was back on the streets of Warsaw in April 1978 whereupon he immediately set about sexually assaulting women and girls. In the remaining months of 1978 alone, he carried out 15 rapes. Often his method was to hide in quiet lanes where he would ambush women and children as they walked home, choking them with rope or threatening them with knives. At other times, disguised in a wig, he would stop his car, wind down the window and call his victims over. As they leant in to hear what he was saying, he quickly wound up the window, trapping them by the neck. Then he would jump out of the car and haul them into woods, often subduing them by hitting them over the head with a spade.

In 1980 he was nicknamed 'The Beast' by Polish newspapers and was jailed for 15 years. He had served 11 years when he was freed as part of an amnesty to prisoners after the collapse of communism. But after a few years of stability, during which he had a daughter, his attacks resumed.

In 1995 Kunowski preyed on a 10-year-old as she returned home alone from school in Warsaw. He said he was a friend of her father's and asked if he could wait in the house until her parents returned from work. Once through the door he pounced on the girl, repeatedly raping her while throttling her with a telephone cord.

He was charged with that rape and with the rape of another schoolgirl but, instead of keeping him behind bars as he awaited trial, the judge made the inexplicable decision to grant him bail to have a hip operation. As police built up a strong case linking him to other rapes in the city, he escaped. It is believed he simply got out of his hospital bed and walked away.

Kunowski sold his house in Mlava, bought a fake Portuguese passport and made his way to Acton, West London, pretending to be a tourist. Using skills he acquired in prison in Poland, he got a job working as a tailor at a dry-cleaning company and soon blended in among millions of anonymous faces.

When the Polish authorities realised that he had fled the country, they issued an international warrant through Interpol. His fingerprints and photograph were available via Interpol's crime database to its 125 members, the UK included, but he was not fingerprinted when he arrived in the UK so he had a clean slate to find new victims in a new country.

The day after murdering Katerina Konev, Kunowski took a job at a strawberry farm in Ledbury, west of London. Unable to control his genetic propensity to steal, he was sacked for thieving from the office. He was held for the crime and handed over to Immigration. Officials discovered he was an illegal 'over-stayer' and he spent two months in a detention camp in Oxfordshire. While there, he applied for citizenship on the grounds of economic hardship in his homeland and, as his application was being considered, he was once again allowed to walk free. His petition was denied in the autumn of 1997 but by then he was back in London, untraceable as neither his fingerprints nor DNA were taken after his arrest.

Astonishingly, even though he was a hunted killer and illegal immigrant, he was given a life-saving NHS heart bypass in 2001 at a hospital around the corner from where he killed Katerina. That year he stopped a woman in West London and told her: 'I know where you live. I murdered a young girl in Iffley Road, four years ago.' In July 2002 he was arrested again for trying to claim benefits using a forged Portuguese passport in the name of Jose Marco Da Dias, but once again the immigration authorities failed to establish his true identity. While under investigation, he disappeared again. A few days later, he was arrested for the rape of the Korean student at his bedsit.

The Home Office said: 'It's a matter of great concern that a criminal with such a serious history managed to get into this country and that his background was not uncovered when he came to our attention. Our system has been completely over-hauled since then. All asylum-seekers are now electronically fingerprinted. The details are fed into an index which alerts us to crime.'

Katerina's father, Trajce, believes his daughter opened the door to Kunowski that day because she thought it was 'Daddy' coming home and she couldn't wait to tell him that she was top of her English class. 'We found about how well she'd done afterwards – she never got to tell us herself,' he said.

After the verdict, Katerina's mother said: 'I find it impossible to understand how he was allowed into the UK to commit this crime. I am aware that he had serious criminal convictions and impending prosecutions in Poland. Something must be done to ensure such a thing does not happen again. I do not feel that justice has been done.'

Detective Chief Inspector David Little, the senior detective investigating Katerina's murder, was asked if Kunowski was likely to have committed offences during the time when his whereabouts was unknown. He said: 'When he wasn't incarcerated he was committing offences. I would suggest he is probably the most dangerous sex offender I have ever come across. Certainly, he is the most prolific.' DCI Little admitted that the 1997 murder investigation had been exceptionally thorough and had thrown up everything the police needed to secure a conviction but, because he was an illegal immigrant, Kunowski had been forensically invisible. He said: 'If the person doesn't exist, you can't bring him to justice.'

Polish lawyer Waldemar Smarzewski prosecuted the 1979 trial, following which Kunowski was sentenced to 15 years imprisonment. Mr Smarzewski, who is now Warsaw's Chief Prosecutor, said: 'When he appeared in court there were about 70 charges, made up of rapes, attempted rapes, lechery with children, endangering a child's life and attempted murder. I wanted to get him 25 years, but there was no evidence for the attempted murder.

'This was a very important and dangerous case because of the number of victims and what he did to them. I wanted to put him away for longer because he was very dangerous. I was sure that if he left prison he would go back to rape and maybe even kill.' Of Kunowski's

9

crimes in Britain, Smarzewski said: 'This is no surprise to me. I knew he would strike again. I think he should remain behind bars for the rest of his life. I am sorry this psychopath ever came to Britain.'

Meanwhile, Kunowski is impressed with life at Her Majesty's Pleasure in Wakefield Prison. In letters, he tells his mother that the food is 'good, with lots of vegetables' and he is happy to admit that for him, incarceration on UK soil is better than liberty in Poland.

2

'CAPTAIN CASH'

*'The cold-blooded murder of an eight-week-old baby, an
18 month-old toddler, not to mention the murders of their mother,
father and grandmother, provide a chilling insight into the
utterly perverted standards by which you have lived your lives.'*

Trial judge Sir Stephen Mitchell

Names: Kenneth Regan and William Horncy
Crime: Mass murder
Date of Conviction: 1 July 2005
Ages at Conviction: 56 and 53 respectively

For at least a decade, Kenneth Regan, nicknamed 'Captain Cash', was a very successful gangster who smuggled drugs, laundered money and sold fake passports on a huge scale. In 1996 business was so good that he had a submarine custom-built so that he could smuggle 15 tonnes of cannabis, worth £40 million, into the UK, but he had to abandon his plans at the last minute. He then muscled in on London insurance firm Serez International, using it as a front to launder upwards of £10 million of drugs money between 1996 and 1998. Working with fellow career criminal William Horncy, he made a fortune supplying more than 1,000 passports to drug traffickers and other international criminals.

But Regan's life of fast cars and Monte Carlo holidays came to a sudden end in June 1998, when armed police pounced during a massive heroin smuggling deal in North London. He tried to escape in his car, knocking over and injuring a policewoman in the process. Detectives found 25kg of the drug in the boot of his Mercedes and he was charged with heroin smuggling and assaulting the officer. Faced with 20 years in jail, the unscrupulous crook turned supergrass to secure a lighter sentence.

In the following few months he was interviewed 15 times by detectives from the National Criminal Investigation Squad and gave information about a £100 million cocaine smuggling ring, which led to the conviction of a dozen top-level criminals and the confiscation of millions of pounds of drugs money. Regan knew about the ring because he was the one who sold the dodgy passports. Investigators estimate that between 1996 and 1998, the gang smuggled cocaine into Britain with an estimated street value of £2 billion. The information provided by Regan led to a total of 15 convictions in a case involving five separate trials.

His co-defendants in the heroin-smuggling case for which he was busted pleaded not guilty when it came to trial. But thanks to Regan's evidence, they all received lengthy prison sentences. The judge told him: 'As a result of your co-operation you will never again be trusted by your former colleagues, so you can't go back and the enmity of those will make your future life precarious... Those who turn against former associates should receive a very great reduction in their sentence.' Regan was given eight years, but he was a free man three years later, in 2002.

With contracts on his life and very few remaining friends in the criminal world, Regan was desperate to be rich again. He had been stripped of all his cash and assets when he was jailed for heroin smuggling and he longed for the trappings afforded by organised crime, so he devised a plan that would leave a shipping tycoon, his wife, her mother and their two infant children murdered in the course of what was later described as 'a crime utterly beyond the comprehension of decent society.'

Amarjit Chohan ran CIBA Freight, a fruit import and export business near Heathrow airport. The multi-millionaire, who started out selling fruit and veg from a shed, was known to be something of a chancer with a fast-and-loose attitude to business. He served a prison sentence for tax evasion and his business, though lucrative, was run chaotically, with staff wages often paid in a combination of cash and cheques. Later, he was referred to in court as 'a charming, but rather feckless boss'.

Kenneth Regan had experience working in the freight industry and was introduced to Mr Chohan – known as Anil – through a friend who worked at CIBA. Towards the end of 2002, Regan began frequenting Mr Chohan's offices, at all times quietly plotting to steal the company and use it to import hard drugs.

Mr Chohan made no secret of wanting to sell his business and one day Regan came to the CIBA offices with the news that he had found a Dutch company who would buy it for £3 million. Following this, Mr Chohan was lured to a meeting near Stonehenge, Salisbury, on 13 February 2003, to discuss a deal. At the meeting, Mr Chohan and Regan were joined by two others: Regan's former passport dealing partner William Horncy and their underworld acquaintance Peter Rees, who posed as the potential purchaser. Amarjit Chohan, 45, was never seen alive again.

After the meeting, Mr Chohan was kidnapped and taken to Regan's home in Salisbury, which he shared with his senile father. Once there, he was tied up, gagged and tortured until he signed over his firm. He was also made to sign several sheets of blank paper on which his captors later typed fake letters from him, informing his staff that Regan was their new boss.

Regan's plan was to kill Mr Chohan, after making it look like he was fleeing England. But Regan and Horncy knew the businessman's disappearance would not have seemed credible if it looked like he had left behind the family he adored. So his wife Nancy, 25, their sons Devinder, aged 18 months, and Ravinder, eight weeks, plus his wife's 52-year-old mother, Charanjit Kaur – who was visiting from India – would all have to be killed too.

The following day, 14 February, Nancy rang her brother, Onkar Verma, in a frantic state after hearing from CIBA staff that her husband had flown to Holland on business. She knew something was wrong because his passport was at the Home Office for a residency application. She also had a phone message from her husband, in which he spoke in English rather than Punjabi (the couple always spoke Punjabi on the phone). His mobile, which he always diligently answered, was switched off.

On Saturday, 15 February, while Rees guarded Mr Chohan, Regan and Horncy drove to their captive's family home in Hounslow, West London, where they tricked Mrs Chohan into letting them in. Once inside, they killed her, her sons and her mother before driving the bodies to Regan's Salisbury home. That night, Mr Chohan was forced to leave several phone messages saying he was leaving England. He was then murdered.

Two days later, Kenneth Regan arrived at CIBA Freight, with a handwritten letter from Mr Chohan and a signed document giving him Power of Attorney to take over the running of the company. Employees recalled the letter, which later disappeared, as saying something like: 'Greed has got the better of me. As you are aware, I've been doing some exports to the USA described as magazines, but in fact this was khat [a drug], which is illegal in the USA. I've got myself in serious trouble. Some people are after me and I have to escape. I fear for the safety of my family.' CIBA staff believed the story and Regan assumed his new role as boss. Everything was going to plan for the man willing to do anything to restore his once-lavish lifestyle.

On 19 February, the five bodies were loaded into a hired van and driven to a farm near Tiverton, Devon, owned by Belinda Brewin, an innocent friend of Regan's, who was away. When Ms Brewin returned unexpectedly to her 50-acre estate and saw a trench and men with a digger, she 'went ballistic'. Regan – who had for years been trying to romantically woo Ms Brewin – said he was fixing a long-standing drainage problem as a 'gift' to her. In fact, they were making a thorough job of burying the Chohan family. Two days later, Regan took Mr Chohan's car to a criminal friend in Southampton, who disposed of it.

Nancy Chohan was very close to her brother, who lived in New Zealand, and they spoke over the phone almost every day. So when Regan claimed that she, Amarjit and the rest of the family had fled without letting him know, he simply did not believe the tale. He spent weeks pestering the Metropolitan Police by phone and email and on 5 March, he flew over to England to find out what was being done to find his family.

At Onkar Verma's insistence, police searched the Chohan home in Hounslow. It was like the Mary Celeste. The washing machine was full of wet clothes and food was half-eaten on plates. Police found Mrs Kaur's out-of-date return ticket to India and her prayer book, which she was known never to be without, was on the bedside table in the spare room. Furthermore, the family's bank accounts had not been touched for more than three weeks. Thanks to Mr Verma's tenacity, the case was handed over to Scotland Yard's Serious Crime Group.

Regan and the rest of the staff at CIBA were interviewed and police became suspicious of the letters signed by Mr Chohan. Alarmed by the police investigation, Regan returned to the farm, accompanied by Horncy and Rees, to dig up the bodies. The following day, Easter Sunday, they bought a boat for cash and dumped the bodies in the sea off Dorset.

Two days later, a father and son canoeing off Bournemouth Pier found a body. A week later, it was identified as Mr Chohan.

Realising the game was up, Regan and Horncy fled by ferry to France. Rees also went on the run, hiding out with a friend in Gloucestershire.

Meanwhile, detectives were building their case. Regan had given Ms Brewin, whose land was used to bury the bodies, a £72,000-a-year job, working just two days a week. Police say he was 'utterly bewitched' by her looks and class. When she heard about the discovery of Mr Chohan's body, she told police about the diggers at her farm. The following day the field was excavated.

On 15 July, Nancy Chohan's body was caught up in fishermen's nets off Poole, Dorset. Her mother's badly decomposed body was washed up on a beach on the Isle of Wight on 7 September. The two boys have never been found.

By September, Regan, Horncy and Rees had all been captured or given themselves in, and on 8 November 2004, they appeared at the Old Bailey where all three denied murder and false imprisonment. Richard Horwell, QC, prosecuting, said post-mortem reports revealed Mr Chohan had been drugged and possibly strangled, while his wife's skull was smashed, probably with a hammer. He told the court that Mrs Kaur's body was too badly decomposed to provide any conclusive information.

The barrister went on to list the damning evidence against the accused. He said analysis of mobile phone records showed that calls from Nancy Chohan to her husband stopped on 15 February. Mr Horwell said: 'It is a certainty that Mrs Chohan and her family were imprisoned or murdered that afternoon and it is of great significance that on that afternoon the mobile telephones of Regan and Horncy were used [in the vicinity of] the Chohan family home.' He said that mobile phone evidence also proved 'beyond doubt' that Regan and Chohan met near Stonehenge on the day that the businessman vanished, adding: 'Within days of Mr Chohan's disappearance, Regan had replaced the carpet and the furniture from the front room of his home address. At some point the room had been redecorated... Something happened to Mr Chohan [there].' Forensic officers testified that the place was 'unfeasibly spotless'.

But the killers left a macabre clue: a drop of blood was found on Regan's garden wall which was conclusively proven to have come from 18-month-old Devinder. It was 4ft above ground level and described as a 'downward drop' by a forensic scientist, suggesting the toddler was being carried at the time. The court also heard that traces of Amarjit Chohan's blood were found on the speedboat used by the three men to dump the bodies.

However, the prosecutor still had the ace up his sleeve. He told the court how Mr Chohan had left a piece of paper in his sock designed to lead police to his killers. The paper – a letter bearing Regan's name and address – had been folded so many times that it had survived days in the sea. 'When it was unfolded it became apparent that it was a letter addressed to Kenneth Regan and his father at their home,' Mr Horwell said.

The QC said the letter's contents were unimportant, but the date was significant. It was dated 12 February 2003, the day before Mr Chohan disappeared. He added: 'It is not just, of course, the fact that in folding the letter and placing it in his sock, Mr Chohan had intended to leave a clue as to the identity of his captors and the place of his incarceration. It also means that Mr Chohan had known that he was going to be murdered.'

The prosecutor then turned his attention to the trench dug by Regan and his accomplices to bury the bodies: 'Horncy told Ms Brewin that Regan had asked them to come and sort out the drainage problem. It was supposed to have been a surprise. A drainage ditch is hardly a conventional gift. The element of surprise is not just unnecessary, it is positively unwelcome as far as the recipient is concerned.'

Mr Horwell said that when the trench was excavated months later by police, they found human hair matching Mr Chohan's: 'The DNA of Mr Chohan was found in the grave, but the entire family was murdered as part of a single plan and it is beyond belief that two or more separate graves would have been used. The grave these men dug was very large. It was a grave for five bodies, not one; it was only too clear what they had been up to – the trench had been dug as a communal grave for the Chohan family.'

By then, Mr Chohan had agreed to sell his business but he underestimated Regan's 'duplicity and ruthlessness,' said the prosecutor in his closing speech. The barrister added: 'Regan was penniless. He had no legal right or interest in CIBA; there were no backers. Regan did not have the collateral to buy a minority interest in CIBA, let alone the entire company. Regan's motive and intentions are obvious: he was desperate for a return to the days of "Captain Cash" – banknotes in the boot of a Mercedes and the luxury home.

'There was only one way he could realise such an ambition and that was through drugs. That meant the means or disguise under which drugs could be imported into the UK in large quantities. CIBA was the perfect vehicle.'

The defence team in the £10 million, eight-month murder trial – one of the longest in British legal history – had a difficult job arguing against the evidence. In his closing speech to the jury, Regan's defence counsel Paul Mendelle, QC, had little to offer: 'The prosecution have invited you to speculate – there is not a scrap of evidence. Regan would have had to be desperate beyond belief to slaughter an entire family for the sake of a business.'

After 12 days of deliberations, the jury found Regan and Horncy both guilty of all five murders. Rees was convicted of false imprisonment and the murder of Mr Chohan, but cleared of the other four killings. He was handed a life sentence, with a minimum recommendation of 23 years.

Judge Sir Stephen Mitchell jailed Regan and Horncy for the rest of their lives, telling them: 'Your crimes are uniquely terrible. The cold-blooded murder of an eight-week-old baby, an 18-month-old toddler, not to mention the murders of their mother, father and grandmother, provide a chilling insight into the utterly perverted standards by which you have lived your lives.'

Detective Chief Inspector Dave Little of the Metropolitan Police led the investigation. He said outside court: 'This is a crime utterly beyond the comprehension of decent society. A young family, a new family, was entirely wiped out at the hands of these murderous men in an attempt to line their own pockets. I hope they reflect on their crimes long and hard for the rest of their lives, which will be spent in prison.'

3

'MISTAKEN IDENTITY'

*'Glen had established himself the credentials that made him an
ideal recruit for a contract killer. He had murdered before.'*

Prosecution Counsel Rex Tedd, QC

Name: Paul Glen
Crime: Contract killing
Date of Conviction: 29 July 2005
Age at Conviction: 34

At around 7.55pm on 8 June 2004, builder Robert Bogle was in the
kitchen of the house that he shared in the quiet, picturesque
village of Farcet, Cambridgeshire. He was cooking a bolognaise sauce for
himself and his girlfriend Angelina Walker when a man wearing a hooded
top, heavy overcoat and black gloves kicked down the kitchen door.

Without saying a word, the stranger brandished a foot-long kitchen
knife and began stabbing Robert, who tried desperately to defend
himself. As he fought for his life, Robert was knifed 10 times – to his
hands, his arms, through his right cheek and his heart.

The 25-year-old struggled to keep his balance as he slid through
his own blood to the doorway, leaving red handprints along the
kitchen units. While his girlfriend hid behind a sofa in the living
room in shock – she was so traumatised by what she heard and saw
that she could not properly give evidence at the subsequent trial –

Robert made it out of the kitchen and to the pavement outside, clutching his chest.

It was just after eight o'clock and his desperate plight was witnessed by a group of teenage girls, who were ambling along with bags of chips from the village takeaway. Robert, with his clothes wet with blood, told the frantic, screaming girls to call an ambulance. As one of them dialled on her mobile phone, he staggered to a nearby shop and the house next door, banging on the windows. But no one came out and he collapsed on a patch of grass.

A recording of a 999 call, made by a 14-year-old girl, went: 'It's right in his heart,' while in the background the victim was heard to shout, 'Get help!' and 'Get off, get off, get off!' as people desperately tried to stem the flow of blood.

Seconds later, the terrified group saw his attacker stroll down the alleyway adjacent to his house. One of the teenagers would later testify in court that she was 'really scared' by 'a large man who wore black gloves'. She said: 'I thought, "Why wear gloves in warm weather?"' Another recalled: 'We thought it was all a joke at one point because the other man just walked away like nothing had happened.'

It would later transpire that the calm stranger who strolled off was Paul Glen, a 33-year-old contract killer, hired by a wealthy local businessman with underworld connections who wanted to 'sort out' a village argument. Unfortunately for Robert, Glen didn't bother to ask his victim's name before stabbing him to death. Had he done so, he would have realised that he had got the wrong man and Robert would still be alive today.

The man Glen was sent to 'sort out' was Robert's friend and housemate, Vincent Smart, who was not at home that night because he was house-sitting for his parents, a few streets away. What makes this case one of the most notable bungled 'hits' in British criminal history is that Vincent Smart was white-skinned and the murdered man was black.

'MISTAKEN IDENTITY'

Glen was hired by millionaire Robert Lotts, who wanted to end a long-running feud between Smart and his three sons: he believed Smart had been bullying them. Lotts was, for the most part, a legitimate businessman who did not want Smart killed – just hurt badly enough to ensure that he left his children alone. The builder was not used to employing men who commit acts of violence for cash but luckily his brother-in-law, Wayne Wright, was able to put him in touch with Glen, a brutal thug from Fleetwood, Lancashire, who had just the criminal CV Lotts was looking for.

At the trial at Norwich Crown Court in June 2005, Prosecutor Rex Tedd, QC, explained why Glen was more than up for the job. He said: 'Glen had established himself the credentials that made him an ideal recruit for a contract killer: he had murdered before.'

Glen had previously been jailed for 13 years for viciously bludgeoning to death Ivor Usher, a Blackpool guesthouse owner, on 21 February 1989. He and an accomplice went with the intention simply to rob the gay bachelor of the £5,000 in his safe, but after tying him up Glen got carried away and smashed his skull to pieces with a bar stool and a wrench. In an effort to cover his tracks, he set light to the building. It was this reckless disregard for human life that would lead Glen to go way beyond Lotts' original plan to scare Smart, and as the prosecution put it, to stab him to death in an 'explosion of unanticipated violence.' Robert was caught in that explosion.

Mobile phone records proved Glen was in Farcet village at the time of Robert's killing and showed how he fled to Blackpool immediately afterwards. They also showed Glen, Lotts and Lotts' brother-in-law had called each other in the build-up and aftermath of the bloody murder. This, and other forensic evidence placing Glen at the house at the time of the killing, meant that he could not deny being there. So, in a desperate attempt to save his skin, Glen claimed in court that the murder was committed by a shadowy figure named 'Steve', whose last name or address he did not know.

Glen told jurors he'd met 'Steve' to arrange a cannabis drug deal on the day of the killing and that he came to the house because it 'seemed convenient.' He insisted he was only going to the house to 'have a word' with Mr Smart, adding that he was there simply as a mediator and that Steve was meant to remain quietly at his side. He told the court: 'I'm a sucker for a hard luck story – I don't like to hear of people being subjected to violence or bullying. I planned to take some cannabis round as a peace offering. If I could reason with the guy, I'd sit down and reason with him. I was a peacemaker.'

According to him, his 'peace-making' efforts were scuppered because while he was upstairs, looking for the intended target Smart, his criminal acquaintance was busy knifing the man's housemate. Glen testified: 'When I got to the bottom of the stairs I saw Steve going through the back door. He [Robert] was trying to follow and I pulled him back. He fell down on the floor and slipped. The blood was everywhere on the floor – I stepped back and saw it all. He shot out of the door. It was all over in a matter of seconds. I was there, but I didn't stab him; I wasn't alone. That's the truth.'

Despite his efforts, Glen's smokescreen was torn apart by the prosecution. Barrister Tedd QC remarked that, as no unidentified footprints were found in the kitchen or indeed the rest of the house, 'Steve' would have had to have been wearing identical trainers to the dead man or identical footwear to Glen's, whose size-10 Timberland prints were, according to the Forensic Sciences Service, imprinted in the blood which covered the kitchen floor. He said: 'Otherwise this man, Steve, is not just a man with no surname, no address, no mobile phone – he is a man with no feet.'

Forensic technicians also found a shred of skin underneath one of Robert's fingernails containing a DNA profile that matched Glen's.

The prosecution argued that Bogle scraped away a piece of Glen's skin as he fought off the blade pounding into his body. The murderer was not Steve, said Mr Tedd, but 'a professional killer, who had travelled to an area where his identity and appearance was completely unknown. That man on the mission was Mr Paul Glen.'

At the end of the five-week trial, the jury of four men and five women was unanimous in their guilty murder verdict. Lotts was later jailed for four years and his brother-in-law, Wayne Wright, to five years in prison after they admitted conspiring to cause Mr Smart grievous bodily harm.

Judge Sir John Blofeld told Glen: 'As a result of your actions a young man, who had a future before him and a devoted family, lost his life in circumstances which were terrible.' He added that it was 'immaterial' to consider a release date as Glen would never be free. Outraged, the killer protested, 'Do I not get a chance to say anything?' as he was led from the dock by police.

Outside court, Robert's father, Linford, his mother Joyce, brother Paul and sister Donna and close friends grouped together as Linford read out a statement about his much-loved child. He said his son's killer had 'got what he deserved' but that the murder had had a devastating affect on his family. 'It's been very difficult,' he told reporters. 'My wife is only here in body, her spirit has disappeared somewhere. We will never forget Robert.'

Robert's older brother Paul remembered a time when he had attempted to emulate his television hero Evel Knievel by riding his tricycle off the patio in the garden of their childhood home in Yaxley, Cambridgeshire. Paul said: 'He went flying and cut his head open. He had to be taken to hospital, and of course, I got the blame as I was supposed to be looking after him. That has always stuck in my head.

'He was just a wonderful person. It's just a shame that he's not here. There isn't anything else I can say or do – he isn't coming back. We will try to get ourselves together; try to move on with our lives as best we can. Robert's death has left a huge void. It's just a hole, a chasm, which just can't be filled. They say time is a great healer. We'll just have to test that theory for ourselves.'

After his whole life sentence, Glen stewed on the prospect for three months and then, in September 2005, his legal team launched an appeal with the Royal Court of Justice, in London, in a bid to have it reduced. But his sentence was ruled fair because not only had he committed a second murder, he'd again done it for profit.

On 3 February 2007, in an extraordinary ceremony performed by a Catholic priest, Glen was married inside the chapel at Whitemoor High-Security Prison in Cambridgeshire. The bride – 41-year-old Paula Kelly from Liverpool – stayed with friends and family at a three-star hotel prior to the service. Glen gave his address on the marriage certificate as 300–310 Longhill Road, March – the postal address of Whitemoor Prison. Under occupation he described himself as a 'builder'. On the wedding night, the newlywed Mrs Glen and her entourage gathered again at the hotel, with only the bridegroom absent from the wedding breakfast.

The following month, it would appear Glen was missing his bride because he made an audacious bid to escape from prison. Along with cop killer David Bieber and another prisoner Keith Stewart, he aimed to break out by holding guards hostage with a gun smuggled into a prison wedding. The trio planned for a guest to secretly hand over the weapon at the ceremony of a prisoner to a former jail worker. They would use the gun to negotiate their release and then be picked up by a getaway car. But prison bosses somehow got wind of the plan and Glen, Bieber and Stewart were dragged from their cells and taken to solitary confinement by officers in riot gear.

All three were made to wear striped prison uniforms, only issued to convicts who have tried to escape. A fourth prisoner was placed on a protection wing, suggesting the three were 'grassed-up'.

Glen was never to consummate his marriage and, under current legislation, never will.

4

'PAPERBOY PREDATOR'

*'In 30 years of police service, this is the most distressing case
I have ever been associated with.'*

Detective Chief Superintendent David Cole, former Head

of West Mercia CID

Name: Victor Miller
Crime: Rape and murder
Date of Conviction: 3 November 1988
Age at Conviction: 34

'It was an ideal set-up, really,' said Victor Miller, explaining to police why he chose paperboys to rape and abuse. 'It was an ideal time when nobody is about and they are boys of the age I go for.'

For 15 years, Miller – described by doctors as 'an especially dangerous sadistic sexual psychopath' – roamed the West Midlands looking for boys to attack. Powerfully-built and wild-eyed, he abused countless terrified youngsters, many of them on paper rounds, who he overpowered with brute strength.

Detective Chief Superintendent Allen Mayo of Mercia Police saw first-hand the effect Miller had on his victims. 'They were stupefied, like snared rabbits in the grip of a snake,' he said. 'He [Miller] says the same about all his victims – they were terrified into immobility.' Though he subjected the boys to violent, degrading assaults, he stopped short of killing them until 17 January 1988.

At around eight o'clock on that bitterly cold Sunday morning, 14-year-old Stuart Gough walked into Higgins newsagents near his home in the quiet village of Hagley, Worcestershire. He had two rounds of deliveries to make, comprising just 14 houses situated within a few hundred yards of the shop. But after leaving with his first round of papers, Stuart failed to return for his second.

Miller, 33, pounced on the fair-haired asthmatic at knifepoint. He then bundled him into his car and drove him, blindfolded, 50 miles to a country lane known as 'Cuckoo Pen' in Bromsberrow, Hertfordshire. There, he brutally raped the boy at the secluded beauty spot and stayed with the shivering, partially-naked youngster while he decided whether to kill him. After his arrest, he told police: 'I was for 20 to 25 minutes in a lot of turmoil over what I could do. If I had been on my own, I would have taken him back, but in this particular instance I was not on my own. There was Trevor [Miller's boyfriend] to consider and that is all that was going through my mind. If I was caught for this offence he wouldn't cope with the mortgage and everything. He's the one person that I know loves me – he's the dearest person that I've got in my life.'

His mind made up, Miller tried strangling Stuart with a shoelace. Finding this too awkward, he found a 7lb rock and smashed it over his head seven times. After the savage attack, Miller left him lying dead in a ditch and drove off. When Stuart's body was eventually found, he was so badly disfigured that police had to identify him by matching his fingerprints to those found on his desk at school.

A week before the murder, Miller fell out with his lover and, desperate for sex, went off alone to pursue his deviant interests, spending the following days roaming the countryside, stalking young men and boys. The day before Stuart's death, a black man in his car approached another Hagley paperboy, 14-year-old Anthony Dingley. The motorist asked for directions to Birmingham and, after chatting for a few minutes, drove away. But he returned four times, forcing the alarmed teen to run and hide behind a bush until he was gone.

However, it was a victim who escaped 48 hours before Stuart's murder who provided the clues that would nail Miller. Cyclist Richard Holden, 18, was attacked by a man while riding down a country lane near his home in Wellington, near Hereford, four miles from Hagley. At knifepoint, he was forced into Miller's car and driven to a secluded orchard, where he was partially stripped. But the teenager managed to fight off his attacker by kicking him in the groin.

Police put Richard under hypnosis in a bid to establish more details of the 'dark-skinned' man he had described and the distinctive silver car he was driving. The horror he relived was so realistic that despite the heat in the interview room, he was freezing cold and shaking. So vividly did he remember the attack that when he awoke from the trance he was rubbing the backs of his hands as he recalled falling into a ditch of icy water. The information provided by him proved invaluable: he described Miller's car (a silver Datsun) and also gave police a clear description of his Afro-Caribbean attacker.

Linking Stuart Gough's case with those of Anthony Dingley and Richard Holden, Detective Chief Superintendent David Cole, Head of West Mercia CID, announced police were looking for a man of Afro-Caribbean mixed-race, aged about 30, 5ft 7in tall, stocky, with short hair and a 'strong, unusual body odour'. They said he may have been wearing a grey woollen hat and that he was believed to own a silver Datsun.

Hagley, with a population of just over 6,000, became the focus of national media attention as one of the largest manhunts ever conducted by the West Mercia force got underway. Aircraft with thermal imaging cameras joined more than 150 police officers and 600 villagers and other volunteers. Detectives from the Regional Crime Squads of Telford and Birmingham supported the search teams and the surrounding district was combed in a bid to find Stuart, who had by then been missing for five days.

Police conducted house-to-house inquiries throughout the village and surrounding areas, and a reconstruction of Stuart's last movements was staged – but nothing was forthcoming. Richard Holden was re-interviewed and was able specify to police that the vehicle being driven by his attacker was in fact a silver Colt Sappora. Soon afterwards, it was discovered that local man Miller, a convicted paedophile, owned such a vehicle.

Tyre marks found at the scene where Richard Holden had been attacked matched those on Miller's car. Also, footprints discovered nearby were identical to those found in dust at the West Bromwich paint factory where Miller was a computer operator. It was also established that his boyfriend, Trevor Peacher, was a convicted sex offender with previous convictions for sex crimes committed against young boys.

Miller and 46-year-old Peacher – who met in prison – had been sharing a maisonette in Pennfields, Wolverhampton, for two years. Visited by detectives, Peacher gave his lover an alibi at the time of Stuart's disappearance. Police weren't convinced and on 27 January, 10 days after Stuart's disappearance, Miller and Peacher were arrested.

Detectives soon realised that Peacher had not been involved in the abduction and he was released, though later jailed for three years for attempting to pervert the course of justice. Then, on 31 January, after four days of questioning, Miller confessed to Stuart's abduction and murder. The following morning, a convoy of police vehicles left Hereford police station and were directed by Miller to the area where he had killed Stuart. He refused to go near the boy's body, but pointed to a drainage culvert where, in driving rain, police made the grim discovery beside a tree stump. Half-covered by leaves, Stuart's battered, broken body was laid on a bed of bracken. The next day, Miller – dressed in red trousers and an open-necked blue shirt – confessed to Hereford's crowded Magistrates' Court that he had murdered Stuart. He also admitted four other charges, including those against Richard Holden and Anthony Dingley.

In a statement read out by his solicitor Anthony Davies, Miller said he wanted to avoid further distress to Stuart's family. 'I have been charged with the murder of Stuart Gough,' read Mr Davies. 'I do not intend to defend the charge. I fully accept what I have done. I have co-operated fully with the police. I can never make up for taking Stuart from his family. I would ask and, indeed, trust that justice will be done and that I will receive the maximum sentence available to the court. I am making this public statement through my solicitor to save speculation and further distress to Stuart's family and all concerned.'

Hours after the hearing, Stuart's father Geoffrey, 58, wept as he told of the effect of his son's murder on the family. He told reporters: 'It gets worse. Whatever the sentence it is too good for him. I have got no mercy for an adult who kills a child. If I could get my hands on him, I'd break his neck.' Geoffrey, sat at home with his wife Jean, 44, added: 'I go to bed every night, mentally and physically shattered. I see Stuart every morning when I go up the road past the spot where he was kidnapped, and every day it gets worse.

'I wish I could turn the clock back. I pray every night to die so I can be with him. His last words haunt me. He said: "Goodnight, Dad" when he went upstairs to bed on the Saturday night. He was always in bed early because of his paper round.'

On 4 November 1988 Miller was jailed for life at Birmingham Crown Court. Passing sentence, Mr Justice Otton told him: 'The charges reflect sadistic sexual attacks on young men and boys. You deliberately chose in some instances newspaper boys because they were particularly vulnerable and without any hope of assistance or escape.

'You have a previous record of offences, which has escalated from relatively minor indecent assaults on young boys to sadistic torture and killing. The opinion of the doctors is that your preoccupation with sex and violence, progressing from fantasy to actuality, is characteristic of a sadistic sexual psychopath.

'You used and abused the body of that 14-year-old boy for your sexual gratification. You then considered deliberately whether to take him back to where you brought him, to let him live or take his life.'

The judge added: 'You are described as a highly-motivated psychopath and you will remain dangerous for the rest of your life. In view of the compelling, overwhelming and unanimous medical opinion, and your own wish to remain in prison for the rest of your life, I anticipate that you will stay in prison for the rest of your life. The public deserves to be assured that you are unlikely ever to be released.' Miller nodded in agreement and smiled from the dock.

The judge said that he would recommend to the-then Home Secretary Douglas Hurd that Miller should die in prison. Hurd agreed and the prisoner was handed a whole life tariff.

After his killer was jailed, Stuart's shattered father Geoffrey said that he 'dies a thousand deaths' every day, imagining his son's final moments at the hands of his killer. 'My mind keeps going back to what Stuart was saying in his last few minutes – was he shouting to me to help him? I just can't get it out of my mind, and I don't think I ever will.'

Miller had a disturbed childhood. His white mother Joan was embarrassed about her son's dark skin and she made no effort to hide her feelings, often making him walk a few feet in front of her in the street. His boyfriend Trevor Peacher revealed: 'Vic felt he had been rejected by his family. Even as a small child his mother used to make him wait for her away from work so her work mates would not know she had a half-caste son.'

In fact, she disowned him when he was five and he spent most of his formative years in care. As a child Miller would lock himself in cupboards and wardrobes for hours, curled up in the foetal position.

Miller had his first homosexual affair at the Bodenham Manor School for maladjusted children in Hertfordshire, where he lived for eight years in the 1960s. When he was 15, Bodenham Manor closed and Miller was moved to Eastfield Special School in Wolverhampton. One of his teachers there from 1970–72 was Fran Oborski, who remembered: 'He struck me as a very disturbed psychopath – intelligent and scary. I was aware he could be a very dangerous character, but I was not aware he was a latent homosexual rapist, or that one day he might kill.'

Miller was 21 when he was jailed for four years in February 1976 for indecently assaulting a 15-year-old boy at knifepoint in Wolverhampton. The boy and his 17-year-old friend were crossing a field when he struck. Miller grabbed the younger boy by the jumper and held a carving knife to his throat. When his friend ran for help, he dragged the boy to a ditch beside a railway and indecently assaulted him.

He did not complete his sentence and weeks after his early release in December 1978, Miller attacked two boys in another field in Wolverhampton. He stripped them and dragged them into a ditch and stabbed one of them in the chest. For this, and an indecent assault on a teenager in Brighton, he was jailed for seven years. It was while serving this sentence in Gloucester Prison that he met his lover Peacher, who was imprisoned for similar offences against boys.

The pair were freed within a few weeks of each other in spring 1983 and set up home in Penn Fields. The following year, Miller was employed at a community project in Wolverhampton, where he drove youngsters in a transit van which was used in attacks in Staffordshire to abduct a 13-year-old newspaper boy at Pattingham, and a 22-year-old man in Lichfield. He accosted another newspaper boy in the grounds of a school at Aldridge, West Midlands, but was frightened off by the caretaker. It was only after his photograph appeared in newspapers and on television that it became clear Miller was the man behind those three attacks.

DCI Mayo, who led the investigation into Stuart Gough's murder, said Miller was the most prolific and dangerous sex offender that he or any of his colleagues had ever come across, adding: 'Besides those crimes he admitted to in court, Miller has confessed to 20 more similar offences, which were never reported.' His colleague, Detective Chief Superintendent David Cole, said: 'In 30 years of police service, this is the most distressing case I have ever been associated with.'

5

'THE BUS STOP KILLER'

'He hated women. He hated blonde women.'

Prosecution barrister Brian Altman

Name: Levi Bellfield
Crime: Double murder
Date of Conviction: 25 February 2008
Age at Conviction: 38

Woman-hater Levi Bellfield was born in Isleworth, West London, on 15 May 1968. He was one of six children and when he was eight, his dad, Joe, died of a heart attack, aged 37. The young Levi went off the rails and by his early teens he was already displaying sadistic and deviant tendencies. When he was 13 he tortured and killed his sister's pet rabbit. Former school friends recall a rumour that he had tried to have sex with the animal.

By August 2004, Bellfield – whose first name is an anagram of evil – had murdered at least two young women. Police believe he may have killed others, including schoolgirl Milly Dowler, who disappeared outside Walton-on-Thames railway station in Surrey, in March 2002 while on her way home from school. Six months later, the 13-year-old's body was found in woodland in Hampshire. Despite a massive police investigation, detectives are yet to charge anyone with her murder, though Bellfield is the prime suspect.

On 25 February 2008, Bellfield – who throughout his trial at the Old Bailey pulled faces, yawned and mouthed obscenities from the dock – was found guilty of murdering students Amelie Delagrange, 22, and Marsha McDonnell, 19, and the attempted murder of schoolgirl Kate Sheedy, 18.

Bellfield trawled bus stops and followed buses late at night, looking for young blondes on their own. He would follow them, offering them lifts, drinks, drugs and sex, and, if they turned him down, he would react with rage. Brian Altman, QC, prosecuting, told the court: 'He hated women. He hated blonde women.' He added: 'These women were targeted victims of a predatory man who stalked bus stops and bus routes in vehicles looking for young women to attack.'

In February 2003, Marsha McDonnell was just feet from her home in a quiet residential area of Hampton, West London, when she beaten over the head with a hammer and left to die on the pavement. Bellfield had followed her bus in his van.

The former nightclub bouncer stalked convent school head girl Kate Sheedy when she got off a bus near her house in Isleworth, in May 2004. When Kate crossed over to avoid the snarling brute, he aimed his vehicle at her and ran her over. He then reversed back over her to make sure she was dead and unable to identify him. His young victim said goodbye to her parents as she lay on the road, waiting to die, but the brave teenager survived to be the prosecution's star witness.

Amelie Delagrange had been out with friends when she was battered over the head three times with a hammer in August 2004. After getting off at the wrong bus stop, she was followed by Bellfield as she walked back towards her home in Twickenham Green, West London and attacked after she refused to talk to him as she cut across the local cricket pitch.

Following the guilty verdicts, judge Mrs Justice Rafferty deferred sentence until the following day but Bellfield refused to attend court, blaming adverse accounts about him in the newspapers. His barrister, William Boyce, QC, announced: 'He has waived his right to be in court today. Overnight, there has been what some consider to be a quite extraordinary explosion of bad publicity. There has been a welter of accusations of other crimes by him.'

Every national tabloid on the news stands the next morning carried the Bellfield verdict on the front page, alongside various damning stories about him, varying from allegations of rape to murder. The *Sun* pulled no punches and splashed the words: 'HE KILLED MILLY TOO' alongside his smug, bloated police mugshot.

Sentencing Bellfield in his absence, Mrs Justice Rafferty said: 'You have reduced three families to unimagined grief. What dreadful feelings went through your head as you attacked and in two cases, snuffed out a young life is beyond understanding. You will not be considered for parole and must serve your whole life in prison.'

Explaining the whole life tariff, the judge added: 'Aggravating features are the chronicle of violence directed towards lone vulnerable young women during the hours of darkness and substantial premeditation and planning. There are no mitigating factors.'

DCI Colin Sutton, who led the investigation, said outside court: 'Levi Bellfield is a predator, who preyed on women over a period of time. He targetted his victims at random, attacking those much smaller and weaker than him. Only he knows why he did what he did.'

Survivor Kate Sheedy and the families of the dead girls held hands with friends and supporters as the verdicts were delivered. They burst into tears of relief when the man who had wrecked their lives was found guilty.

Kate, by then a 21-year-old university student, faced reporters outside court, saying of Bellfield's absence at the sentencing: 'I am disappointed that he was not in court to hear the judge's words, which were so strong. I think it shows the type of person he is – a complete coward.

'It means so much to me that he got a full life term; it's what I wanted. The fact that he will never see the light of day again is brilliant. Even if it had been 40 years' time, I would not feel safe if he was let out again. I have waited for nearly four years for this day.'

Amelie's mother, Dominique Delagrange, paid tribute to her daughter and said of Bellfield: 'We would like to have heard from Bellfield a confession of sorts, some evidence of remorse. In this we were disappointed. This guilty person has showed an unbelievable level of arrogance.'

A female officer who worked on the case said: 'Bellfield has deprived us of the pleasure of seeing his face when he was told he will never leave jail, but at least we can be satisfied that this is the last time he will be in control.'

Bellfield, who had 11 children by five women, was arrested in November 2004. The jury found him unanimously guilty of murdering Amelie Delagrange and convicted him by a 10–2 majority of Marsha McDonnell's killing and the attempted murder of Kate Sheedy. After deliberating for six days, the jury was unable to reach verdicts on charges that Bellfield attempted to murder hairdresser Irma Dragoshi, 33, who received head injuries, and kidnapped Anna-Maria Rennie, 17. Those offences, which all occurred at bus stops, were ordered to lie on file.

The judge ruled that a great deal of the evidence gleaned while Bellfield was under suspicion was too prejudicial for the jury to hear. But once he was jailed, much of this evidence came to light. Several women who had earlier given statements to police about Bellfield have since told of the full shocking extent of his loathing and predatory attitude towards females. His former friends, work colleagues and prison acquaintances came out to speak of a psychopath who thought he was above the law.

Paul Jarvis met Bellfield while he was on remand at Belmarsh Prison, South-East London, in 2005. He said: 'He was like a caveman. He treated women like dogs.' Bellfield told him: 'You feed them and keep them – you can do what you want.' Jarvis also revealed that the thug confided in him that he murdered Amelie Delagrange after she refused his offer of cocaine. This evidence was not allowed at the killer's trial.

Bellfield was renowned in his hometown of West Drayton, Middlesex, for trying to pick up teenage blondes, who he followed in his Toyota Previa people carrier. The car had blacked-out windows and he kept a mattress and blankets in the back – they came in handy when girls were drunk or naïve enough to fall for his propositions. Those who resisted his advances were sometimes drugged and raped.

As the years passed, fuelled by steroids, cocaine and mental instability, Bellfield's violent obsession with young blondes worsened. His ex-girlfriend Johanna Collins, with whom he had a son and a daughter, described him as, 'Six-feet-one of pure walking evil'. Johanna suffered three years of 'hell' with the killer, telling of how he ruled her with the fear of beatings and systematic rapes. She also admitted how he would return home from his work as a club bouncer and boast about the girls he had raped that night.

She said: 'When he came in late at night after working on a club door, he would tell me how he had "another little slut" in the back. Levi took great pleasure in telling me how they fancied a kiss and a cuddle, but when he got them where he wanted them, he just took them.

'I would be told to get out of bed and scrub the cars out so there was no trace left of whatever he had done. He would tell me straight out if he had raped a girl – or even two – on an evening. He'd laugh and say they deserved what they got.

'When he finished he told the girls to 'F**k off back into the nightclub' or just to 'F**k off'. He warned them what would happen if they went to police. I was just too scared to even think of saying anything.'

Johanna revealed how she had once found Bellfield's 'stalking kit' in a bin bag when she was tidying the garage. She said: 'I pulled out my dad's old donkey jacket. There was also what looked like a bobble hat and a magazine, Cosmopolitan. The coat felt heavy and something was in the lining. The left-hand pocket had been cut out so your hand went right the way down to this hunting knife.

'Then I realised the "bobble hat" was a full-face balaclava. I opened the magazine and all the pictures of pretty girls or models with blonde hair had been slashed or hacked-up.' When she mentioned her shocking find to her husband, Bellfield flew into a rage. Johanna said: 'He beat me and forced my face over the pictures of the blondes, shouting, "I f**king hate blondes, they should all f**king die!"'

Becky Wilkinson, mother to four of Bellfield's children, said she felt safe for the first time in years after he was jailed. Becky, who was with the brute from 1989 to 1995, told: 'For those years I went through a traumatic, violent relationship with Levi that I couldn't escape. When I eventually did, he would stalk me.

'For the time we were together he would hit me, rape me. I wasn't allowed to speak to my family or see them – he wouldn't let me do anything. It is a big relief to know he will die behind bars.'

Bellfield, overweight with a squeaky, effeminate voice, told a colleague at the wheel-clamping firm where he worked that girls who dyed their hair blonde were: 'Impure sluts who deserved to be messed around with.' He boasted that he regularly shaved his entire body to avoid leaving DNA evidence, saying he was 'untouchable'.

A former bouncer friend recalled how Bellfield spiked a young blonde's drink with date-rape drug Rohypnol at a club in Maidenhead, Berkshire. He raped the girl in the car park and stole her mobile phone. Later that night the girl's mother called the phone and Bellfield taunted her with details of what he had done to her daughter.

Bellfield suffered wild mood swings and went from friendly and affable to murderous in a heartbeat. In 2004, he turned on his former friend Peter Rodriguez, hitting him three times in the head with a hammer and stabbing him with a screwdriver in the stomach and kneecaps.

The wheel-clamping business Bellfield ran was known for its

bullying methods. He and fellow clampers demanded £250 in cash to release vehicles and those who argued were threatened with violence. Motorists who would not pay up were warned they would receive a visit at home. Bellfield told them he had police contacts that could trace addresses from car number plates.

Ricky Brouillard, who worked for the thug, told police that Bellfield once offered to sell him sex with his 'naïve' 16-year-old girlfriend and her sister, 14. 'I would describe Levi as an animal,' Brouillard said. 'I remember being disgusted. I met his girlfriend on one occasion and he said, "Do you want to buy her off me?"'

Bellfield boasted that he made more than £70,000 in cash every year from his various jobs and he regularly flashed thick wads of money. He thought he was above the law and he was arrogant and reckless. But that recklessness was to prove his undoing. Bellfield had been clever on his nights out hunting down and beating women, being careful to dispose of vehicles and clothing used in the attacks. But he did not consider the CCTV cameras that caught him on film or the evidence of mobile phone records placing him at the scenes of his crimes.

Cameras on buildings and on buses captured detailed footage of four of Bellfield's vehicles and placed him at the scene of the murders of Amelie Delagrange and Marsha McDonnell, and at the attempted murder of Kate Sheedy. The day before his arrest, police were following his car when he pulled up and started chatting to two young girls who were waiting at a bus stop. Later, the girls told police how he had offered them a lift and asked how old they were. When they said they were 14, Bellfield said: 'You must be virgins – I bet you are nice and tight.' He then drove away, laughing to himself.

Emma Mills – mother of three of his children – was living with Bellfield when police arrived at their West London home to arrest him. She recalled: 'It must have been four or five in the morning when they came. The house was lit up with torchlights and I thought he must be in trouble with the police – he'd been in trouble before, for fraud.

'But this was different. There were about 30 policemen with guns; there were dogs, all surrounding the house. They were banging on the door and screaming his name. I thought, "What the hell have you done now?" We were in bed and he turned, and he just looked at me and he looked so scared. It was complete fear. I've never seen him look like that before.

'He said, "I'm sorry," and then he ran out onto the landing, pulled out a chest of drawers and used it to jump up into the loft – that's the last time I ever saw him. I went downstairs just as the door flew open and a load of police officers pushed past me, calling his name.' Police found Bellfield naked in the loft, crouched behind a roll of insulation. Ironically, officers noted that the prolific sexual predator was anxious to hide his private parts that had shrunk after years of steroid abuse.

Police believe the three hammer attacks for which Bellfield was jailed are just the tip of the iceberg. They suspect he may be responsible for many more, similar attacks on women. Officers are currently working through cases where victims have no recollection of being attacked because of their horrific injuries. In many cases, their injuries were put down to falling over drunk or fainting.

DCI Sutton said: 'There is a group of 20 or so other offences that we will be looking at because we feel they may be offences which Bellfield had something to do with. They are not 20 murders, they are 20 attacks on women.'

After the trial, it emerged that Bellfield's first girlfriend, Patsy Morris, was murdered in 1980. The 14-year-old was found strangled in undergrowth on Hounslow Heath, 48 hours after going missing from a playground. Bellfield, then just 12, was said to have been fascinated by the unsolved killing – it is just one of the many crimes that police have said they will be questioning him about.

6

'DEATH IN THE DRAINS'

'One would have to say that anyone committing these crimes must be out of their minds.'

Defence counsel Ivan Lawrence, QC

Name: Dennis Nilsen
Crime: Multiple murder
Date of Conviction: 3 November 1983
Age of Conviction: 37

Respected civil servant Dennis Nilsen sat in the bath with his lover, a 16-year-old called Martyn Duffey. It was bizarre that a dog-loving, nerdy pen-pusher was soaking in the suds with a handsome, streetwise young man, and it was especially odd because Martyn was dead.

It was May 1980, and Martyn had made his way from his home in Merseyside to London, looking for work. There, he found a sex-crazed serial killer.

The pair met by chance in the capital's West End. At that time the deal was simple: if you were a young man who asked for money, there were men who would give you money – so long as you did as they requested. Nilsen asked and Martyn said yes. For a roof over his head and a hot meal, he accepted Nilsen's offer of a bed to sleep in at his house in Melrose Avenue, Cricklewood Hill, a suburb of North London.

It was the costliest deal of the young man's life.

As Martyn slumbered, Nilsen strangled his guest, but as he withdrew his hands he realised he didn't have a corpse in front of him, but an unconscious 16-year-old youth, who would scream down the neighbourhood if he woke up. So Nilsen dragged him to the kitchen, filled the sink with water and plunged his head underneath until he was sure no life remained. He then filled the bathtub, added a splash of bubble bath and placed Martyn's cooling body in the water... Then he got in himself.

In a journal written in prison, and quoted in the Nilsen biography *Killing for Company* by Brian Masters, the killer recalled the macabre episode:

I remember sitting astride him (his arms must have been trapped by the quilt). I strangled him with great force in the almost pitch darkness with just one side light on underneath. As I sat on him, I could feel my bottom becoming wet. His urine had come through the bedding and my jeans. I pulled him over my shoulder and carried him down. He was unconscious, but still alive. I put him down, filled the kitchen sink up with water, draped him into it, and held him there, his head under the water. I must have held him there for about three or four minutes. I then lifted him into my arms and took him into the room. I laid him on the floor and took off his socks, jeans, shirt and underpants. I carried him into the bathroom. I got into the bath myself this time and he lay in the water on top of me. I washed his body. Both of us dripping wet, I somehow managed to hoist this slipping burden onto my shoulders and took him into the room. I sat him on the kitchen chair and dried us both. I put him on the bed, but left the bedclothes off. He was still very warm. I talked to him and mentioned that his body was the youngest-looking I had ever seen. I kissed him all over and held him close to me. I sat on his stomach and masturbated. I kept him temporarily in the cupboard. Two days later, I found him bloated in the cupboard. He went straight under the floorboards.

It was a new experience for Nilsen: he'd never bathed with a corpse before, but he'd killed before. And now, as the pale, prune-like body of Martyn Duffey lay between his legs, he knew he'd kill again.

Dennis Nilsen was born in November 1943 at Academy Road, Fraserburgh, Aberdeenshire to a Scots mother and a Norwegian father, Olav Magnus Moksheim, who had adopted the surname Nilsen to seem less German at a time when Britain was battling Hitler. His father was an alcoholic, as were many seafaring men at that time in the North-East of Scotland. Nilsen's parents divorced when he was just four. Later in life, his mother remarried and the boy's new family warned him of 'impurities of the flesh'. This advice was to give him an unhealthy view of human relationships and a murderous conception of sex.

Between 1961 and 1972 Nilsen served in the British Army with the Royal Fusiliers. He loved drinking with his comrades and was a regular in the bar. Like many young soldiers of his time, he saw action in the conflict in Aden, which raged in what is now Yemen from 1963–67. Later serving in the Persian Gulf, where he became a cook, he was popular with colleagues because of the amount of meat he could cut from a bone. It was reportedly in the Middle East that he discovered his homosexual tendencies with an Arab boy. There followed a short stint in the Metropolitan Police, but he was unhappy with the prevalent homophobic, macho atmosphere at Willesden Police Station, where he was based, and after a year, he resigned.

Nilsen the copper became Nilsen the civil servant, securing a place as a clerk at Kentish Town Job Centre. Colleagues viewed him as diligent, almost workaholic. They also respected his commitment to the Trade Union Movement. By this time, he was about to begin another career: as a killer. On 30 December 1978, he was drinking alone in a pub called the Cricklewood Arms, popular with the area's large Irish community. There, he met a young, anonymous Irishman, who looked about 18. The lad accepted his older friend's invitation back to the flat at Melrose Avenue for more alcohol. Afterwards, the pair went to bed, but fell asleep without having sex. During the night Nilsen woke with a desire to kill – he took a cord from the end of the bed, wrapped it round the young Irishman's neck and pulled. There was a struggle, but within a minute the victim was still.

To make doubly sure he had actually killed, Nilsen fetched a bucket of water and held the youth's head in it. In what was to become a repeated trademark, he then carefully washed him and put the body to bed. The next day, he placed it under the floorboards, only to retrieve it a day later for another hot bath. Following this, the body remained under the floorboards until August 1979, when the killer burned it on a bonfire of fence posts at the bottom of the garden.

The next attack, in October 1979, did not prove fatal. Andrew Ho, a young student from Hong Kong, was lured back to Melrose Avenue. But the killer's attempts at strangulation were half-hearted and his victim escaped. Police were alerted and quizzed Nilsen, but the investigation was dropped as Ho, 19, did not want to go through with a prosecution and admit in front of a public court that he had intended to sleep with a strange man twice his age.

Nilsen's second murder came on 3 December 1979. He took a day off work to go Christmas shopping. At the time no one perceived it as odd that such a loner would need time to buy gifts for anyone, but the clerk had other items on his shopping list and as he sat drinking in the Princess Louise pub in Holborn he came across Canadian Kenneth Ockendon. Kenneth, 19, had just completed a technical course and was holidaying before flying home for Christmas. His final destination was Melrose Avenue, where he accepted an offer of a heavy boozing session with Nilsen.

As Kenneth drank whisky and listened to music through headphones, Nilsen strangled him with the flex from his stereo. Once more, the victim was given a hot bath before being taken to bed. The next day, the corpse was hidden under the floorboards, only to be disinterred several times over the next fortnight to 'watch' TV on an armchair next to the whisky-swigging murderer. Kenneth was one of the few victims to be reported missing. His frantic parents in Canada contacted police in London, who found his unused airline ticket home in his hotel room. But there was little more they could do. Kenneth Ockendon was placed on Scotland Yard's Missing Person's Register.

There followed the killing of victim number three, Martyn Duffey, whose murder is described earlier. The fourth victim was Billy Sutherland, a 27-year-old from Edinburgh, who was working as a male prostitute in London's West End. Nilsen insists he had no intention of taking Billy home, but the rent boy followed him on the Underground. His insistent manner sealed his fate. Strangled with Nilsen's bare hands at Melrose Avenue, his body went under the floorboards along with the others. But here Nilsen's own recollections – the only details available of his crimes with few witnesses – become vague. During this time, he was drinking more and more, traipsing around the gay bars of early 1980s London in search of liquor, sex and victims.

Victim five was an Asian prostitute, 'probably Thai or Filipino'; six was an 'Irish labourer', while seven a 'hippy type' found in a doorway at Charing Cross. Of victim eight, the killer had no recollection apart from that he'd cut him into three pieces before hiding him under the floorboards. Nine and ten were later described to police as merely young Scots picked up in Soho's gay Dean Street area.

But Nilsen did manage to recall his eleventh victim. Little wonder, as he was a skinhead with a tattoo ironically reading 'Cut Here' around his neck. The lad boasted how he liked fighting and how tough he was. Not so tough after a dozen cans of beer and several large whiskies, though. Nilsen strangled him and hanged his corpse from a bunk bed to admire it for an entire day.

On 10 November 1980, Scottish barman Douglas Stewart met Nilsen at The Golden Lion in Dean Street. He was to have a lucky escape. As usual, large amounts of alcohol had been consumed and the younger man fell into a slumber. He woke up in the nick of time to find his host strangling him. Nilsen was also carrying a large knife. Stewart literally fought for his life and managed to fend off his attacker. Almost immediately after the attack he called the police, but no action was taken because the officers, it is reported, considered the incident to be a 'domestic'.

Murder victim twelve – prostitute and pickpocket Malcolm Barlow – was discovered slumped in a doorway by Nilsen. Suffering from epilepsy, he had collapsed from the effects of the drugs he was taking for his condition. The killer called an ambulance and Malcolm was taken to hospital. After treatment, he returned to Melrose Avenue and waited on the doorstep of his 'rescuer's' home. He was invited inside, plied with drink... and throttled. His corpse was hidden under the kitchen sink until the killer had time to put him under the floorboards.

The disposal of bodies at Melrose Avenue was a task Nilsen – using butchery skills acquired in the Army Catering Corps – approached with apparent relish. As the space beneath the floorboards filled up, he removed the corpses. Stinking rotten, they would be dissected by him, wearing only his underpants. Heads were cut off, main organs removed and torsos cut into three. Then the parts were packed into suitcases and hidden in a shed at the rear of the property, covered in rubble. Other body parts were dumped in a narrow space between a fence and wall, where London's dogs, cats and foxes acted as undertaker. Yet more body parts ended up on the bonfire, tyres covering up the smell of burning flesh.

In his journals, Nilsen describes in revolting detail the process of chopping up one of his victims:

I had to have a couple of drinks before I could start. I removed the vest and undershorts from the body. With a knife I cut the head from the body. There was very little blood. I put the head in the kitchen sink, washed it, and put it in a carrier bag. I then cut off the hands, and then the feet. I washed them in the sink and dried them. I made a cut from the body's naval to the breast bone; I removed all the intestines, stomach, kidneys and liver. I would break through the diaphragm and remove the heart and lungs. I put all these organs into a plastic carrier bag. I then separated the top half of the body from the bottom half. I removed the arms and legs below the knee. I put the parts in large black carrier bags. I put the chest and rib cage in a large bag and the thigh/buttock/private parts (in one piece) in another. I stored the packages back under the floorboards.

In October 1981 Nilsen moved to Cranley Gardens, Muswell Hill. There, he had a problem: there was no garden in which to dump or burn the remains of bodies and the floorboards could not be pulled up. He would have to take another route.

Nilsen's first known guest at his new address was student Paul Nobbs. He awoke after a drinking session with Nilsen, suffering bruises to his throat. Paul, 25, consulted a doctor, who told him that he had probably been strangled. The man, who met Nilsen in Soho's Golden Lion, refused to go to police – he was afraid his homosexuality would be discovered. Another hair's breath escape was by drag queen Carl Stottor – who went by the name of Khara le Fox. After meeting Nilsen in the Black Cap pub in Camden, he awoke submerged in Nilsen's bath. His attacker explained to Carl that he had passed out and it was only a revival attempt.

In December 1982, John Howlett became the first to be murdered at Cranley Gardens. There was a tremendous struggle, during which John even tried to strangle Nilsen back. Eventually he was drowned after having his head held underwater for five minutes. He was to become the first victim of a ghastly end – being flushed away in pieces down the toilet into London's Victorian sewerage system.

Nilsen's next victim was drunken drifter Graham Allen. Taken home from his haunt on Shaftesbury Avenue, Graham was given a meal. As he tucked into an omelette, the homeless man was strangled from behind and left in the bath for three days while Nilsen planned his disposal. Body parts were boiled on the stove and the flesh either flushed down the lavatory or put in black-liners and left out for refuse collectors.

Nilsen's unwitting nemesis was drug addict Stephen Sinclair. The youngster dropped into a booze and drugs-fuelled stupor at the killer's home, where he was stripped and strangled. His body was cut up and flushed down the drains.

The slow-burning massacre that stalked London's gay and homeless young men since 1978 was brought to light by a cleaning company responding to a blocked drain – blocked, it turned out, by pieces of Stephen Sinclair's body. The company found the drain was packed with a flesh-like substance, resembling chicken.

Suspicious, the drain inspector summoned his supervisor and they called police. Upon closer inspection, some small bones and what looked like human flesh were found in a pipe leading off from the drain. DCI Peter Jay was called to the scene with two colleagues and waited outside until Nilsen returned home from work. As they entered the building, Jay introduced himself with the now-famous words: 'Mr Nilsen, we've come to talk to you about the drains.'

As they entered the flat DCI Jay immediately smelt rotting flesh. Nilsen asked why the police would be interested in his drains and the officer told him they were filled with human remains. 'How awful!' Nilsen exclaimed. 'Don't mess about, where's the rest of the body?' snapped Jay.

Dennis Nilsen came to trial at Court No. 1 at the Old Bailey on 24 October 1983. He was charged with the murder of six of the seven men that police had been able to identify: Kenneth Ockendon, Martyn Duffey, Billy Sutherland, Malcolm Barlow, John Howlett and Steve Sinclair. The defendant was also charged with the attempted murder of Douglas Stewart. To each count, he pleaded not guilty.

He told the court: 'By nature I am not a violent person. You can look at my school reports, Army and Police Service, and nine years in the Civil Service and you'll find not one record of violence against me.' Questioned by the prosecution as to why he murdered, he replied: 'Yes, it is a great enigma. These things were out of character. I killed people over a period of five years and it got worse.' He denied that during his time on remand he had taunted fellow prisoners about his crimes, saying: 'I've never gloried in their publicity, never given interviews to the press, not received any money for anything.' He added: 'Since I have been in prison I have felt no irresistible urge to kill someone else.'

Defence counsel Ivan Lawrence, QC, argued Nilsen was not guilty on account of being mentally ill. He told the jury: 'One would have to say that anyone committing such crimes must be out of his mind.' But the prosecution, led by Alan Green, QC, had already told the jury that Nilsen killed simply because he enjoyed it. After 24 hours, the jury returned a ten to two majority verdict. Nilsen was guilty on all counts and he was sentenced to life, with a recommendation that he serve at least 25 years. Home Secretary Leon Brittan later imposed a full-life tariff.

In his summing-up, judge Mr Justice Croom-Johnson said: 'There are evil people who do evil things. Committing murder is one of them. A mind can be evil without being abnormal.'

7

'ROT IN HELL!'

'He was so evil that no restriction such as a curfew or tagging would have stopped him. You would literally need a policeman at his side at all times to stop him.'

Detective Inspector Tim Grattan-Kane

Name: John McGrady
Crime: Serial rape and murder
Date of Conviction: 16 May 2006
Age at Conviction: 48

The mum of murdered schoolgirl Rochelle Holness will never forget 25 September 2005 – the last day she saw her daughter. 'It was a Sunday,' Jennifer Bennett recalled. 'I'd been to my sister's and when I got back I was shocked because all the dishes in the kitchen had been washed up. I went up to Roch's room to thank her and she just said "OK" like a typical teenager.'

Rochelle stayed upstairs, sorting through her clothes and texting her boyfriend. About 20 minutes later, she came down when the credit ran out on her phone. Jennifer said: 'She came to me and asked for money for the payphone. I didn't have any money, but a friend gave her 30p and off she went. Rochelle left the house at 7.30pm. It was still light outside and I didn't think anything of it. She was 15 and she was always going to the phone box – it was only a three-minute walk away.'

At around the same time that Rochelle left her home in Lewisham,

South London, alcoholic serial rapist John McGrady was at his council flat on the nearby Milford Towers estate, attempting drunken sex with his girlfriend, Margaret Arif. Since waking up hungover at lunchtime, the former butcher had been downing cans of strong cider and now, unable to perform in bed, he became frustrated. Margaret knew what was coming so she dressed before her lover's mood worsened. As she left the shabby seventh-floor flat, McGrady asked: 'What am I going to do? That means I will have to go out to look for someone.' Margaret thought he was joking and laughed as she walked past the empty cider cans strewn across the floor. She had no idea what was to come.

The phone box Rochelle Holness used that night was on the outskirts of McGrady's estate and just a few minutes' walk from her home. CCTV footage shows her walking away from there at 8.03pm, at which point she was alone. As she made her way home, Rochelle crossed paths with McGrady, a psychotic sex offender, who had already served two life sentences for attacks on young women.

In a drunken, sexually frustrated rage, McGrady abducted the young girl from the street and marched her up to his flat with the intention of raping her. No one but McGrady knows for sure, but police believe he threatened the teenager with a knife. His previous sex assaults involved knives and unless her life was in immediate danger, Rochelle would never have gone off with a scruffy stranger who stank of stale booze. Furthermore, she and her friends knew to stay away from Milford Towers, a run-down, crime-ridden 1960s estate despised by residents, a place that the local deputy mayor conceded was 'ghastly'.

That night, Rochelle's mum went to bed expecting her daughter to return at any time. When she checked her room at 11 the next morning and saw she wasn't there, she simply assumed she had gone off to school. But that evening she didn't come back and Jennifer started to worry. She tried ringing Rochelle's mobile, but it just rang and rang.

In an interview with the *Mirror*, Jennifer said: 'At 10pm her boyfriend Seb called to check Rochelle was alright. He said she was supposed to see him, but she never turned up. I thought that was weird, so I immediately started ringing around her friends to see if she was with them, but of course she wasn't. I couldn't sleep that night.'

The next morning she called the police and reported Rochelle missing. When she still hadn't returned the following day, Jennifer went to a photocopying shop and made hundreds of flyers, each bearing Rochelle's picture.

That afternoon – Wednesday, 28 September – Jennifer was handing out the flyers close to where Rochelle disappeared when her son Michael, 22, rang her mobile. Jennifer recalled: 'Michael said, "Mum, there are loads of police outside the flats across the road." I rushed home and when I got there, my other son Richard said he'd heard someone had been murdered.'

Together with her ex-husband, Denroy – Rochelle's dad – Jennifer ran over to Milford Towers to see what was going on. Denroy, 45, said: 'When I got there they were carrying a stretcher out with a body bag on it. As they walked past me I tried to open the bag. I wanted to see if it was Rochelle inside, but the police stopped me. I thank God now that I didn't see what was in it, because if I had, I think I would have died there and then.'

Inside was the couple's treasured daughter. 'I grabbed a police officer and gave him a flyer with Rochelle's photo,' Jennifer said. 'I asked, "Can you tell me if that's my daughter in there?" He took it and said he would go and check. He came back down half an hour later and it was the look on his face I will always remember. He said he couldn't confirm anything except to say that it was a girl and that they would like me to go to the police station to answer questions.'

The next day, a police liaison officer arrived at the house. Jennifer said: 'I just looked at him and said, "It's my daughter, isn't it?" and he said, "I'm so sorry." I immediately said, "I want to see her." But then he added, "I have some other bad news. Her body was dismembered into nine parts – we found her in black bin bags." He was very factual, but I was in hysterics, a complete mess.'

Forensic scientists were unable to tell whether Rochelle was sexually assaulted, but three deep scratches down McGrady's arm proved she fought him as he tried to have his way with her before choking her to death. Police believe she died within an hour of being at McGrady's flat and that she lay there dead overnight.

The following day, McGrady was caught on security cameras in a nearby hardware store buying hacksaw blades. Back at his flat, he used knowledge gained as a butcher's assistant to cut her up into pieces, which he stuffed into five black bin-liners. He then loaded the bags into a Tesco trolley and transported them to a rubbish chute nearby, leaving a trail of blood along the way.

Two days after Rochelle went missing, McGrady's girlfriend Margaret visited his flat, where she found him shaking and repeating the words, 'I have killed a man.' She noticed there were bloodstains on the carpet, but she assumed both the blood and his ramblings were down to a drunken fight between him and any number of fellow violent alcoholics living on the estate.

When she returned the next day, she found that he had cut his wrists and other parts of his body. There was a bloodied steak knife on the arm of his chair and scattered around him were suicide notes he'd written, confessing to Rochelle's murder. One was addressed to Margaret and another to the police. In the letter to the police, he claimed that he'd been 'told what to do by a greater force.'

His wrists still dripping with blood, McGrady took Margaret to where he had dumped the body parts. After composing herself, the sickened woman phoned the police. Within minutes, four police officers and an ambulance were at the scene. An hour later, Milford Towers was cordoned off and according to witnesses at least 40 police were in attendance. Questioned after his arrest, McGrady admitted killing Rochelle, but claimed he could not remember any details about the girl's abduction, murder or the subsequent dismemberment and disposal of her body.

On 16 May 2006 Belfast-born McGrady – who hails from a family of IRA killers – was jailed for the rest of his life at the Old Bailey. Judge Stephen Kramer told him: 'You cruelly took the life of a young girl and you have left her family, and especially her mother, bereft. I am driven to the conclusion that you must have been motivated by sexual desires.

'I am also satisfied that, particularly when you have been drinking, you are – and continue to be – a dangerous predator on women, especially young women. Just punishment requires me to pass a sentence which means you never have the opportunity to prey on young women again.' As he was led to the cells, Rochelle's mum screamed at him: 'Rot in hell!'

John McGrady had a long history of violent sexual crimes against young women. In 1988 he was jailed for six years for raping two 19-year-olds at knifepoint in Greenwich, South-East London. He forced the pair to commit humiliating sex acts on each other before raping them in turn.

In 1993 he pulled a knife on a woman who he had followed off a bus. He bundled her over a wall and was ready to assault her when a police patrol car stopped and disturbed him. This time, he went back to jail for five years. He had also been acquitted of rape three times in 1984, telling juries that the women had consented. In one case the alleged victim said he had worn a balaclava and used a knife.

Outside court, Rochelle's mum voiced her family's outrage at the system's failure to monitor such a dangerous man: 'The system has let us down. We feel terrible anger and upset that a man with such predatory instincts was allowed to live with us.'

Rochelle's murder led to huge criticism of the system of monitoring sex offenders in Britain. Despite his appalling history of attacks on young girls, McGrady was one of thousands of ex-convicts left off the Sex Offenders' Register because their crimes took place before it was created and inclusion was feared to be in breach of their human rights.

But Detective Inspector Tim Grattan-Kane, head of the Specialist Crime Directorate unit that investigated the murder, believes McGrady was too despicable and devious to stop, even had he been monitored. He said: 'McGrady has not been brought to our attention since his release in 1997, but whatever systems may have been in place, he is so evil I do not think anything could have prevented him doing what he did.

'Since his last spell in prison, he has used different permutations of his family names to disguise his identity. He has worked as an odd-job man and as a butcher for a time, but latterly, heavy drinking marked his life and he did not stray far from his flat. He was so evil that no restriction, such as a curfew or tagging, would have stopped him. You would literally need a policeman at his side at all times to stop him.

'Although he pleaded guilty, he has never told us what happened, especially how Rochelle came to go to his flat. It was clear that the motive was sexual, but at no time has he admitted why he did it. His mind went completely blank when he had to admit anything.'

This refusal to tell what happened is hard for Rochelle's family to bear. 'I'm never going to hear the proper story of how that beast killed my baby,' says Jennifer Bennett. 'I've been left in the dark. I want to know why he took her up there and I'm never going to know.'

In January 2007 McGrady's lawyers appealed against his whole life sentence, claiming it was 'manifestly excessive'. His barrister, Thomas Smith, asked Sir Igor Judge, sitting with Mr Justice Gray and Mr Justice Henriques at the Court of Appeal, to reduce his sentence and give him a chance of release before he dies.

Declining the appeal, Sir Igor said: 'The sentencing judge was satisfied that the seriousness of what he did in murdering the victim was extremely high and must have been motivated by sexual desires.

Particularly when in drink, the judge said he was, and would continue to be, a dangerous predator on women, especially young women.

'The judge concluded that he must pass a sentence which would mean that he would never prey on women again. He concluded that he must impose a whole life sentence. That decision is criticised before us today by Mr Smith. It is argued that a whole life term, whilst it was an appropriate starting point, was only a starting point, and doesn't represent an end point. He also submits that intent to kill was not proved, and that too great an emphasis was placed on the danger posed by this applicant and the protection of the public.

'It is also argued that there was evidence of genuine remorse, sustained by the guilty plea, and we are also asked to bear in mind Mr Smith's client's age. We are extremely doubtful as to the basis of his remorse.

'We are prepared to accept that he felt and feels sorry for himself, but we are not prepared to accept that he has no recollection of how this unfortunate young woman died. If he was truly sorry, he would have something to say to the parents and family of the victim, who have repeatedly expressed their profound disturbance at their lack of real knowledge and facts about the events which led to the death of this precious member of their family.

'This was the murder of a child, a teenage girl, who was chosen by McGrady because she was a teenage girl, for his own sexual purposes. Whatever he may have intended when he first targeted and abducted her, there is no doubt that he must have known exactly what he was doing when he strangled her.

'This was not the first time he had applied manual pressure to the throat of a young woman. Strangling involves serious force and as we know in this case, a struggle. At some stage he intended that this girl should die. After she was dead, her body was subjected to the gross indignity of dismemberment in a bid to escape detection.

'This case fell, rarely, within the category where the starting point is a whole life order. We can see no reason whatsoever for interfering with the sentencing judge's conclusion, with which we entirely agree. This application is refused.'

8

'THE FOX'

'Put the light on, scream and you're dead.'

Hutchinson (to victim as she cowered in bed)

Name: Arthur Hutchinson
Crime: Triple murder and rape
Date of Conviction: 14 September 1984
Age at Conviction: 43

On the morning of 28 September 1983, Arthur Hutchinson arrived at Selby's antiquated police station in North Yorkshire where he was due to appear at the Magistrates' Court in the same building that afternoon. The charges against him were theft, burglary and rape.

There was only one officer on duty at the station that day, PC Fred Jackson, who was just two weeks away from retirement. He already had his hands full in dealing with two juvenile absconders, when psychopathic Hutchinson, 42, turned up at the ground-floor reception, flanked by two warders from Armley Jail in Leeds. He was taken to the station's only interview room and searched. While PC Jackson logged the contents of the prisoner's pockets, Hutchinson made his move to escape.

He told the prison officers that he needed to use the toilet and they took off his handcuffs to allow him to do so. But while PC Jackson signed various forms accepting responsibility for his visitor, all three officers heard heavy footsteps as Hutchinson sprinted up the staircase leading to the court rooms above.

He thundered into Court No. 1, where a stunned decorator watched as he vaulted the rail surrounding the dock, jumped onto the Press bench and dived through a window, shattering the glass and slicing his knee open. Outside, he landed on a barbed wire fence but worked himself free, hobbling anonymously through the town's bustling streets.

Three-and-a-half weeks later, at around midnight on 22 October, Hutchinson entered the home of solicitor Basil Laitner, 59, and his doctor wife, Avril, 55, in Dore, Sheffield, 42 miles from Selby Magistrates' Court.

That day, the Laitners had hosted a wedding reception for their eldest daughter, Suzanne. The reception was held in a marquee in the garden from 4pm until around eight that evening. Once the guests had gone, the Laitners went with their son Richard, 28, for supper at a nearby relative's house, leaving an 18-year-old bridesmaid at home because she felt tired. They returned home at about 11.15pm and were joined shortly afterwards by Hutchinson, unshaven and filthy after many days on the run. He had broken in through a patio window.

Sometime shortly before midnight, the bridesmaid was awakened by Avril Laitner's screams. When her eyes adjusted to the darkness in the bedroom, she realised someone else was in there with her. The intruder left and the girl, who Hutchinson would later rape, was so petrified she was unable to move from her bed.

As she sat frozen and gripping her bed sheets, the girl heard Basil Laitner arguing with a man whose voice she did not recognise. Next, as prosecution counsel would later say in court, she heard a 'gasping, choking sound and then all returned to deathly quiet'. She then heard Avril saying, 'Just take the money and go, leave us alone!' before the sound of 'terrible screaming'.

Basil was murdered on the landing. He was stabbed twice in the throat and then, as he slumped on the banister, Hutchinson rammed the knife into his back. His wife was stabbed to death in her downstairs bedroom and Richard was similarly killed in his room.

At Hutchinson's trial at Durham Crown Court in September of the following year, the jury was shown a video recording made by police when they arrived at the house. The film began with the outside of the Laitner home and then the camera moved inside. Avril Laitner was lying face down on the floor of her downstairs bedroom, surrounded by her scattered jewellery and credit cards. A pathologist would later reveal that she had 26 marks of violence on her body, including four stab wounds to her left arm and 13 wounds in the palm of her left hand, which were received as she tried to fend off her attacker. The fatal wound had been inflicted down the left-hand side of the neck, severing her jugular vein.

The camera then moved to the stairs and the dead body of Basil Laitner came into view. He was laid out on the top two steps, his head down and his hands resting on the top step in front of him. Blood was spattered on the carpet and walls.

His son Richard, a promising young barrister, was in his bedroom, half on and half off his bed. He was covered in blood and his hands were folded, gripping his chest where he had been stabbed twice.

Prosecution counsel Robin Stewart, QC, said the defendant probably went to Richard's bedroom first because a bridesmaid's dress hung on the outside of the door, leading him to believe that he would find a girl there to rape. But on discovering Richard, he 'speedily despatched' him. Mr Stewart said Basil Laitner was most likely killed next, followed by his wife.

The court heard that after the killings, Hutchinson went back into the bridesmaid's room, where she remained terror-stricken in the dark. He flashed a torch in her face and said: 'Put the light on, scream and you're dead.' At knifepoint he ordered her out of the room, warning her to hide her eyes otherwise she would see 'something horrible' on the stairs. He walked her through the pool of blood next to Basil's body and into the wedding marquee, where she was forced to sit on a chair while Hutchinson handcuffed her hands behind her back. The girl, the prosecution's chief witness, told the court: 'I said, "Please don't kill me." He said that he would not if I did as he said. He walked me up to the other end of the tent and said he wanted to screw me.'

She said Hutchinson, at all times brandishing a knife, had sexual intercourse with her three times, once in the marquee and twice in her bedroom. During the assault he told her that he was on the run from an open prison and boasted of how he had killed everyone in the house. Throughout, he affected a Scottish accent. As dawn was breaking, he left her bound with ties securing her hands and feet. Before walking out of her bedroom, he whispered to her: 'I am going now, don't suffocate yourself.' He left the shattered girl to be discovered hours later by horrified workmen who came to the house to dismantle the marquee.

When police arrived, the bridesmaid's foot was caked with Basil Laitner's blood and her nightdress stained with Avril's blood from her killer's hands. Despite the ordeal she had been through, the teenager was able to give a detailed description of her attacker and a police artist drew a sketch of the suspect, which bore a remarkable resemblance to the man who had escaped from Selby Magistrates the month before.

Hutchinson evaded arrest for 16 days, making his way north to Darlington and his home town of Hartlepool, about 120 miles north of the Laitner home. Finally, he was caught in a field at High Stotfold Farm in Dalton Piercy, near Hartlepool, on 5 November. As he was taken in, he said to the arresting policeman: 'I'm not a murderer. I should have stayed down my fox hole, shouldn't I?' After his arrest, police found a tape recording in a Darlington guest house, where he had stayed under the name 'A. Fox'.

On the tape, Hutchinson said: 'Because I was able to get this tape recorder, transistor, I've been able to listen to everything that's been going on – where they have been waiting for me, where they have been looking for me, so I knew exactly which way to head out of the way from 'em. Like playing cat and mouse, or should I say fox on the trot.

'I'm making no comments on the triple killings. Let the police do what they want, I'm saying nowt. I'm not telling anybody nothing about that business. Mebbes I'm a bit daft in the head like people think I am. Let them think what they want – I am still free, that's the main f**king thing.'

When questioned by police, Hutchinson agreed that he had escaped from custody in Selby in September, but denied that he had been anywhere near the Laitner home. Asked about the murders, he said: 'I did not kill them people.'

As his trial approached, however, he changed his story after learning of the vast amount of evidence found at the Laitner home which proved he had been there. 'A forensic expert's dream' is how police privately described the murder scene. Hutchinson has a rare blood group, shared with only one in 50,000 people in Britain, and his blood was discovered all over the bridesmaid's bed sheets. The blood had come from the wound to his knee, sustained when he escaped from Selby.

Hutchinson also left a palm print on a champagne bottle in the wedding marquee and twice bit into a piece of cheese that he found in the Laitners' fridge. A dental expert made casts of the bites and they matched a cast of Hutchinson's teeth taken after his arrest. He duly revised his story in court, claiming the bridesmaid had invited him to the house, where they had consensual sex. He denied any involvement in the triple murders.

By pleading not guilty, Hutchinson forced the rape victim to go through the ordeal of cross-examination by his defence counsel, James Stewart, QC. Mr Stewart suggested she had met Hutchinson in a Sheffield pub on Friday, 21 October, the day before the wedding and arranged a rendezvous at the house after the reception. She denied this, and further claims that she left the patio door unlatched and told Hutchinson that a bottle of champagne would be waiting for him in the kitchen.

Visibly shaking, the girl answered 'No' to a series of questions in which the defence said that she had taken the man to the bedroom, danced with him, kissed, petted, undressed, had intercourse and then taken a white powder drug. She acknowledged that there was a stage where she tried to appear that she was enjoying sex with Hutchinson. Explaining why, she said: 'Because I didn't want to die – I was acting as though I was enjoying it.'

Next, Mr Stewart asked her if she had consented to all the sexual acts and she broke down and sobbed into both hands. The trial judge, Mr Justice McNeill, offered to adjourn the court when the witness sobbed: 'I want to go home!' She regained her composure, but when the defence barrister asked her to bind her hands with the grey spotted tie Hutchinson had allegedly used to tie her up in her bed, she refused.

When Hutchinson gave evidence, prosecution counsel said: 'I'm going to suggest to you a number of things. I suggest that you have lied through and through, and in particular that you lied repeatedly to the police throughout the preparation of this case and that you have lied in court today.'

When the QC asked him if he had repeatedly lied to police, Hutchinson agreed. Mr Stewart continued: 'I suggest that you are lying now. You have changed your defence to admit being in the house and whatever nasty things you have said against [the rape victim] are because you are a desperate man who realises the evidence nails you to that house that night. Bluntly, I suggest you have told a tissue of lies about [the rape victim].' In his closing speech, he said Hutchinson was a 'deliberate and repetitive liar' who had 'no concept of the truth.'

The jury of six men and six women took just over four hours to reach their unanimous verdicts of guilty on all three murder counts and the rape. During the announcement, Hutchinson showed no emotion.

Passing sentence, Mr Justice McNeill made no direct reference to the ordeal endured by the bridesmaid. He told Hutchinson: 'You are interested in weapons, are arrogant, manipulative, have a self-centred attitude towards life, and a severe personality disorder, which is not amenable to any form of treatment.

'It seems to me only right in the public interest that I should recommend a minimum period of imprisonment, and I do recommend that that should be 18 years. You will be over 60 years of age, if that period is served.'

After the trial, Hutchinson's mother, Louise Reardon, said she believed his crimes were the result of an accident he had as a child. He was just four years old when he rode his bicycle into a lamppost. For three days young Arthur – described by his mother as her 'little angel' – lay in a coma. The accident left him with meningitis, a fractured skull and a split personality.

Speaking days after her son was jailed, Louise, then 79, said Hutchinson's violent side began to show at the age of seven when he stabbed one of his sisters with a pair of scissors. 'I had five girls and they made life hell for Arthur,' she recalled. 'They called him a bastard, which was true.' Hutchinson was one of two illegitimate children by Arthur Hutchinson, Louise's lodger. She also had four children by local pitman Cuthbert Reardon.

By the age of 11, Hutchinson made his first appearance at Juvenile Court, charged with indecent assault. There followed 19 further appearances, including four charges of sexual intercourse with girls under 16. At 18, he married neighbour Margaret Dover, who was pregnant with his child. Three years later, they separated. A year after that, he was jailed for unlawful sexual intercourse.

He was 27 when he met his second wife, Hannelore, at a staff Christmas party at Hartlepool's Buxted chicken factory. She remembered: 'He just stood and watched me for two hours without saying a word. I suppose it flattered me.' Five months later they were wed and Hutchinson was both unfaithful and violent. Hannelore said: 'Anything could provoke him, sometimes nothing. He used to boast about his conquests. The day he left me, he beat me up in the street. He knocked me to the ground and put the boot in. I once saw him knock his mother out of a rocking chair, halfway across the room. Anyone who can do that must have a split personality.'

Despite his brutality, Hutchinson's mother refused to forget her fond memories of her son. She remembered how her country-loving lad took home an injured rabbit and bandaged its leg, and of the day he saved a drowning budgie and fed it whisky; of the little Arthur who collected all her lettuces to give to local pensioners, and of the sensitive boy who would nearly faint at the sight of blood.

The doting mother – who died in 1985 – added that no matter how cruel, violent and dishonest he became as he grew up, she still loved him. She said: 'I saw him the night they caught him. You could see in his eyes he was sorry. He's been a bad lad and it has split the family because I stand by him. They accuse him of being my favourite, but I love them all. Arthur just needed the same.'

Ten months after he was jailed, Hutchinson failed in an appeal against his conviction at London's Court of Appeal. Lord Justice Watkins said he had been convicted on 'devastating evidence.' He had, the judge said, been convicted of 'outrageous and almost unbelievably horrid' killings.

For two decades after his incarceration, owing to his mindless brutality, Hutchinson – a martial arts fanatic with an obsession for knives – was feared by fellow inmates. One officer at Wakefield Prison where he is held described him as 'like a bomb about to reach the end of its fuse.'

He is in his late sixties now and not the physical force he once was, but his twisted nature has not changed. His half-brother Dino

Reardon, whom Hutchinson once tried to shoot, told the News of the World in 2004 that he has been plagued with threatening phone calls from the killer, hinting he'd hunt down the surviving Laitners if he ever got out. Taking the threats seriously, Dino said: 'I know he would go for them first and me afterwards. He has regularly made threatening calls to me, leaving coded or cryptic messages. What I can't believe is that his calls are not vetted. The really frightening thing is that he's hinted at going after the surviving Laitners. He never forgets a grudge. No matter how old he is when he comes out of prison, I know that he will still be coming after me.' Hutchinson's sentence was increased from the judge's minimum recommendation of 18 years to a whole life tariff by Home Secretary Leon Brittan, meaning Dino need have no such fears.

9

'THE GAY SLAYER'

*'He was unable to stop killing – he was under a form of
compulsion. He was not in control. He was on a roller-coaster –
it was becoming easy for him.'*

Ireland's Defence Barrister, Andrew Trollope, QC

Name: Colin Ireland
Crime: Serial murder
Date of Conviction: 20 December 1993
Age at Conviction: 39

The burly, bull-necked man with the military haircut was careful to avoid the CCTV camera as he walked into The Coleherne pub on Old Brompton Road, Kensington, South-West London, on 8 March 1993. He looked cautiously round the well-known gay haunt and caught the eye of Peter Walker, a theatrical director and choreographer. Peter – a regular at the bar – had no idea the rucksack carried by the tall stranger contained a murder kit comprising gloves, duct tape, a knife, lengths of sailing cord and a change of clothing. The stranger's name was Colin Ireland, a warped survival fanatic, soon to be nicknamed 'The Gay Slayer' by the tabloid press.

Ireland, 39, walked over to his admirer and they got chatting. During the course of their conversation, Peter admitted that he liked being beaten up during sex. Unfortunately for him, he was being picked up by a man at the start of a carefully prepared mission to kill gay sadomasochistic men.

'I had gone there [the pub] with the idea that if someone approached me, something would happen,' Ireland later told police. 'It would be some kind of trigger.'

With two failed marriages behind him and the recent loss of his job, Ireland was disgruntled and bitter about life. He wanted to 'be a somebody' and made the decision to be a serial killer. He read the FBI handbook, The Crime Classification Manual by Robert Ressler, and learned that to be recognised as a serial killer he had to murder 'one over four' people. Peter Walker was about to be the first.

The pair finished their drinks and caught a taxi to Peter's Battersea flat. As they walked towards the building, Ireland carefully pulled on a pair of gloves. Once inside, 45-year-old Peter shut his two dogs, a Labrador and a German Shepherd, into the living room and led his new acquaintance into the bedroom.

With his consent, Peter was tied naked to his four-poster bed. As he lay there, spread-eagled, Ireland slapped and punched him with gloved hands and whipped him with a dog lead. He then fetched a plastic bag from the kitchen, placed it over his victim's head and began to suffocate him. But he pulled the bag off at the last moment as Peter thrashed his head about, gasping for air. Later, Ireland told police: 'I took the bag away and told him how easy it was to end it all. It was a fate thing and he said to me, "I'm going to die." And I said, "Yes, you are." I think in a way he wanted to die – there was a lack of desire to carry on; he was quite controlled about it. In the end I killed him with the plastic bag.'

Once Peter was dead, Ireland burnt his pubic hair to see what it smelled like. Then, while rifling through his victim's belongings, Ireland came across a letter informing him that he was HIV-positive. This disgusted him into further defiling the man's body. He stuffed knotted condoms into Peter's mouth and nostrils, and arranged two of his teddy bears next to the body in the '69' position.

All night long, Ireland stayed at the flat watching TV and eating from the dead man's fridge. He meticulously cleaned away all evidence of his visit and left during the morning rush hour to be less conspicuous. For his next four killings, he followed the same pattern. Later, he said: 'After killing Walker, I walked down the road and thought that anyone who looked at my face would be able to see I had just murdered somebody. I thought they would be able to tell just by looking at me. I remembered losing my virginity and I remembered the same feeling – you're always buzzing.'

Two days after the first murder, he phoned the news desk at the *Sun* and said: 'I have murdered a man.' He then told the reporter where the body was located. In his gruff London accent, he continued: 'I am calling you because I am worried about his dogs: I want them to be let out – it would be cruel for them to be stuck there.'

For a few moments he was silent, but then he added: 'I tied him up and killed him, and I cleaned up the flat afterwards. I did it. It was my New Year's resolution to kill a human being. He was homosexual and into kinky sex. You like that sort of stuff, don't you?'

The paper contacted the police, who went round and found Peter dead on his bed. Detectives also discovered his cash card was missing and that £200 had been withdrawn from his account after his death. Despite a detailed forensic search of the flat, they had no clues as to the identity of his killer.

More importantly, the police inquiry involved a sub-group of the gay population who indulged in what many regarded as bizarre practices. In a twist that was to hamper the investigation, the day after the body was discovered, the Law Lords ruled that sado-masochistic practices between consenting adults were illegal in what became known as the notorious 'Spanner Case'. Gays were concerned that, by co-operating, they could be prosecuted.

Almost three months later, police had the body of another tied-up gay man on their hands. On 30 May, Christopher Dunn, a 37-year-old librarian, was found dead by a colleague who was concerned that he had not turned up for work.

The previous evening, Christopher met Ireland at The Coleherne, where he confided to the killer that he liked to be dominated. The ever-charming Ireland was soon at Christopher's flat in Wealdstone, North-West London, drinking wine and watching an S&M video.

Christopher was found bound and gagged, wearing a black leather harness and belts. Before strangling him with a nylon cord, Ireland asked him for his bank PIN number. To ensure he told him the right one, he set fire to his genitals with a lighter. He then stole £200 from the dead man's account. Again, he spent the night with the deceased before leaving the next morning.

Speaking of the hours he spent alone with the bodies of his victims, Ireland later told police: 'It's strange but now I remember overwhelming things... death and what it smells like. When people have been strangled, they break wind; that's what it smells like. I think if I had just killed these people and gone, I wouldn't have been affected mentally so much, but sitting with these bodies like five or six hours on some occasions, watching them gradually blotch as they go cold... it wasn't something I think I could cope with, quite honestly.'

Detectives investigating Christopher's death concluded that he died accidentally during an extreme sado-masochistic sex act. They believed the burns to his genitals were caused in the process. As such, no connection was made with Peter Walker's death and inquiries into the second murder ceased.

Next to die was Perry Bradley, a 35-year-old American sales director, who was again a regular at The Coleherne. The pair met at the pub on 4 June and after a brief flirtation, both men went to Perry's Kensington home.

Perry was wary of being tied up but after Ireland explained that he could not perform sexually unless there was sado-masochism, he relented and agreed to it. Ireland told the trussed-up Perry that he was a thief and that he intended to torture his PIN number from him. The killer later revealed that the American simply replied: 'I'm quite happy to give you anything you want to know.' Ireland did not kill his latest victim straightaway. Instead, he told him: 'It's going to be a long night – I suggest you get some sleep if you can.'

Ireland recalled to police: 'I just sat and listened to the radio and he actually went to sleep.' Around an hour later, as Bradley slept face down on his bed with his hands trussed behind his back, Ireland killed him. He said: 'I put a noose around his neck and tied it to something. I sat there, thinking, and at one point I thought of letting him go. Then I thought, "It's easier to kill him." My plan was to kill. He hardly struggled.' He stole £100 from the dead man's wallet and later withdrew £200 from his bank account.

Despite the money being stolen from the bank accounts of the dead men, police had still not managed to link the three killings. Each death was investigated by different local teams of detectives and there was no co-ordination between them.

Three days later, on the evening of 7 June, Ireland was back in The Coleherne, where he met Andrew Collier, a care worker in a nursing home. A similar pick-up pattern ensued and the men were soon at the 33-year-old's flat in Dalston, East London. Andrew readily agreed to being tied up and was soon dead by strangulation. While rifling through his belongings, Ireland discovered his latest victim was, like Peter Walker, HIV-positive and decided to express his disgust at not being told of his condition when sex was clearly on the cards.

Furious, Ireland hanged Andrew's pet cat, Millie, using a rope thrown over the bedroom door. He then draped the animal over the dead man's naked body: he put Andrew's penis in the cat's mouth and the cat's tail in the victim's mouth. Both the tail and the penis had condoms pulled over them. Later, he told detectives: 'I was the killer and he had AIDS; that annoyed me. He never told me – he thought there was going to be a normal sexual encounter. I wanted him to have no dignity in death.'

Ireland admitted the obscene ritual with the cat was 'part anger and part of an increase in the thrill of killing.' He said: 'I wanted to know how you would react when you came across the scene: you're not thinking normally when you do something like this. But it was almost like a signature, to let you know I'd been there. I was reaching that point, you know, where you feel you have to step up a stage at a time.'

Ireland stole £70 from Andrew and left the next morning, but by then he had made his first mistake. During the evening, he and Andrew looked out of the window when they heard a police siren and he left a fingerprint on the frame that escaped his later, usually meticulous, cleaning efforts.

On the afternoon of 8 June, Ireland rang the police at Kensington to claim responsibility for all four murders. He said: 'If you don't stop me, it will be one a week. I pissed myself when I read that I was an animal lover. I thought I would give you lot something to think about, so I killed the cat.' Hours later, he called Battersea police and asked: 'Are you still interested in the death of Peter Walker? Why have you stopped the investigation? Doesn't the death of a homosexual man mean anything? I will do another.'

It was the murder of his fifth victim, Maltese chef Emmanuel Spiteri, which led to his capture. On the evening of 12 June, Emmanuel was in The Coleherne with a handkerchief hanging from his rear pocket, a telltale sign on the gay scene that he liked to be dominated.

Ireland bought him a drink and, via two trains, they went to the 41-year-old's flat in Catford, South-East London. Once there, he handcuffed his victim to the bed and tied his feet together with sailing cord. He then put a noose around the bald man's neck.

The killer takes up the disturbing tale: 'I bound him, but he was becoming suspicious. The word had got around about the gay murders and he was getting a bit worried. By then it was too late, but he was a very brave man. I told him I wanted his PIN number. He refused to give it to me, even though I threatened to kill him. He said, "Do whatever you are going to do. You will just have to kill me."' Ireland's police statement continued: 'He was a very brave, strong-minded man, but I couldn't allow him to stick around and recognise me so I killed him with the noose.'

As usual, Ireland – now officially a serial killer – stayed the night, but he changed his pattern by setting fire to the murder scene before he left. Shortly afterwards, the fire went out. Asked after his arrest why he had started the fire, he told police that he used to be a fireman, adding: 'There's a bit of arsonist in all firemen. There's an element in me that's highly destructive, very cold. In some moods I'd be quite happy to burn the world down.'

By the time Emmanuel's body was found later that morning, the Metropolitan Police knew they had a serial killer on their hands. Although they had Ireland's fingerprint left at the scene of the fourth murder, there was no one to compare it to. They traced Emmanuel's movements from The Coleherne the previous night and obtained CCTV footage of him walking out of Charing Cross station with a tall, bulky man with cropped hair. Detectives released the video to the press.

Fearing the 'Gay Slayer' would strike again, Detective Chief Superintendent Ken John appealed to him directly on national TV news. He said: 'I need to speak to you. Enough is enough – enough pain, enough anxiety, enough tragedy. Give yourself up.'

Seeing his CCTV image, albeit blurred, made Ireland panic. For a few days, he pondered his situation, then on 19 July, he walked into a solicitor's in Southend, Essex, where he admitted that he was the man with Emmanuel. However, he claimed that he left the victim alive with another man, who must have been responsible for his death.

Within minutes of interviewing Ireland, police knew they had their man. He let slip the detail about Andrew Collier's dead cat – something that had not been made public. Furthermore, his fingerprints matched those found at the flat. Faced with the case against him, he confessed to all five murders.

On 20 December 1993, Colin Ireland appeared at the Old Bailey for sentencing, having pleaded guilty at an earlier hearing. Prosecution counsel John Nutting told the court: 'These murders were premeditated and meticulously planned. It would seem the defendant set out to be a serial killer. He told others that in order to be so classified he knew he would have to commit at least five murders. He chose a vulnerable group as his intended victims – homosexual men who indulged in sado-masochistic sex, thus enabling him to tie them up with no resistance from them before killing them.' He added that at no point was Ireland under the influence of drink or drugs during the murders.

Andrew Trollope, QC, defending, said: 'Ireland himself advances no mitigation or offers any kind of excuse or justification for what he did. He accepts total responsibility for his thoughts and actions during the weeks he was committing these killings.' Mr Trollope stated that Ireland was neither insane nor suffering from diminished responsibility and offered no medical excuse for his actions: he had simply chosen homosexuals as his target because he could 'readily prey upon them'. The barrister added: 'He was unable to stop killing – he was under a form of compulsion. He was not in control; he was on a rollercoaster – it was becoming easy for him. He reached a point where he wanted to be caught. These calls to police were not taunts, they were acts of a perpetrator asking to be arrested.'

Ireland yawned frequently, stretched and played with his bottom lip as Mr Trollope told how he had 'bitterly resented' the loss of his job as a relief manager at a night centre: 'That occupation was his last attempt to lead an ordinary, stable life. Once the killings began, there was an excitement and that drove him on.'

Passing sentence, Mr Justice Sachs told Ireland: 'In my view it is absolutely clear you should never be released. To take one human life is an outrage, to take five is carnage. No one who had read the papers or listened to today's hearing can be anything other than revolted by your wickedness, which is almost beyond belief.'

He added: 'By any standards you are an exceptionally frightening and dangerous man. In cold blood and with great deliberation you have killed five of your fellow human beings. You killed them in grotesque and cruel circumstances. You expressed a desire to be regarded as a serial killer – that must be matched by your detention for life. In my view it is absolutely clear you should never be released.'

Ireland acknowledged the judge's words with a nod, accepting that he was going to die behind bars. As he said to police after his arrest: 'I wasn't forced to do it. I should be placed where I can't inflict harm on others.'

10

'THE SHOPPING SPREE'

'I didn't intend Peter any serious harm. I was later shocked to hear that he had died.'

Smith (to police)

Name: Michael Smith
Crime: Murder
Date of Conviction: 15 May 2007
Age at Conviction: 52

In August 1975, Michael Smith met Sheila Deakin at a party and he could not believe his luck when she agreed to go out with him. He was 21, and had spent much of the previous decade in approved schools and borstals; Sheila was 18, and in his eyes the prettiest girl in Stoke-on-Trent. From the start, he was besotted, but two days before Christmas that year, Sheila burst the bubble and ended up dead.

On the morning of 23 December, Sheila went to pick up her two-year-old daughter, Debbie, from her mother's house two miles away. When she failed to return to their two-bedroom flat by late afternoon, Michael became agitated. Recently, she had been going out a lot with a girl who lived in a flat near to theirs in the city's Penkhull area. Her new friend took her for the occasional night out to pubs and clubs, much to Michael's annoyance. He assumed she was out with her again and spent the night on the sofa, drinking cider. When she came home, he killed her.

At his trial at Stafford Crown Court in April the following year, Smith gave his version of the events that led to Sheila's death. He explained that she had gone out in the morning to 'fetch her child from her mother's home and collect her social security. But she did not come back all day, and I guessed she had gone out with this girl and some men. I went to bed that night and she had still not returned.'

He told the jury that he woke up just before midnight to loud knocking on the front door. When he answered it, a man was standing there with Sheila by his side: 'The bloke told me to hand over the keys and get out of the flat because it was Sheila's flat. Sheila kept saying that she hated me – it was like a slap in the face coming from her. The man hit me and kicked me, then left.'

Smith said that once the man had gone, he tried to talk to his girlfriend and 'calm her down.' He told the court: 'She said that other men were better than me – I took that to mean they were better in bed than me.' Those were to prove her last words.

'I put my hands around her neck,' Smith said. 'I did not mean to harm her; I have never felt like that before. I can vaguely remember putting part of her tights round her neck.'

After killing Sheila, Smith stripped her body. Judge Mr Justice Melford Stevenson asked him why he did so and Smith replied: 'I have thought about it since, but I still don't know why I did it. I put a cushion under her head and put a coat over her. I sat there until morning, just staring at her: I knew she was dead.'

He then went to his parents' house nearby and told his father that Sheila had dumped him for another man and that he felt suicidal. After about an hour, he said he was going to try and talk things through with her, promising his father that he would not do anything stupid and would return by lunchtime. When he had not shown up by 8pm, his father phoned the police, fearing he might have harmed himself.

Officers went to the flat and broke down the door. Sheila's naked body was laid out on the living room floor with Smith beside her. The gas taps in the kitchen were turned on and the flat was full of fumes.

Smith denied Sheila's murder, but admitted manslaughter on the grounds of provocation. Prosecution counsel Peter Weitzman, QC, told the jury: 'Provocation means a sudden and temporary loss of control. The question is, was the defendant subject to such passion that he was not in control of himself?'

The jury of three men and nine women took two hours to find Smith guilty of murder. In tears, his mother was helped from the public gallery before the judge told him: 'The jury have convicted you of murder and I cannot see how they could have avoided that conclusion… You will go to prison for life.' He was then told that he would be eligible for parole after 10 years but, far from being released after that time, Smith spent 30 years inside after escaping from various prisons.

In July 1982, he was one of six inmates who escaped from Nottingham Jail. He spent 12 days on the run before being caught while drinking in a pub in Hanley, near Stoke. In 1987, he escaped from Ashwell Open Prison, in Leicestershire with another inmate. He absconded from Sudbury Open Prison, near Uttoxeter in 1991, and then went on the run from Leyhill Open Prison, in Gloucestershire, in 1993. Finally, he was given parole on 26 August 2005. Almost a year to the day, he killed again.

The battered body of his former drug addict friend Peter Summers was found on 24 August 2006. The dead man's mother, Stella Parson, called police when he failed to return her calls for more than a week. Officers entered his flat in Squires View, Stoke, and found him lying face down under a double bed. He had been beaten about the head with a champagne bottle and his bedroom was covered in blood.

A pathologist said the 35-year-old was probably attacked on 17 August. In his view, the victim could have lived for up to four days before he died. Trails of blood across the floor and handprints on the bed suggested he had been able to crawl around the room during his slow death.

A week before he attacked Peter, Smith broke the terms of his parole when he tested positive for controlled drugs. Recall to prison was inevitable and this gave him a devil-may-care attitude during his last few days of freedom.

Peter's former partner Sarah Welch had taken their nine-year-old son Liam on holiday to Turkey and left Peter in charge of the Squires View flat. On 16 August, his friend Smith went round to the flat to take drugs. In a heroin-induced moment of madness, Peter showed Smith a toolbox containing £8,000 in cash that Sarah had hidden in the loft. He even counted the money in front of him.

That afternoon, Smith sent a text to his friend Mark Johnson, boasting that he had pulled off a drugs deal and asking him if he 'wanted a grand'. At some point during the next 24 hours, Smith walked into Peter's bedroom armed with an empty champagne bottle and repeatedly bludgeoned his defenceless victim around the head. He then picked up the cash and fled, leaving him bleeding on the floor.

On 18 August, Smith travelled 16 miles to Stafford and took his ex-girlfriend, Caroline Hulme, out on a shopping spree. Caroline later told police that her boyfriend had a red bag that was full of cash and he was 'jittery'. He told her that he was in 'big trouble' but would not say why. She said he spent lavishly on them both.

At his trial at Stafford Crown Court in May of the following year, prosecutor Nigel Baker, QC, said around £800 of jewellery had been recovered, but the rest of the money was still missing. He added: 'The defendant was partying and enjoying himself in the days after coming into this money from the deceased.'

The barrister read out the statement that Smith gave to police: 'I didn't intend Peter any serious harm. My intention was to leave him dazed and make my escape with the money. I didn't think he needed emergency treatment; I was later shocked to hear that he had died.'

Anthony Barker, QC, defending, said Smith admitted the murder shortly after being recalled to prison on 25 August. He added: 'He is resigned to the fact that he will spend the rest of his life in prison. This is the picture of a man who has effectively thrown his life away. He is not asking the court for mercy.'

Mr Barker told the court that his client had a dreadful early life, suffering physical and sexual abuse. It made him a deeply disturbed boy and by the age of 11 he was at an approved school, where experts tried to control his violent urges. But his temper worsened and when he was 13, he was locked up in a borstal. During the next five years he enjoyed fewer than 12 months of freedom.

On 31 July 1974, he was jailed for two years for beating up a man who disturbed him while he was burgling his house. He was back on the streets in November 1975, and within weeks he had committed his first murder.

Sentencing the double killer, Mr Justice Nelson told Smith: 'You have pleaded guilty to the brutal killing of a former friend. You struck his head with a bottle to enable you to steal a substantial amount of money you had seen him counting. He may have lived between one and four days before he succumbed to injuries you inflicted. This was a terrible crime. You have taken a life and caused terrible grief and loss to his relatives and his friends.'

The judge added: 'Murder is a dreadful crime, but what is truly shocking is that this is the second time you have committed it. You were released and committed this murder about one year after. The law requires me to pass a life sentence, but I am also required to pass a minimum term. I have considered whether there is any mitigation which might affect that starting point. The case remains exceptional and that minimum term should be one of a whole life order. This was a brutal attack on a man for the purpose of theft, the victim was left to die and afterwards money was spent by you on a shopping spree.'

After the sentence, Peter's former partner Sarah Welch paid tribute to him: 'We were together since I was 13 and I spent my teenage and adult years with him until the age of 29. We had two children. Our first son, Kieran, died suddenly when he was just seven weeks old. Liam, our second, is now nine.

'Peter's death means that Liam has missed out on the chance of having his dad there as a teenager and as an adult. I'm still too angry to have an opinion about Michael Smith. He knew Peter had a son, and must have understood that his actions would have consequences for Liam. Our son will now have to grow up, knowing that a person could be so evil as to murder another human being, purely and simply out of greed.'

Peter's mother, Stella Parsons, said: 'I will never understand how or why anyone could do such a thing, how they could take someone's life in such a horrible and vicious way. I'm still as angry with Smith as I was then. His sentence will never be enough.'

11

'THE HIGHLY-
INTELLIGENT
PSYCHOPATH'

*'I unsheathed a short sword stick and stabbed him in the belly,
running the blade up into his heart.'*

Childs on killing one of his victims

Name: John Childs
Crime: Mass murder
Date of Conviction: 4 December 1979
Age at Conviction: 40

On 28 November 1980, East End hard man Henry MacKenney, known in the London underworld as 'Big H', was found guilty of four gruesome murders at the Old Bailey. Standing at 6ft 5in tall, the 48-year-old snarled down from the dock as the verdicts were read out. Many of the jurors looked away to avoid his intimidating stare.

The ruthless villain, whom notorious gangsters the Kray Twins had failed to recruit, stood with his fists tightly clasped by his sides. Five prison guards surrounding him in the dock could see that he had his fingers tattooed: those on his right hand had the letters 'LTFC' and those on the left said 'ESUK'. When he intertwined them, it spelt: 'LETS FUCK'.

As the judge began sentencing him, MacKenney moved forward in the dock and shouted: 'I think you are a hypocrite. Bring this farce to a close. Do your worst!' In response, Mr Justice May said to him: 'The court has listened to a story the like of which I have seldom heard, even in these violent times.' With his face red with fury, MacKenney interrupted: 'I killed nobody! I have saved lives. You forbade me to bring those people here. You hid a psycho report from the jury!' He then turned to the jury of ten men and two women, who had unanimously convicted him, and yelled: 'You are mongols and right mugs!'

MacKenney had every reason to be angry: he was completely innocent of all four murders. His conviction was based exclusively on the testimony of John 'Bruce' Childs, a psychopathic self-confessed killer with a serious mental disorder that compelled him to lie repeatedly in a way that would have been undetectable to a jury. The 'psycho report' that was kept from the jury would have destroyed Childs' credibility as a witness. Because of Childs' lies, MacKenney spent 23 years in prison for crimes he did not commit.

On 15 December 2003, MacKenney and his friend Terry Pinfold — wrongly jailed for his involvement in one of the killings — walked free from the Court of Appeal when their convictions were quashed. Both men were frail and gaunt after suffering ill health in prison. Pinfold, 70, had suffered six strokes and had serious heart and bowel problems. MacKenney, 73, was pale and weak after contracting emphysema and a near-fatal dose of pneumonia. The best years of their lives were a long way behind them.

More than 25 years earlier, in September 1978, the man behind their ruin was arrested in connection with a £500,000 robbery in Hertfordshire. During police questioning, Childs — well known among London's East End criminal fraternity as an oddball fantasist — told detectives that he had something much bigger to admit than anything they already had on him. In a statement lasting many hours, the wiry, bearded crook told how he and two associates, MacKenney and Pinfold, had been in the business of murder. He said they had killed six people for profit between October 1974 and October 1978. Their victims were haulage contractor George Brett and his son Terry, nursing home proprietor Fred Sherwood, roofing contractor Ronald Andrews, teddy bear manufacturer Terry Eve and prison absconder Robert Brown.

Childs boasted to police that they would not find any bodies because they had been chopped up and disposed of. Checks quickly proved that all six people were missing and Childs was charged. The police could not have dreamt of an easier result.

On 4 December 1979, Childs, of Poplar, East London, pleaded guilty to six counts of murder at the Old Bailey. John Mathew, QC, for the prosecution, briefly outlined the details of the crimes before the judge, Mr Justice Lawson, sentenced him to life imprisonment on each count, to run concurrently. The full macabre and horrific details of the murders – among the worst any Old Bailey jury has heard – were saved for November the following year, when Childs took to the witness box to turn Queen's Evidence against his 'accomplices' MacKenney and Pinfold.

Childs, who had spent 15 months in solitary confinement for his protection in the run-up to the trial, told the court how he needed to come clean about every detail of the murders because he found it increasingly difficult to stomach what he had done. Indeed, until his confession to the six killings, his criminal record did not include offences of serious violence.

Prosecution counsel, David Tudor Price, told the jury that Childs' confession led the police to MacKenney, who had been brought up in the Elephant and Castle area of South London, and had convictions for taking cars, lorries and causing actual bodily harm. Pinfold, a former amateur boxer, was in prison for his part in an armed robbery when Childs confessed. The police also arrested Leonard Thompson, 41, and Paul Morton-Thurtle, 34. The prosecution said they had taken out contracts to kill with the central conspirators. Both were later found not guilty.

Mr Tudor Price warned the jury of ten men and two women: 'The details of this case are extremely unpleasant. It will be necessary for you to steel yourself to listen to descriptions, which are really revolting.'

In his first of four days in the witness box, the star – and only – witness for the prosecution, said he lived in fear of his life because he had broken the professional criminals' code by testifying against his fellow killers. Childs, 41, admitted: 'I'm scared of the damage Mr MacKenney can do to me and my family because I have had the audacity to stand here and give Queen's Evidence. I am open to being killed myself.'

He went on to relate the story of what he and his murder gang had done. The tale began, he said, when he was released from prison in 1972 and went to work for Pinfold, who was manufacturing lifejackets, designed by MacKenney, at a factory in a former church hall in Dagenham, Essex. The three had had serious discussions about killing people for money, but nothing came of it until they came across Terence 'Teddy Bear' Eve, who made soft toys on the balcony of the hall. Childs said Pinfold wanted to take over Eve's business and the three would-be killers had various schemes for getting rid of him. They discussed the idea and it was decided that Eve, 35, would be killed by MacKenney and Childs at the church hall with Pinfold absent – as he would be the one taking over Eve's business and so needed an alibi.

Childs told the court that at around midnight on Friday, 1 November 1974, MacKenney led Eve into a covered alleyway where Childs was hidden behind a curtain. He bolted the door behind him and started to beat him with a length of hydraulic hose which had two heavy nuts attached to it. Childs emerged from his hiding place and hit Eve twice in the face with a hammer. As Eve lay unconscious on the floor, MacKenney strangled him with a rope. The alleyway was covered in blood so Childs threw buckets of water over the floor and walls. Both men stripped off their bloodied clothes and MacKenney used his jeans to block the gap at the bottom of the door to prevent the bloodied water from seeping out into the car park.

They continued cleaning up until the following morning, when they called Pinfold and asked him to come to the factory. Arriving between 8 and 8.30am, Pinfold said he did not wish to know the details, but asked where the body was located and whether the factory was clear as he had employees attending for work that morning.

Childs said that on the Saturday evening he and MacKenney had put Eve's body, wrapped in a tarpaulin, into the boot of MacKenney's car and had taken it to Childs' council flat in Poplar. They bought an industrial mincing machine and lined the floor with plastic sheeting to catch the blood, but the household electric current was not strong enough to get the machine to work properly so they used an axe, a saw and knives to cut up the body. Relishing the attention he was getting in the witness stand, Childs went into graphic detail, telling the court how MacKenney had sawn off one of Eve's legs before deciding to complete the dismemberment in the bath.

At all times avoiding the eyes of the accused men who glared at him from the dock, Childs told how MacKenney called him to watch as he put a butcher's knife to the dead man's throat and, 'with about three motions', cut his head clean off. Once Eve was chopped up, they tried flushing parts of him down the toilet, but it took too long. Instead, Childs said that he spent 24 hours incinerating the body on a grate in his living room fireplace. He told the court how he sat 'relaxed and having a drink' as the flesh burned and that the bones were crushed with a mallet and disposed of with the ashes around the East End. The same method of disposal was adopted for each of the killings.

Childs said that after the success of their first murder, the three men held a 'policy meeting and the result of that was that we were going into the murder business.' He told the court: 'Mr Pinfold would be our agent, Mr MacKenney would kill, and in any trouble I would assist him to kill. Disposals would be at my place, and in the case of anyone cracking up, the other two would get rid of that member.'

He told the court how they had their first contract to kill within two months: they were paid £1,800 by Leonard Thompson – known as 'Big Lenny' – to kill haulage contractor George Brett. Thompson held a grudge against Brett because he had given evidence against him in a court case after the two men had fought. Thompson had received a suspended prison sentence for malicious wounding.

They hatched a plan to lure Brett from his home to the church hall on the pretext that Childs, calling himself 'Mr Jennings', wanted some haulage work done. Childs said he went to Brett's home on 2 January 1975, dressed as a City businessman, complete with bowler hat, and Brett agreed to follow him in his car. When his car would not start, Brett got a rope to tow it and, tragically, it provided an opportunity for his 10-year-old son, Terry, to go along for the ride.

On arrival at the hall, Childs said he gave young Terry a teddy bear to hold. MacKenney brandished a stengun and twice shot Brett, 35, through the back of the head. As he did so, Childs held the boy with his hand over his mouth. The court heard how MacKenney then put the gun to the boy's head and killed him with a single shot.

Childs described how he and MacKenney had rowed over Terry's 'heartless and unnecessary' killing. He told the court: 'Had I had a gun when MacKenney killed that young boy I would have shot him to pieces. Afterwards it was too late – we were in schtuck.' He turned to the jury and said: 'As God is my witness that is right. I would not willingly become a child murderer.'

The court heard that Pinfold was summoned to the factory and asked to deal with the disposal of Brett's Mercedes. The two bodies were taken to the compressor shed at the back of the factory, where MacKenney sawed Brett's legs off. Both bodies were put in dustbins and transported to Childs' flat in his van. Childs said that before the bodies were removed from the hall, he had smeared Pinfold with blood to symbolise his involvement in the killings. Once at the flat, they laid plastic sheeting, where needed, and dismembered both bodies, burning them in the grate. The ashes were emptied into a canal. Childs said MacKenney kept one of Brett's eyes as a souvenir. He told the court: 'He washed it in my sink, then wrapped it in toilet paper.'

Next to die, in January 1975, was Robert Brown, an ex-wrestler who was on the run from Chelmsford Prison. He was living on a camp bed at the factory and he had seen all the blood after the murder of Eve. Childs told the court that he had been asking too many questions and that he and MacKenney agreed he needed 'taking out'. Childs said he lured Brown to his flat, where MacKenney shot him twice in the back of the head. But the bullets did not kill him and so they hacked away at him with axes. When even that failed, Childs said that he had 'unsheathed a short sword stick and stabbed him in the belly, running the blade up into his heart.'

According to Childs, the fifth killing was commissioned by builder Paul Morton-Thurtle in July 1978. (The jury later found him not guilty of procuring the murder trio's services.) Childs said Morton-Thurtle had hired him and MacKenney to kill Frederick Sherwood because he owed Sherwood money and was finding it difficult to repay it. He told the court that they agreed to kill Sherwood for £4,000, with payment being made by a deposit of £1,500 and then fortnightly instalments of £500.

After learning that Sherwood was trying to sell his car, Childs told him he wanted to buy it and arranged to make the purchase at MacKenney's home. When Sherwood arrived, Childs hit him across the head with a 21b hammer, and then MacKenney shot him.

The final victim was, according to Childs, murdered for a different motive. He said MacKenney was having an affair with Gwendoline Andrews, the wife of his friend Ronald. Childs told the court: 'MacKenney explained to me what a nice house she had and that altogether her and the money were an attractive parcel. He told me he intended to kill the woman's husband.'

Childs said he was paid £400 by MacKenney to assist in the killing in October 1978. He claimed that MacKenney told Andrews that he suspected his wife was having an affair and recommended a private detective who could check on her. Childs posed as the detective and Ronald went to his flat to meet him. Childs said: 'I offered him a drink and he sat down and was shot in the back of the head by MacKenney with a revolver fitted with a silencer.' He said they put the body in the bathroom and later MacKenney expressed grief at the killing. Childs testified: 'He said, "Ron forced me to kill him by not walking out and giving me his wife and his house."'

When Childs finished giving evidence, defence counsel Michael Mansfield called IRA prisoner Patrick Guilfoyle to the witness box. Guilfoyle told the court that Childs had admitted to him in prison that the men in the dock were innocent. He added that Childs had told him that he feared the police would charge his wife, Tina, with murder and said that he had 'botched it all up'. He said Childs had told him that his wife was the 'best butcher in London'. Guilfoyle said Childs often spoke about hating Henry MacKenney and that he had told him that the people he had 'squealed' on were innocent.

A second prisoner, Philip Cartwright, who was inside for theft and wounding, said Childs had indicated to him that MacKenny was innocent and that he was naming the wrong people involved in the killings.

Cross-examined by Mr Mansfield, Childs denied that since being in custody he had told fellow prisoners that he wanted to 'do Mr MacKenney down' or that he had delighted in telling people about the cutting-up and burning of bodies. In his closing speech, defence counsel said: 'The case against MacKenney rests almost entirely upon the word of one man, Childs, a man who is maniacally obsessed in thoughts and actions by violence.'

Despite the defence witnesses casting grave doubt on Childs' evidence and the absence of any concrete evidence, the jury believed much of what they had heard and found MacKenney guilty of murdering George Brett and his son Terry and of killing Frederick Sherwood and Ronald Andrews. He was found not guilty of the murders of Terence Eve and Robert Brown. Mr Justice May sentenced him to concurrent terms of life imprisonment on each murder, with a recommendation that he should serve 25 years.

Pinfold was sentenced to life imprisonment after being found guilty of murdering Eve. He was found not guilty of killing George Brett and Mr Brown and of helping to assist in the disposal of the body of Terry Brett. Paul Morton-Thurtle was found not guilty of murdering Mr Sherwood, and as he walked from the dock, MacKenney patted him on the back. Leonard Thompson was found not guilty of the murder of George Brett and his son.

At the Court of Appeal on 30 October 2003, Lord Chief Justice Lord Woolf was told that after giving evidence at the original-trial, Childs changed his story on numerous occasions. David Somekh, a consultant forensic psychiatrist, said Childs suffered from personality disorders. During the three-day hearing, it emerged that attempts to tell the trial jury about Childs' mental state were blocked. The court also heard revelations about the trial: although Pinfold was found guilty of having procured MacKenney to murder Eve, MacKenney was acquitted at the Old Bailey of having committed the murder. It didn't make sense.

It also emerged that before their trial, there were doubts within the Metropolitan Police about whether Eve had been murdered at all. James Harrison-Griffiths, a retired Detective Chief Inspector, said that he had attempted to investigate Eve's disappearance in 1976, but was warned off by Commander Bert Wickstead, Head of the Serious Crimes Group. Mr Harrison-Griffiths said: 'There was a conflict between senior officers. My Chief Superintendent was encouraging me and Commander Wickstead was discouraging me. There was politics involved.'

He added: 'Commander Wickstead told me that Terry Eve was living under an assumed name in South London. He told me that the future of the CID would be short-lived if I didn't stop this inquiry.' It was also revealed that Eve had every reason to disappear because there was a warrant for his arrest in connection with the hijacking of £75,000 worth of stereo equipment. Eve was facing five years in jail. Lawyers for MacKenney and Pinfold said the credibility of Childs as a witness would have been 'shot to pieces' had the jury had heard this evidence at the original trial.

Edward Fitzgerald QC, for MacKenney, called psychiatric evidence to show that Childs, who had since retracted his accusations against the pair, was a skilled fabricator and 'highly intelligent psychopath' who would 'say anything, at any time, when it suited him'. Mr Fitzgerald added: 'The jury did not know he was a person who suffered from a serious psychotic personality disorder. No one should be convicted on this man's word.'

Even his own confessions of murder were thrown into doubt by the evidence of Eve being alive after his supposed death.

Mr Fitzgerald revealed that Childs had admitted to more murders from prison, confessions which had been discredited. He said this showed him to be either a fantasist, who made up elaborate tales of gruesome murders for which he claimed responsibility and whose evidence should therefore be disregarded – or, if the confessions were true, the jury at the original trial had been 'profoundly misled'.

The barrister said that Childs had written a series of letters to various people, including Pinfold, admitting he had perjured himself at the trial in order to secure early release from prison. Mr Fitzgerald also challenged Childs' claim that he had disposed of victims' bodies by dismembering them and burning them on his domestic grate. At the original trial, the prosecution sought to prove the claim by producing evidence of a police experiment in which a dismembered pig carcass was burnt on the grate, but Mr Fitzgerald said the experiment was flawed. It involved having to hold a board in front of the fire no fewer than 37 times to maintain a sufficient draught. Yet Childs had testified in court that incinerating the victims was easy and that he was 'in a chair, having a drink, very relaxed' while the body parts were burning.

Lord Woolf said that when he read Childs' account of how he disposed of bodies, 'My common sense told me it was a pretty unlikely story.' When their convictions were formally quashed on 15 December 2003, Lord Woolf said fresh evidence showed that Childs was a 'pathological liar.'

Sitting with Mr Justice Aikens and Mr Justice Davis, the judge said they were 'unable to say where the truth lies as to these terrible murders' and that the evidence of Childs, although corroborated to some extent, was 'not capable of belief.'

Outside court, Pinfold and MacKenney hugged everyone in sight. MacKenney said: 'I'm shattered at the moment; I'm very relieved. It's been a long time coming – it's 23 years too late. The case should never have got to court in the first place. It was a fiasco.'

Pinfold said: 'Childs gave his story, and looking at the evidence, he was proved a liar.'

12

'I WAS MAD'

*'I wanted to get out of there in one piece. I was terrified
and scared.'*

One of Ayre's victims, aged 10

Name: Stephen Ayre
Crime: Rape and murder
Date of Conviction: 26 April 2006
Age at Conviction: 44

On 9 September 1984, loner Stephen Ayre met his on-off girlfriend, Irene Hudson, at the Mississippi Nightclub in Shipley, West Yorkshire. Irene, who had severe learning difficulties, left the club with him at around 9.30 that evening. She was never seen alive again.

Ayre, 23, took the vulnerable girl, who was just 5ft 3in tall, to a nearby field for sex, but as they kissed, Irene laughed and pushed him away. Ayre lost his footing and went sprawling onto the grass. As he got to his feet, Irene pushed him over again, only this time he went tumbling into a ditch full of nettles and he lost his temper.

Seething, he climbed up from the ditch and pushed Irene, 21, so hard in the chest that she fell flat on her back. By the time she got to her feet, he had a metal bar in his hand and he hit her across the head with it. She fell back to the ground, where Ayre battered her at least 20 more times until her head was a pulp and the surrounding grass was submerged in her blood. Ayre's white shirt was soaked red so he took it off, wiped his blood-spattered face with it and sprinted home to bed. Witnesses described seeing him running through the streets half-naked.

After his arrest, he recalled to police: 'Suddenly, she gave me another push and I slid down the banking into the nettles and then I was mad. My hand was on the metal bar. I suddenly hit Irene on the head with the bar – I don't know how many times.'

Irene, who had a mental age of 13, was reported missing when she failed to return home that night. The following day, her battered body was found dumped on a bridle path near Shipley railway station. Ayre was soon arrested. Several witnesses had seen him with Irene on the night of her murder and his blood-soaked shirt was found near her body.

Faced with the overwhelming evidence against him, Ayre pleaded guilty when his case came to court in March 1985. The judge heard how he had consumed a 'vast amount' of alcohol on the night of the murder and had told police: 'I was mad. I wanted to hurt her, but not to kill her.'

Before sentencing him, the judge heard how Ayre had recently received a suspended prison sentence for having sex with an underage girl. In mitigation, his lawyer told the court that Ayre had a disturbed childhood that had left him with 'a very low tolerance threshold and an extremely quick temper.' He was sentenced to life with a recommendation that he should serve at least 13 years before being eligible for parole.

Ayre remained in prison for 20 years after his first four requests for release were refused. His eventual release in April 2005 proved to be one of the most controversial parole mistakes in British history.

After he was released, Ayre moved into a probation service hostel. Within weeks, he broke the terms of his parole when he was caught drunk and disorderly in a street outside the area he was permitted to enter. The factors involving alcohol in Irene Hudson's murder seemingly ignored, he was given a conditional discharge.

He spent six months in the hostel and started work as a labourer at a Bradford factory in September of the same year. Peter Batty, works manager at the firm, said he was misled about Ayre's past by a probation officer. He recalled: 'I interviewed him and he came across as a nice, polite, quiet person. He told me he had served 21 years for murder. He said he had repeatedly hit his brother-in-law with a dustbin lid because the bloke was hitting his sister and he had died.

'We contacted his probation officer, who confirmed what he had told us and said he was not a danger to our employees. We knew what he said he had done was wrong, but because the bloke had been beating up his sister and he said it wasn't his intention to kill him, we didn't see him as a cold-blooded murderer and decided to give him a chance for a future.

'We employed him on 5 September and he was a very polite, obliging and hard-working employee. Everyone, including the women staff, thought he was a smashing fella.'

Such was Mr Batty's confidence in Ayre that he gave him a reference and paid his deposit when the Probation Service deemed him fit to live in society. In early October 2005 he moved into a flat on Bingley Road, Saltaire, West Yorkshire. His landlady, who asked not to be named, said Ayre rang her after seeing an advertisement in the local paper. She added: 'He seemed all right. He said he would take the flat and he came back with a reference from his employer, who paid the £200 bond and £330 for the first month's rent. Ayre gave me his contact numbers and sister's address, and everything seemed OK.'

The following February, Ayre took a 10-year-old boy to his rented flat, where he brutally raped him. Within hours he was back in police custody and he admitted that he had raped the youngster. He said he did it because he wanted to go back to prison.

Two months later, on 26 April 2006, Ayre appeared at Leeds Crown Court for sentencing. Prosecutor Gavin Howie told how Ayre – who had 'a psychopathic disorder, but not a mental illness' – spotted his victim playing in the street with a friend. He lured the child back to his place with the promise of a BMX bike. Mr Howie continued: 'He prevaricated at first at the door of the flat. He then physically picked up the boy and dragged him into the flat.'

The court was told that during the 30-minute ordeal the youngster was threatened with a Stanley knife. Throughout the horrific assault, the child was told that he'd have his throat slashed if he did not comply with his abductor's demands. Ayre turned the volume up on his television to drown out the lad's screams. The boy told police: 'I wanted to get out of there in one piece. I was terrified and scared.' After the attack, he ran back to his father's house and told him what had happened. The sickened parent sprinted to Ayre's flat to discover that he had fled.

At around 8.30 that night, Ayre handed himself in to police, telling them that he wanted to be back behind bars. He said: 'If it hadn't been that boy, it would have been someone else but I saw him and something fell into place.'

In mitigation, defence counsel Michelle Colborne said her client was deeply sorry for what he had done and had pleaded guilty at the earliest opportunity. Referring to the attack on the boy, she explained: 'It was a way out of the depression and inability to cope with life as it was for him at that stage.'

Sentencing him, Mr Justice Tugendhat said that Ayre posed a particular risk to young people if he was ever allowed back into the community. The judge told him: 'You have committed very serious offences. I have no doubt there is a high risk you will commit other serious and violent offences, if you were free to do so.' He said that Ayre had used a degree of planning to lure the youngster to the flat where he had carried out the 'gross indignities', adding: 'You do not understand the gravity of what you have done. You are extremely dangerous, and a particular risk to children and young people and other vulnerable people of both sexes.' The judge told how he had taken into account all the aggravating features, including the fact that a knife was used, the age of the victim and the nature of the offences, to come to the conclusion that Ayre should spend the rest of his life in prison.

He added: 'This is not an inquiry into how you were free to commit them [the offences]. It would not be appropriate for me to comment on that. I understand the family and the public will be concerned about certain aspects of this case.'

After the sentence, prosecutor Mr Howie said outside court: 'We welcome the sentence. This was a brutal and sadistic crime, carried out with the deliberate aim of being sent back behind bars. The sentence reflects the vile nature of the offences committed and the significant danger he continues to pose to the public.'

The case of Stephen Ayre brought about huge criticism of the parole and probation systems in the UK. The nature of his original crime and his prison record meant that he had four requests for parole refused before his release. He served 20 years against his recommended minimum tariff of 14 years laid down in 1985.

Yet when he was finally released, the Probation Service was far from rigorous in its supervision. When Ayre was caught, drunk and disorderly, in an area from which he was banned, he was given a conditional discharge when it was well within the powers of parole officers to send him back to jail. Furthermore, there is the question of how he was deemed safe to live in the community from which he abducted and raped the 10-year-old.

Despite the public outcry, it was announced in June 2007 that two inquiries into the circumstances surrounding his release by the Parole Board and the monitoring of him by West Yorkshire probation service were to be kept secret by the authorities. The reason, the Parole Board explained, was to protect Ayre's data protection rights. As a result the public do not know the background to how he was approved for release by the Parole Board at his fifth attempt. It is also not known how the West Yorkshire Probation Service monitored Ayre after his release and whether his probation officer understood that he was depressed, having difficulty coping with life and wanted to go back to prison.

It is also not clear if the Probation Service knew that Ayre had breached the terms of his parole when he was caught drunk and disorderly in an area from which he was banned. Whether probation officers faced disciplinary action is also not known.

Norman Brennan, Director of the Victims of Crime Trust, believes that the Probation Service should be held accountable. 'The public have an absolute right to know the details and the authorities have a duty of care to tell them what went wrong,' he said. 'People's lives are being devastated because of their mistakes.'

In June 2008, the father of Ayre's 10-year-old rape victim was informed by Secretary of State for Justice Jack Straw that the report would remain a secret, despite his repeated appeals. Appalled, he said: 'The police, the courts and the Probation Service failed my son and ruined his life and they have not done anything to put it right, and I really think they should.'

He added: 'For a lot of people this has passed on, but for me and my son it happened yesterday. He is a strong kid and I am very proud of him, but he deserves a lot better than this.'

13

'TONIGHT'S THE NIGHT'

'I find it difficult to foresee whether it will ever be safe to release someone who can shoot two little boys as they lie asleep in their beds.'

Trial judge Mr Justice Drake

Name: Jeremy Bamber
Crime: Mass murder
Date of Conviction: 28 October 1986
Age at Conviction: 25

At about 3.25am on Wednesday, 7 August 1985, an officer at Chelmsford Police Station answered a call from a terrified young man called Jeremy Bamber, who told him: 'My father's just phoned me, he said, "Please come over, your sister has gone crazy and has got a gun."'

So began the case of the White House Farm Murders, one of the most controversial in British criminal history – and one that still makes headlines today.

After his call to police, Bamber drove to the farm in Tolleshunt D'Arcy, Essex, from his home in the village of Goldhanger, three miles away. When he arrived at about 3.50am the 24-year-old was met by three policemen who were waiting outside. He told them: 'My sister's a nutter. I think something terrible has happened – there are guns inside.'

Armed police arrived at 5am and at just after 7.30, they smashed down the back door with a sledgehammer. Inside the 18th-century farmhouse, they found five dead bodies. Nevill Bamber, 61, was lying on the kitchen floor. He had been shot eight times in the head and body; he had also been badly beaten. Near to him was the telephone, lying off the hook.

June Bamber, also 61, was upstairs in the doorway of her bedroom. She had been shot once in bed and a further six times as she tried to escape her attacker. One of the bullets hit her right between the eyes. Meanwhile, Sheila Caffell – Jeremy's 'nutter' sister – was sprawled on the floor beside her parents' bed with an Anschutz semi-automatic rifle in her hands. The gun was laid across her chest and she had been shot twice in the throat. A Bible lay on the floor beside her.

Across the landing, Sheila's six-year-old twins, Nicholas and Daniel, were murdered while they slept. Nicholas was shot three times in the head and Daniel five times. Daniel still had his thumb in his mouth when police found them. When officers outside the farmhouse told Jeremy Bamber of the slaughter of his family, he threw up and went into a state of shock.

Essex police were convinced they had an open-and-shut case. Sheila, a 28-year-old former model nicknamed 'Bambi', had a history of mental illness. Two years earlier, she was diagnosed paranoid schizophrenic and underwent treatment at a psychiatric hospital. Her condition worsened after her recent split from the twins' father, sculptor Colin Caffell. She had expressed thoughts of killing herself and her children and she had a very difficult relationship with her strict, God-fearing adoptive parents (both she and Jeremy were adopted). Sheila was also in the habit of forgetting to take her medication.

Detectives were convinced she had lost control and had acted on her schizophrenic urges. All the evidence pointed to her killing her family before finally turning the gun on herself. When police checked the doors and windows after finding the bodies, they discovered that they were all locked from the inside. As far as they were concerned, the killer's identity was not in question.

Consequently, the house was not treated as a proper crime scene and much forensic evidence was obliterated or never gathered in the first place. Some 20 police officers were allowed to traipse in and out of the house and bloodstained bedding and carpets were destroyed.

At his family's funeral, nine days later, Jeremy Bamber was a mess. 'He was terribly distraught through the service and could barely walk behind the coffins,' recalled his cousin, David Boutflour. 'But when we were 100 yards down the road, out of sight of the [press] cameras and other people, Jeremy looked back at us and gave us the biggest grin. It was chilling. Peter, my brother-in-law, turned to me and said, "He did it, didn't he?"' Earlier that day, Bamber had commented that he hoped the press cameras would capture his good side.

After a tearful display at the graveside, Bamber took his friends out for a meal to celebrate. At the party afterwards the champagne and drugs were on him. He continued partying for several weeks, selling off his parents' furniture at London antique shops to fund his playboy lifestyle until his inheritance came through. Later, he treated a group of friends to a £6,000 holiday to Holland and flew one friend out to St Tropez for a five-star jaunt. As the funds from his parents' furniture ran dry, Bamber even touted soft-porn photos of his dead sister around the Sunday newspapers.

There were four people who, from the very outset, refused to believe the murder-followed-by-suicide story. Pamela Boutflour, June Bamber's sister, her husband Robert, and their children, David Boutflour and Anne Eaton, were convinced Sheila was not responsible. Their tenacity helped change the course of the inquiry.

On the evening of Friday, 9 August 1985 – three days after the slaughter – Essex police gave David and Anne the keys to the farmhouse. They went there the next morning, mainly to retrieve valuable items before Jeremy had the chance to sell them. But, as Anne

Eaton would later say, they had another reason for visiting the crime scene: 'I wanted to look around the house because I didn't believe the story that was going around. I wanted to look for myself, I wanted to look for clues.'

Her brother found a silencer, neatly wrapped in cloth, in Nevill Bamber's gun cupboard. He recognised it as belonging to the murder weapon and he was stunned. 'I thought every inch of the house would have been turned over and anything of relevance removed,' he said. 'It was a huge surprise to us to find such an essential piece of the gun left behind.' It would later turn out that no fewer than six police officers had checked the gun cupboard without noticing the silencer.

David saw that the silencer's outer plating had been damaged and that a small particle of red paint was lodged in the end of the barrel. The paint matched exactly the crimson paint on the kitchen mantelpiece where a recent indentation had been made. He deduced that the silencer had come into contact with the mantelpiece during some kind of struggle in the kitchen, probably while Nevill was fighting for his life.

Meanwhile, Anne was carrying out a thorough check of the upstairs rooms. She discovered that the fanlight of the kitchen window could be opened from the outside of the house, allowing an intruder access to the catch on the main opening section of the window. Her discovery flew in the face of Essex Police's assertion that all the doors and windows had been locked from the inside when the killings took place. 'Anyone could have got in there,' she said.

That afternoon, David noticed what appeared to be a tiny speck of blood on the muzzle rim of the silencer. There was also a grey hair attached to the device. Excited by the find, he immediately rang the police but it was two days before an officer came to collect it. The grey hair stuck to the silencer was lost on the way to the forensic laboratory. Home Office tests on blood found inside the barrel proved that it was of the same type as Sheila's. With the silencer fitted, the rifle would have been too long for anyone to have used it to commit suicide. In any case, Sheila could hardly have shot herself once in the throat, removed the silencer, taken it downstairs, wrapped it, put it in the gun cupboard and then made her way back upstairs to lie down close to her mother's corpse and shoot herself a second time.

The post-mortem examination of her body found that she had in her system a drug called Haloperidol, a tranquiliser with which she was being injected as part of her treatment for schizophrenia. The effects of the drug would have severely impaired her ability to accurately fire the gun no fewer than 25 times. Furthermore, the paint on the silencer matching the mantelpiece in the kitchen suggested her father had at one point grabbed the barrel of the rifle and struggled desperately before he was killed. Although 61-years-old, Nevill Bamber was a fit man and would have overpowered his waif-like, sedated young daughter with ease. The prospect of her battering the 6ft 4in farmer to death seemed remote.

A fortnight after the funerals and a month after the killings, Jeremy Bamber finished with his girlfriend, Julie Mugford. Soon afterwards she discovered that he had slept with one of her best friends. Fuelled by hurt and anger, she went to the police and told them that Bamber hated his parents and had repeatedly told her how he wanted them dead. She said he had made murderous threats – which she had previously dismissed as fantasies – about his 'old' father, his 'mad' mother and his sister who 'had nothing to live for'. On the night of the massacre, Bamber had phoned her and said simply, 'Tonight's the night.' She said he rang her again at around the same time as he called the police, saying: 'Everything is going well.' When she arrived at the farmhouse after the killings, Bamber took her to one side and said: 'I should have been an actor.'

After Julie Mugford's testimony and the detective work by Bamber's family, senior investigating officer, DCI Thomas 'Taff' Jones, was taken off the case for what were described as 'operational reasons'.

The new police team took a different view, believing Bamber had killed everyone to claim his inheritance and then tried to frame his sister for the murders.

The original investigation team appeared to attach no significance to the condition in which Sheila Caffell's body had been found. Despite blood being all over the floor in the kitchen, on the stairs and in the master bedroom, her bare feet were spotless. The ex-model's long, manicured fingernails were in salon-perfect condition – hardly those of a woman who had pulled a trigger 25 times and reloaded a magazine, holding 10 rounds, at least twice during the course of the killings. Forensic tests on her hands and nightdress found no significant traces of lead or gun oil, which would have been in abundance had she been the killer.

The Boutflour family told police that Sheila had no experience of firearms. 'She didn't know one end of a gun from another,' said Anne. In fact, only one person said she had used a gun before, and that was her brother.

Jeremy Bamber was arrested on 8 September 1985 as he returned from his holiday to St Tropez. In October of the following year, after 13 months on remand, his murder trial began at Chelmsford Crown Court.

Anthony Aldridge, QC, for the prosecution said that the blood inside the rifle silencer found at the farmhouse was the 'giveaway damning evidence' that Sheila Caffell could not have killed herself. He said: 'Sheila can't have taken off the silencer because she would have been dead after the second shot. It's far more likely that someone had shot everyone with the silencer on, then when he tried to fake the suicide by placing the rifle on the body, he realised she could not have shot herself. So, he removes it. There is only a small amount of blood on the outside – the size of a pinhead. He wouldn't have appreciated the giveaway, damning piece of evidence inside.'

Mr Aldridge said that as Sheila was not responsible for the killings, Bamber made a 'fatal mistake' when he rang police to tell them of the phone call he'd had from his father in which he described his sister 'going crazy' with a gun. The barrister explained: 'If the telephone call occurred, it meant Sheila was running amok with a gun. If he didn't get the call and he was lying, it meant it was Jeremy Bamber who did it and he was trying to cover it up.'

Bamber's ex-girlfriend, Julie Mugford, proved to be a star witness. The 22-year-old teacher gave evidence for more than five hours, often trembling and frequently sobbing. Throughout her appearance, Bamber avoided her occasional glances in his direction, but frequently shook his head as she spoke. She told the court that in late 1984 – about a year after they met – Bamber began telling her that he wished all his family were dead and that he had devised a plot to kill them. He told her that his father was getting old, his mother and sister were mad, and the twins were emotionally disturbed by their upbringing. He said that he would be doing the boys' father, who was divorced from his sister, a 'favour' by killing them.

Miss Mugford said that at first she did not take her boyfriend seriously but she was disturbed when his plans grew more elaborate. She told the court that by the summer of 1985, he had decided on shooting them and making it appear that his mentally ill sister was responsible. She said: 'Jeremy killed some rats on the farm with his bare hands to see if he could kill his family, and after doing so, he said he thought he could.'

She described how she spent the next few weeks in Bamber's company. 'He used to ask me if he was behaving OK, particularly in public,' she told the court. 'I said in respect of what had happened he was looking far too happy.' She could not understand how he was coping so well, but he told her that he had done everyone a favour and that there was nothing to feel guilty about.

Cross-examined by Mr Geoffrey Rivlin, QC, defending, Miss Mugford insisted she was not a 'scorned woman' seeking revenge but she agreed that the relationship had deteriorated in the weeks after the killings and that 'a barrier' had gone up between them. Asked why she took a month before going to the police, she said she understood the police were sure Sheila Caffell was responsible and that it was a closed case.

In his summing-up at the end of the 18-day trial, Mr Justice Drake told the jurors that if they believed the blood on the silencer was Sheila's they should convict. After considering the evidence for nine-and-a-half hours, the jury of seven men and five women found Jeremy Bamber guilty of the murders on a majority verdict of 10 to two.

Sentencing him to a minimum of 25 years in prison, the judge said: 'Your conduct in planning and carrying out the killing of five members of your family was evil almost beyond belief. It shows that you, young man though you are, have a warped, callous and evil mind concealed beneath an outwardly presentable and civilised manner.'

He added: 'I believe you did so partly out of greed because although you were well-off for your age, you were impatient for more money and possessions. But I believe you also killed out of an arrogance in your character which made you resent any form of parental restriction or criticism of your behaviour.

'I find it difficult to foresee whether it will ever be safe to release into the community someone who can plan and kill five members of their family and shoot two little boys asleep in their beds.' Douglas Hurd, the Home Secretary at the time, ruled that Bamber should never be released.

Essex police, who were severely criticised for their handling of the initial investigation, admitted after the trial that senior officers had shown a serious lack of judgment in the early stages of the inquiry. Deputy Chief Constable Ronald Stone said that the crime had been 'very cunningly arranged by a very cunning man' and admitted his officers deduced precisely what Bamber had intended. He told reporters: 'With the benefit of that perfect science hindsight, it could be said that judgments made at the scene of the crime by senior officers were misdirected.'

'TONIGHT'S THE NIGHT'

From the moment he was jailed, Jeremy Bamber has protested his innocence and has twice appealed against his conviction. His most recent appeal, in December 2002, focused on DNA evidence from blood on the silencer. Bamber's legal team had the blood tested, using DNA-related techniques not available at the time of the original investigation. The fresh evidence pointed to DNA belonging to June Bamber – not Sheila – being found on the silencer. Yet, when forensic scientists investigated the inside of the silencer still further, they found DNA which matched Sheila's, so flooring his argument. Rejecting the appeal, Mr Justice Kay said: 'In our judgment, the more we examined the detail of the case, the more likely we thought it to be that the jury were right.'

In May 2008, Bamber's lawyers tried and failed to have his whole life tariff reduced. High Court judge, Mr Justice Tugendhat, said: 'These murders were exceptionally serious. In my judgment you ought to spend the whole of the rest of your life in prison.'

A month earlier, Bamber attempted to have his prison status downgraded from category A to B, claiming he posed a lower risk and required a less severe regime inside.

In April 2007, he passed a lie detector test in Full Sutton Prison, near York. He was asked 12 questions, including: 'Did you shoot your family on 7 August 1985?'

He is now campaigning for a third appeal against his conviction and has employed controversial lawyer Giovanni Di Stefano – who has represented the likes of Saddam Hussein and Serbian war criminal Slobodan Milosevic – to head his legal team. Nicknamed 'The Devil's Advocate', Di Stefano says the new case for Bamber focuses on evidence gleaned from graphic police pictures of Sheila, which he claims were undisclosed at the original trial and the two subsequent appeals.

The pictures, taken by a police photographer who arrived at the farmhouse after 9am, allegedly show the blood still red and flowing from Sheila's wounds. Bamber's team say the new evidence puts the case into a fresh light. They argue that if blood was still leaking from Sheila's wounds, then she had died relatively recently, and certainly long after the time that Bamber met with police at around 3.50am. His lawyers also claim to have a police radio log proving that in the hours after meeting Bamber outside the farmhouse, officers believed they saw, through a bedroom window, someone alive inside the house. At the original trial, the officers put the sighting down to 'a shadow' or 'a trick of the light'. Di Stefano believes the new evidence proves they were right the first time.

He said: 'These photographs prove, at the very least, that Mr Bamber could not have killed his sister. Put it all together and it is a very bad picture of yet another possible miscarriage of justice, for which a man has paid with more than 20 years of his life.'

Whether the new evidence turns out to be as overwhelming as Bamber hopes remains to be seen, but his cousin, David Boutflour, insists: 'The fact is the man is guilty as hell. I really wish Jeremy wasn't a murderer and a liar, that he wasn't the one who killed five members of my family. Jeremy has probably convinced himself he didn't do it to the point he passed a lie detector test, but he did it, and he deserves to rot in jail for it.

'The Criminal Cases Review Commission really needs to stop being persuaded by publicity seekers. If Jeremy came out of prison, we're pretty sure he would come after us.'

14

'HANNIBAL THE CANNIBAL'

'It does not matter to them whether I am mad or bad. They do not know the answer and they do not care, just so long as I am kept out of sight and out of mind.'

Robert Maudsley

Name: Robert Maudsley
Crime: Quadruple murder
Date of Conviction: 16 March 1979
Age at Conviction: 25

At 11am on 26 February 1977, Broadmoor patient Robert Maudsley and fellow psychopath David Cheeseman snatched a third inmate, David Francis, from his room. They claimed Francis, a paedophile, had sexually assaulted a friend of theirs.

As they dragged him, kicking and screaming, across the corridor, four nurses intervened but they were threatened with knives fashioned from pieces of a dismantled radio. Maudsley and Cheeseman bundled Francis into an office and trussed him up with flex from a record player.

For more than nine sickening hours, the corridors rang with the sound of his screams. Staff recalled hearing him shout, 'God, no; God, no!' while the sadistic pair took their time in torturing him. Between punches, kicks and knife cuts, he pleaded for his life. After nine hours, just after 8pm, Maudsley garrotted Francis and finally put him out of his misery. He and Cheeseman held the body triumphantly above their heads, moving to the door so that guards and medical staff could see them through the window.

What happened next is the stuff of prison legend. According to one guard, when he and his colleagues entered the room, the dead man's head was 'cracked open like a boiled egg.' A spoon was hanging out of it and part of his brain was missing. It is believed Maudsley ate it.

Bizarrely, considering the crime had occurred inside a secure mental hospital, Maudsley was declared fit to stand trial for the murder and was sent to Wakefield High-Security Prison in West Yorkshire, where his reputation preceded him. The grisly killing earned him two prison nicknames: 'Blue', after the colour his victims turned and 'Spoons' in homage to the utensil he is said to have used to sample Francis's brain. When the serial killer film The Silence Of The Lambs was released 13 years later, the tabloid newspapers described him as the real-life Hannibal the Cannibal.

On 28 July 1978 – just five months after his arrival at Wakefield – a wild-eyed Maudsley strolled into a prison officer's room, placed a homemade knife on the desk and calmly announced: 'There will be two men short on the roll call.'

Shortly before morning exercise, the tall, wiry maniac had stood behind the door of his cell holding a knife crafted from a canteen soup spoon. He was waiting for his fellow inmate Salney Darwood, a 46-year-old sex offender who had been giving him French lessons. As Darwood entered the room, Maudsley pounced, frenziedly stabbing him in the back, neck and head. When his victim fell bleeding to the floor, he knelt over him and hacked away at his throat until he was sure he was dead. He then pushed the body under the bed and washed his blood-soaked hands.

With his weapon tucked into the waistband of his trousers, prisoner 467637 walked out to the yard, where he mixed with other inmates on exercise. An hour later, he spotted his next victim, William Roberts, who was lying face down on his bed. Maudsley – who had never met the man before – lunged at Roberts and stabbed him in the back of his head. When Roberts turned to face his deranged attacker, he was stabbed in his chest and face. Maudsley then lifted his victim and repeatedly banged his head against the wall with such force that chunks of plaster fell into the pool of blood on the floor.

Convicted of double murder the following year, the judge told Maudsley that he would spend the rest of his life in prison and he was inexplicably sent back to Wakefield. Unable to mix with other prisoners for his and their safety, Maudsley – now officially classed as 'Britain's Most Dangerous Prisoner' – was placed in solitary confinement, where he has remained for more than 30 years.

During his time in solitary, he has been moved to a number of high-security prisons, including Woodhill in Buckinghamshire and Parkhurst on the Isle of Wight, but he has spent the vast majority of his sentence at Wakefield. In 1983 a 'cage' was specially constructed for him in the basement of the jail, under F-Wing. A solid-steel door led to a bulletproof Perspex window, similar to the one through which Dr Lecter was observed in The Silence of the Lambs. The only furnishings were a table and chair made of compressed cardboard and a concrete slab, which served as a bed. Like Lecter, Maudsley was passed his meals and other items through a slot at the bottom of the window.

In an article in the *Sunday Express* in 2002, Maudsley described his life inside the cage:

At 8am breakfast is brought to my cage by my keepers and put under the inner gate, which has a gap at the bottom. It consists of cornflakes, a carton of prison milk, a one-inch container of jam and one of butter, two bread rolls and a bottle of hot water.

The milk is often sour, so I throw it and the cornflakes down the toilet and just eat the rolls with a cup of tea. This is the time I make applications to write letters or visiting orders. It is also the time I must request exercise. If I forget to ask, I am deemed not to need it.

If I have asked for exercise, six or seven officers take me out of the cage at 8.30am. First, I stand on a wooden box and spread my arms; then I am required to open my mouth, then stick out and lift my tongue. A keeper then gives me a rub-down, while another keeper uses a metal detector all over my body. I have to lift my feet for inspection.

If I disagree with any aspect of this procedure I am returned to my cage and deemed to have refused exercise. Exercise is for one hour. I am not allowed to smoke or bring anything to drink out into the exercise yard. If another inmate attempts to speak to me from his cell window, he could be given CC [cellular confinement].

The yard has CCTV cameras and is made of concrete or Tarmac. There are no trees, grass or flowers. It is bare, sterile and bleak. I find the enforced silence depressing. When the hour is up, I have to go through the search process and return to the cage. I leave my shoes outside the cage. From 9.30–11am I see no one.

At 11am lunch is placed through the gap. I usually only eat half as it is tasteless, bland and unwholesome. At this time I am usually given any mail and a prison newspaper.

At 5.30pm I am given the last meal of the day. I am given hot water to last until 8am. I am given two loaves of white sliced bread a week. This usually goes mouldy after a few days. No extra butter or jam is provided.

On Wednesday afternoons my keepers bring me my 'canteen' to my cage. These are goods from the prison shop. Usually I can only afford hand-rolled tobacco, plus cigarette papers and a large box of matches.

On Sundays I am meant to be given a kit change. If it happens, I get one pillowcase, two sheets, two towels, two pairs of socks, two pairs of underpants, two T-shirts and a set of one-piece overalls. If it doesn't happen, I have to stay in dirty clothes and sheets for another week.

For many years, Maudsley remained in the cage for 23 hours a day. In 2003 he was moved to solitary at Wakefield Prison's Close Supervision Centre – where he still resides – which was set up especially to house the most disruptive inmates in Britain. Once a day, he leaves his cell for an hour to walk around the 20 x 12ft exercise yard, where the walls are so high that the sun never shines. His every move is watched by at least five guards. It has been three decades since the 6ft 2in prisoner killed anyone, but no one is taking any chances.

The mental and physical effects of solitude have made Maudsley appear far older than his years. He is gaunt and sickly-looking, his skin a ghostly white from a lack of natural light. In letters to *The Times* in March 2000, Maudsley said: 'The prison authorities see me as a problem and their solution has been to put me into solitary confinement and throw away the key; to bury me alive in a concrete coffin. It does not matter to them whether I am mad or bad. They do not know the answer and they do not care, so long as I am kept out of sight and out of mind.'

He added: 'I am left to stagnate, vegetate and to regress; left to confront my solitary head-on with people who have eyes, but don't see and who have ears, but don't hear; who have mouths, but don't speak. My life in solitary is one long period of unbroken depression. All I have to look forward to is further mental breakdown and possible suicide. In many ways, I think this is what the authorities hope for. That way, the problem of Robert John Maudsley can be easily and swiftly resolved.'

Maudsley has a genius-level IQ and loves classical music, poetry and art. He studies the paintings of Claude Monet and Vincent Van Gogh and is keen to do an Open University degree in Art History.

He had a wretched upbringing. On 26 June 1953 he was born in

Liverpool to bad parents, who already had three young boys. His father, also called Robert, was a quick-tempered lorry driver, who had little time for family life. He and his wife Jean struggled to cope with their children and just before the young Robert's second birthday, he, his older brothers, Paul and Kevin, and big sister, Brenda, were deemed 'suffering from parental neglect' and taken into care by social services.

All four were moved to Nazareth House, a Roman-Catholic orphanage run by nuns in Liverpool. Several years later, it was decided that their parents – who had since had more offspring – were fit to take them back and they were moved home. Their new life was to be a relentless nightmare of sadistic physical and mental abuse.

Maudsley's brother Paul recalled: 'At the orphanage we had all got on really well. Our parents would come to visit, but they were just strangers. The nuns were our family and we all used to stick together. Then our parents took us home and we were subjected to physical abuse. It was something we'd never experienced before. They just picked on us, one by one, gave us a beating and sent us off to our room.'

The most brutal treatment, however, was reserved for little Robert. He said: 'All I remember of my childhood is the beatings. Once I was locked in a room for six months and my father only opened the door to come in to beat me, four to six times a day. He used to hit me with sticks or rods, and once he bust a .22 air rifle over my back.'

Eventually, social services took Robert away and his father told his siblings that he had died. He spent the next few years in various foster homes and when he was 16, he made his way down to London and found work as a labourer. Within six months he developed a drug addiction and began supplementing his income as a rent boy. In 1974, four years after his arrival in London, he was picked up for sex by another labourer, John Farrell. Once the deed was done, Farrell produced photographs of children he had abused and Maudsley flew into a rage and garrotted him. Later that year he was found guilty of manslaughter by diminished responsibility and sent to Broadmoor Hospital, where he told doctors he sometimes heard voices in his head, telling him to kill his parents.

At his last murder trial in 1979, Maudsley admitted that during his violent rages he imagined his victims were his mother and father. His lawyers argued the murders were the result of pent-up aggression resulting from his terrible childhood. 'When I kill, I think I have my parents in mind,' he said. 'If I had killed my parents in 1970, none of these people need have died. If I had killed them, then I would be walking around as a free man without a care in the world.'

Paul Maudsley is angry at the lack of treatment offered to his brother by the prison authorities. He said: 'As far as I can tell, the prison authorities are trying to break him. Every time they see him making a little progress they throw a spanner in the works. His troubles started because he got locked up on his own as a kid – all they do when they put him back there is bring all that trauma back to him. All I want for Robert is that he be treated like other prisoners, but it seems that's too much to ask.'

Norman Brennan of the Victims of Crime Trust says Maudsley forfeited his right to be treated like other prisoners when he murdered three of his fellow inmates: 'Maudsley is a psychopath. He's a danger to everyone he comes into contact with and we should not be bending over backwards and spending unnecessary time and resources pandering to his every wish.'

Dr Hugo Milne, a leading criminal psychologist who has spent many hours with other killers, including Yorkshire Ripper Peter Sutcliffe and Black Panther Donald Neilson, once said: 'Maudsley was the only one I've ever been frightened of.'

15

'THE TOWPATH STALKER'

*'We have got to piece our lives together again. Life will never be
the same for any of us.'*

Mother of victim

Name: Anthony Entwistle
Crime: Multiple rape and murder
Date of Conviction: 9 March 1988
Age at Conviction: 38

Walking along a secluded path alone at night, schoolgirl Michelle
Calvey was a dream target for Anthony Entwistle. The predator
was in his car, scouring the quiet roads around Blackburn, Lancashire,
for a vulnerable young female to satisfy his lust for violent sex. It was
Sunday, 10 April 1987 and Entwistle was enjoying his 18th day of
freedom after serving seven years of a ten-year prison sentence for a
string of vicious sex attacks.

Michelle, 16, had been to visit her aunt. She left at 9pm to catch the
bus home for supper with her mum, step-dad, two brothers and sister.
But a sex beast was following her every step.

Entwistle, 37, pounced on Michelle – who was just 5ft tall – on a
canal towpath close to her aunt's house. He bundled her into his car
and then drove her to a more secluded place, where he could abuse her
at will.

The following day, a rural policeman on his rounds found Michelle at Slipper Lowe, a woodland beauty spot on the fells above Darwen, about four miles from where she was abducted. No attempt had been made to hide her naked body, which had been openly dumped in a lovers' lane. She had been raped and strangled with a ligature. Police doctors were able to prove that she had been a virgin before the assault.

'It was a vicious attack,' said Detective Superintendent Bill Hacking at a press conference the next morning. He went on: 'It is possible she knew her attacker. He could have picked her up as she walked home. She was taken to the wooded area near Darwen by car and she would have had to be carried, or would have had to walk to the spot where her body was discovered. There had been no effort to conceal her. It is an area used by courting couples and someone may have seen something on Sunday night, which was a fine night.'

Routine police inquiries soon revealed that Entwistle was back on their patch after his prison stint. Within four days of the murder, he was arrested. The suspect initially claimed he was away for the weekend in Blackpool and did not return until the Monday evening. But he had no alibis and could not account for the several witnesses who had seen him in the Blackburn area during that period.

When told of the weight of evidence against him, he burst into tears and blurted to detectives: 'I didn't mean to harm her. It all went horribly wrong, it's like a nightmare.' He said he saw Michelle crying on the towpath close to her aunt's house and went over to comfort her. Entwistle, who police believe may have attacked upwards of 20 lone women at night, said he was worried about the girl because she was alone in the dark.

At his trial at Preston Crown Court the following March, he said from the dock: 'She was in a secluded area. I felt she was in danger of being harmed by someone or herself.' He said he asked Michelle if she wanted a lift home but she declined his offer and asked him to leave her alone. Entwistle was unable to do so. He admitted to the court: 'I could not get her out of my mind, so I went back.'

Entwistle then spun a story that appalled the police and members of Michelle's family, who sat in the gallery. He said that when he approached the upset girl a second time, she willingly went with him to his car. He claimed she 'needed loving' and they agreed to drive to a 'quiet place' in the nearby hills. Once there, he alleged, they climbed into the back seat of his car, took off their clothes and had consensual sex.

Prosecution counsel Richard Henriques asked him how Michelle ended up dead as a result of this apparently shared passion. Entwistle claimed that as Michelle got dressed, he told her he had to take her home. He said this made her 'hysterical', adding: 'She started crying and screaming, and trying to get out of the car. I was trying to do two things at once – starting the car and holding her back.'

Entwistle recounted that as there were courting couples nearby, he tried to shut Michelle up and in panic put her T-shirt around her face and twisted the ends to hold her firm. He explained to the hushed court: 'I remember putting my hand over her mouth and then around her throat. I had the T-shirt and put it round her neck. She was unconscious and I realised something was seriously wrong with her: she just went still.'

He said he tried to rouse her and when he realised Michelle was dead, he stripped her naked and drove her a short way to the spot where she was found the following morning. Then he drove home and went to bed, but he could not sleep so he washed his car and went to a late-night garage to buy petrol. He said he then panicked and drove to a secluded spot nearby known as Pickup Bank, where he burned Michelle's clothes.

Prosecution counsel told the court that when charged with the murder, Entwistle said to police: 'I did not mean to harm the girl – it was a complete accident.' The barrister then turned to the jury and said: 'This was no accident.' Next, he listed the accused's damning list of previous convictions including how, in October 1973, he attacked a woman who was walking along a canal towpath. He threw her to the ground and raped her while tightening a knotted stocking around her neck. Two months later, he raped a 15-year old girl, who he choked with a cravat.

For those crimes, Entwistle was sentenced to 10 years in jail by a judge who branded him 'an appalling danger' to any woman found alone on the streets at night. The court heard that within weeks of his release for that crime, in March 1980, the accused attacked another woman. He dragged her from the street and over barbed wire into fields, where he indecently assaulted her while tightening a rope around her neck.

In May of that year he jumped on a girl from behind, put a rope about her neck and dragged her into an alleyway behind a pub. The victim's cries alerted passers-by and he fled without going further.

Nine days later he attacked another girl from behind, putting his hand over her mouth and again placing a rope around her neck. A taxi driver saw him standing over the girl with his trousers around his ankles, and Entwistle fled.

On another occasion a 48-year-old woman opened her front door to find Entwistle, wearing a stocking mask and brandishing a piece of broken glass. He rushed into her home, but the woman screamed and he fled. That same night, his perverted desires unsatisfied, he pounced on a 24-year-old housewife on her way home from her supermarket job. Again, her screams saved her.

Days after that assault, he attacked the babysitter of his two young children as she slept in the spare bedroom of the family home. He repeatedly raped the teenager as he chatted to her about his marriage problems.

Another victim was a nurse who was on her way home from a hospital in Blackburn. He put a ligature around her neck and dragged her into bushes before assaulting her. Unlike his previous crimes, he threatened to kill the young woman if she dared scream.

The prosecutor explained that it was while on parole for the latest in a long list of sex crimes that Entwistle picked out Michelle to rape and murder. Obvious parallels between his previous crimes and the evidence against him meant that the jury of seven women and five men took just 90 minutes to reach their unanimous guilty verdict after the three-day trial. Sentencing him, Judge Mr Justice Rose recommended a minimum of 25 years behind bars. He warned him: 'Don't assume you will be released at the end of that time.' At those words, Entwistle, dressed in a brown pinstriped suit, rolled his eyes upwards. The judge added: 'I have no doubt that you killed Michelle in the course of, or the furtherance of rape. It is the most horrifying event in an appalling catalogue of attacks on young women you carried out during the brief time you were at liberty in 15 years. You are now 38. It seems to me that you are likely to be a menace to young women for many years to come.' Home Secretary Douglas Hurd later ordered Entwistle to die in jail.

Outside court, Michelle's mother, Annette Dean, told how she was unable to sit through Entwistle's lies. 'I walked out. I was sick to my stomach', she said. 'It was important for me to be there for my own peace of mind and to see him get as much as they could give him, but Entwistle will still get out again one day. They should bring back hanging for blokes like him, who can do that to a young girl of 16. It has been horrible for us during the trial. We have still got to piece our lives together again. Life will never be the same for any of us.'

Fighting back tears, she continued: 'Michelle was the best daughter I could have wished for. I am heartbroken, and always will be.'

16

'THE MOORS MURDERER'

'Do you believe me now?'

Ian Brady (after his final killing)

Name: Ian Brady
Crime: Serial murder
Date of Conviction: 6 May 1966
Age at Conviction: 28

The tape recording heard at Chester Assizes in 1966 was arguably the most harrowing any British jury has been subjected to. Ten-year-old Lesley-Ann Downey pleaded for her life, calling for her mother as the taunts of her killers rang in the background. She was stripped, gagged and finally strangled with a piece of string.

Hardened reporters wept openly on the press bench in the courtroom. Several needed time off work with stress following what they had heard. One journalist's first act on his return home from court that day was to burn the shoes he wore at Saddleworth Moor as he covered the earlier parts of the case. He figured the once peat-caked shoes would always remind him of that harrowing recording.

The case had become the most notorious in British history: the Moors Murders.

Ian Brady and Myra Hindley met at the office of a small firm called

Millwards Merchandising near Manchester, in 1961. Their first date was to watch the film, Trial At Nuremburg, which was about the prosecution of Nazi leaders following World War II. Hindley was an 18-year-old secretary and Brady, then 21, was a clerk. Up to that time, the bleached-blonde teenager had been described as a normal Catholic girl, who left school at 15 to train as a typist. The impressionable youngster soon became fascinated by Brady's obsession with fascism and the violent pornographic writings of the French aristocrat, the Marquis de Sade. Soon they became lovers and by 1963, they were killers.

Their first victim was 16-year-old Pauline Reade, a neighbour of Hindley's. Pauline had been on her way to a dance in the Crumpsall suburb of Manchester on 12 July 1963. As she walked along the road, Hindley pulled up in a battered car and offered her a lift. Pauline knew the peroxide blonde to be the sister of a girl called Maureen who lived next-door-but-one.

Once Pauline was in the car, Hindley asked if she'd mind helping her to look for a lost glove. She promised she would drive her to the dance afterwards and pointed to a pile of pop records she could choose from as a reward if they found the glove. Pauline agreed – unaware Ian Brady was following them on a motorbike.

The car pulled to a stop on Saddleworth Moor, where Hindley claimed to have mislaid the glove. It was, of course, a trap and Brady pounced, smashing his young victim's skull with a shovel. The Nazi-crazed fiend then raped the girl before slitting her throat with a knife, almost decapitating her. Pauline was buried in a 3ft deep grave on the Moors, where her body remained undiscovered for 24 years.

The killer pair struck again on 23 November 1963, when their victim was 12-year-old John Kilbride. Hindley asked for the youngster's help in carrying some boxes. When he got into the car, Brady was sitting in the back. Terrified, John was driven up to the Moors, where Brady led him away from the road and attempted to slit his throat. He failed, but completed the murder with a shoelace.

Another 12-year-old, Keith Bennett, became the killers' third victim on 16 June 1964. He too was lured into the car and driven up to the Moors. Led into a ravine by Brady, he was strangled with a piece of string while Hindley took photographs from above.

Victim number four was 10-year-old Lesley-Ann Downey, who was lured away from a fair in the Ancoats district of Manchester on Boxing Day, 1964. The little girl was taken to the home that Hindley shared with her grandmother in Wardle Brook Avenue, Hattersley. Brady had recently moved into the house.

Inside, Lesley-Ann was forced to strip and pose for obscene photographs – sometimes bound, sometimes gagged, at one time in a kneeling position of prayer. Throughout the torments, her piteous cries for mercy and pleas to be released were recorded by Hindley on a reel-to-reel tape recorder. It was this recording that so horrified the courtroom less than two years later.

Lesley-Ann was raped and killed. The next day, Brady drove her body to Saddleworth Moor and buried it. Ten months later, her remains were discovered.

The final killing was that of 17-year-old Edward Evans, who was lured to the couple's house and hacked to death with an axe while Hindley's grandmother slept upstairs. Brady later claimed that Edward was gay and had been tempted back with the promise of sex, but this was never proved.

Crucially, the killing was witnessed by Hindley's brother-in-law David Smith, husband of Myra's younger sister, Maureen. For a year, Brady had been 'grooming' Smith, a notorious local thug, to become the third person in the murderous gang. Smith was in the kitchen when he heard screams and was ordered by Hindley to 'run upstairs and help Ian'.

He watched in horror as Brady, in a murderous frenzy, smashed Edward's skull with an axe before strangling him with electrical flex. Smith insisted it was fear for his own life that made him follow the orders to clear the room of the grisly remains and carry the body to an upstairs room wrapped in polythene.

Smith had always dismissed Brady's boasts of earlier murders. When the task was complete and Edward was wrapped tightly in polythene, Brady turned to his accomplice and asked: 'Do you believe me now?'

After agreeing to meet Brady the next afternoon to dispose of the body, Smith sprinted home, where his first act was to be sick in the bathroom. Waking his sleeping wife, he told her of the killing he had just witnessed. Three hours later Smith called the police station at Hyde – a town later made notorious as the base of serial killer Dr Harold Shipman – and reported what he had seen to the duty officer.

The next day Superintendent Bob Talbot arrived at Hindley's home. The sullen blonde answered the door and the senior policeman explained to the pair that he was investigating a violent act that had taken place the previous night and asked to see the upstairs room. Eventually Hindley and Brady relented, and on entering the spare bedroom Talbot and his colleagues found the body of Edward Evans. Brady was immediately arrested. During questioning he insisted that Hindley had nothing to do with the killing and said his sole accomplice had been David Smith.

Hindley's involvement was exposed when a ticket found in her prayer book led officers to a left-luggage locker in a Manchester railway station. Inside were two suitcases crammed with evidence implicating Hindley and her lover. She was arrested and charged. A police search for evidence uncovered photographs, the recording of Lesley-Ann Downey and a photograph of Hindley with her dog, Puppet. The dog was staring into what appeared to be a freshly dug gravesite, which local officers recognised to be Saddleworth Moor. A grim search of the bleak upland area began and within two weeks the bodies of Lesley-Ann Downey and John Kilbride had been found.

On 6 May 1966, after a 15-day trial, Brady was found guilty of the murders of John Kilbride, Lesley-Ann Downey and Edward Evans, and handed down three life sentences. He would have hanged, but just five months earlier Parliament had abolished the death penalty, to the dismay of the furious crowds outside the courthouse who had to be restrained by a police cordon throughout the trial.

Hindley was given two life sentences for the murders of Lesley-Ann Downey and Edward Evans.

Trial judge Mr Justice Fenton Atkinson described the Moors Murderers as 'two sadistic killers of the utmost depravity.' He singled out Brady as 'wicked beyond belief.'

In 1982, Lord Chief Justice Lane imposed a 40-year minimum tariff on Brady and Hindley, making them eligible for parole in 2005. This was increased to a whole life tariff by Home Secretary David Waddington in 1990, a decision confirmed by his successor, Michael Howard, in 1994. Hindley made successive attempts to have her whole life ruling overturned but failed every time.

Part of one bid for freedom, in 1987, was coming clean over the killing of Keith Bennett and Pauline Reade. After months of digging on the Moors, Pauline's body was found but still there was no trace of Keith.

On 15 November 2002, Hindley died of a heart attack, less than two weeks before the House of Lords stripped the Home Secretary of the power to set tariffs on prisoners.

Ian Brady spent 19 years in Parkhurst Prison on the Isle of Wight before being declared criminally insane in November 1985. He was sent to Broadmoor secure mental hospital and then to Ashworth on Merseyside, where he currently resides.

In contrast to his accomplice, Brady has indicated that he does not want to be released and insists on the right to be left to die in jail. He has now been on hunger strike for nine years and is force-fed three times a day.

Ian Brady was born Ian Duncan Stewart at Rottenrow Hospital in Glasgow, on 2 January 1938. Unable to cope with her new arrival, his mother Peggy gave him up for adoption to a couple called John and Mary Sloane. Little is known about the Sloanes, who lived in the tough Gorbals district in the Scottish city. John was a 39-year-old grain storeman, while his wife worked in a cotton mill. They already had four children and the newly-extended family was crammed into a two-room flat with outside toilets. His natural mother made frequent visits and although she was referred to as 'Aunty' Peggy, Brady claims he knew her real relationship to him from an early age.

In an exchange of letters with *News of the World* journalists in 2005, Brady recalled: 'I was brought up as a member of the family and also had many weekly visits from my mother, thus illustrating it was possible to have a happy life in the Gorbals, as well as an exciting one during the War.'

Aged 11, he won a place at Shawlands Academy, where he was described as 'Bright, but lazy'. Two years later, in 1951, he was given five months' probation for housebreaking. During this time he developed his obsession with the Nazis.

His brushes with the law continued, and in November 1954 a sheriff ordered that he should leave Glasgow and live with his natural mother, who had moved to Manchester and married an Irish labourer called Patrick Brady. The young Ian took the name of his stepfather and secured several jobs, including one at Manchester's famous Boddington's Brewery. But the stealing continued and several spells in borstal followed. Eventually he served a three-year sentence in the city's tough Strangeways Prison.

In 1959, Brady found work as a clerk at Millwards Merchandising, where he met Hindley two years later.

Behind hospital bars, Brady has not served his time quietly, almost taunting the families of his victims. Now in his seventies and weighing seven stone, he is campaigning to be moved to a regular prison, where it would be illegal to force-feed him. He spends his time watching TV documentaries (albeit with fading sight) and smoking up to 70 roll-ups a day. As he is being force-fed, saliva has rotted the enamel from his teeth and he is half-crippled by a degenerative back condition. Without the force-feeding – a process that involves inserting a tube into his stomach via his nose – doctors say he would be dead within 10 days.

It would have been impossible to forget Ian Brady because of his crimes, but to ensure continued notoriety, the killer has cultivated contacts with journalists, through whom he issues personal appeals. One, in 2006, read: 'The Home Office has made it clear I will never be released. Therefore I should not be held in a hospital.'

He added: 'In 1998 I chose to stop all social phone calls and visits when Ashworth commenced taping phones and monitoring visits.

'I have had untreated cataracts for seven years as Ashworth considers outside hospital treatment would attract unwarranted public attention to my condition. So my reading is negligible and is added by clip magnification sent by a friend.'

Since 2006, the killer has been advised by controversial and colourful lawyer, the 'Devil's Advocate' Giovanni de Stefano. He consults with his client in Ashworth via video link from his Rome office, while two hospital staff look on.

Di Stefano dropped a bombshell in January 2008, indicating his client was about to confess to the killing of a 14-year-old hitchhiker identified as 'JT', thought to be Jenny Tighe. Jenny disappeared from a children's home in Oldham on 30 December 1964, at the height of Brady and Hindley's murderous rampage.

Jenny was the product of a broken home and when she went missing those close to her believed she had fled to London – she had run away many times before. Police have dismissed Brady's claim as 'hogwash' and a cynical marketing tool by his lawyer. Jenny Tighe remains officially a missing person.

But di Stefano challenged police: 'If it turns out that JT or any more children were murdered by Brady and Hindley, then I would invite

Greater Manchester Police to prosecute my client. If Brady is fit to plead in court, then he is not mad and cannot stay in Ashworth.'

In 2007, it emerged that Brady has been allowed to retain photographs taken on Saddleworth Moor in 1964, potentially giving clues as to the location of Keith Bennett's grave. Frustratingly, because Brady was never charged with Keith's murder, the police have no power to apply for a warrant to seize the pictures and the killer is not about to surrender them.

Brady even wrote a book in 2001 called *The Gates of Janus: Serial Killing and Its Analysis*. To widespread fury, the work was published by an underground American publisher called Feral House. His continued games are a final insult to the memories of his victims and a source of continued anguish to their families. In 2006, he let it be known that when he eventually dies he would like to be buried in his home city of Glasgow. Winnie Johnson, the mother of Keith Bennett, said: 'He should not be allowed a proper burial when his victims didn't get one. Keith is still up on Saddleworth Moor and never got a proper burial, so why should Brady get one?'

Jackie Powell was Brady's Mental Health Advocate – an independent specialist who represents psychiatric patients – at Ashworth. She said: 'The only time I saw Ian Brady cry was when he was talking about the death of his mother, Peggy. His emotions for her came to the surface. He was angry she'd suffered for decades simply because she was his mother.

'He was bitter about not being able to attend her funeral and angry that, when he visited her for the last time, they were not left alone.'

Ms Powell added: 'He believes he has the right to die, and having spent a lot of time with him, I believe he's right.'

17

'THE MAN IN BLACK'

'You are as dangerous a man as it is possible to find.'

Sentencing judge Mr Justice Kerr

Name: Peter Moore
Crime: Quadruple murder
Date of Conviction: 29 November 1996
Age at Conviction: 50

Violent and sadistic predator Peter Moore was the 'Man In Black'. At night, he lurked in the gay haunts of North Wales, attacking his victims in a way designed to cause maximum terror, always dressed in black from head to toe. 'Black was his uniform,' said prosecuting barrister Alex Carlile, QC, at Moore's trial in November 1996 for the brutal murders of four men. 'He was the man in black, with black clothes, black thoughts, and the blackest of deeds.'

Homosexual Moore, 50, had been committing violent assaults on fellow gay men for nearly 20 years. Police believe he was responsible for at least 50 attacks during that period. Each time he used a large knife or truncheon to terrorise, dominate and humiliate his victims before disappearing into the night.

He had an unhealthy interest in Nazism, often wearing Nazi-style caps, leather boots and other black leather apparel. He even sported a moustache like Adolf Hitler's. Mr Carlile told Mold Crown Court: 'He thought it gave him the dominant and overbearing appearance he sought to frighten his victims and for his own sexual gratification.'

Moore lived alone in St Asaph Avenue, Kinmel Bay, Clwyd, after the death of his devoted mother in May 1994. She called him – her only child – the 'miracle son' after having him in her mid-forties. When his father died in 1979, he and his mother became inseparable and did everything together. Mrs Moore was very proud of her Peter, who ran a successful chain of small cinemas, and he returned her praise with expensive treats, from meals out to holidays abroad. Police believe his mother's death in May 1994 may have triggered the change in his criminal behaviour, from sadistic attacks to serial killing.

His first murder victim was Henry Roberts, a 56-year-old retired railwayman, who he killed in late September 1995 with a £25 hunting knife he bought as a 49th birthday present to himself. Henry lived alone in a filthy and ramshackle cottage on the outskirts of Caergeiliog, Anglesey. The loner was well off, courtesy of inheritances and a large redundancy payment from his former employer. His money went on taxis to the Sportsman's Inn two miles away, where he was a virtual fixture, paying for every round with a banknote and feeding the change into the pub's fruit machine. Despite his wealth, he chose to live in squalor, with rubbish piled high on each surface and carpets encrusted with dog faeces.

Henry's cottage stood off the A5 on Moore's route home from his cinema in Holyhead, which he visited late at night, once or twice a week. By coincidence, Henry was also interested in Nazi paraphernalia and had a Nazi flag on the wall of his home.

Fellow drinkers at the Sportsman were unaware of Henry's unsavoury domestic life and he was well regarded by those who knew him. When he failed to turn up at the pub for the third day running, one of the regulars visited his home to check he was OK. He found his body lying face down near an outhouse; his trousers were round his ankles and there was a stab wound to each buttock. The rest of his body was riddled with knife wounds: 14 to the front and 13 to the back. 'He had been killed by an attack of frenzied and sadistic viciousness,' said the prosecutor at the trial. Deep cuts to his hands and arms showed that he'd tried to defend himself against the attack. He died from a single stab wound to the heart. After the killing, Moore took Henry's Swastika flag as a trophy.

Next to die was Edward Carthy, 28, described in court as 'a rather sad figure'. Prosecution counsel added: 'He was a young drug addict and a drunk – a disaster waiting to happen.' Edward, from Birkenhead, was openly homosexual and frequented Paco's gay bar on Stanley Street, Liverpool. One Friday in early October, Moore visited Paco's to scout for prey and met Edward, who he recalled was very drunk.

The young man latched onto Moore, wanting him to drive him home for sex. Instead, Moore drove him to a forest in North Wales. Moore told police that when Edward realised he was not being driven back to Birkenhead, he became suspicious and tried to jump out of the van. 'I think he got a bit frightened, actually,' the killer recalled. In the forest, Moore stabbed him four times, killing him.

After his arrest in December 1995, Moore led police to Edward's badly decomposed body. He drew them a map showing where he had dumped it in the trees. By then foxes had ripped off his head and one of his arms.

His third victim was Keith Randles, 49, from Chester. Keith, who was divorced with two daughters, had lost his long-term middle management job, but managed to find work as a traffic safety officer guarding a set of roadworks on the A5, the main road across Anglesey. On 30 November, Keith bought fish and chips from a local takeaway and settled down for the night in the caravan he occupied on the roadworks' compound. Moore, again returning late at night on the A5 from his Holyhead cinema, knocked on the caravan door, dragged Keith outside and repeatedly stabbed him. Construction workers arriving for work at 7.30 the next morning found him lying dead on his back, covered in blood.

Moore made detailed confessions that were 'disturbing, chilling and callous', describing how he killed Keith for pleasure. On his arrest, he delighted in telling police that Keith had pleaded for his life on behalf of his grandchildren and asked him why he was doing it. He had replied with one word: 'Fun'. Detectives asked Moore how Keith reacted and he replied: 'He looked nonplussed.' A detective asked him: 'Would you say that at that point he accepted the inevitable?' Moore had replied: 'No, he carried on screaming.' Asked if he had enjoyed it, Moore said: 'There was a certain enjoyment from it, but the enjoyment certainly wasn't sexual. Like everything, it was a job well done. You know, the job was done.' This time, he took the victim's video recorder and mobile phone as trophies.

The last man to die was married father-of-two Tony Davies. He lived with his family in the Colwyn Bay area and worked at the local crematorium in Mochdre. On the afternoon of Sunday, 17 December, Tony, 35, had taken his aunt to the cemetery to put flowers on her husband's grave, but she fell and broke her leg and they spent the rest of the day in hospital. At 11pm, he told his wife Sheila that he was going out to his aunt's to check that she was settling down for the night. He never returned and at 4.30 the next morning, Sheila phoned the aunt, who told her that he had left her home three hours earlier.

After leaving, Tony drove to Pensarn Beach, a known haunt for gay men looking for casual sex. At 6.12am a policeman found his blood-soaked body a few hundred feet away from his car. Moore later told police that he had been cruising around, looking for someone to kill, and had ended up at the beach. He said he watched Tony get out of his car, light a cigarette and walk to the water's edge. When Moore got to him, he found him with his trousers round his ankles. 'I just took the knife out and stabbed him,' he told police. 'I think he screamed or shouted a bit.' A duffel coat belonging to Tony was later found in Moore's kitchen and his keys were in the killer's fishpond.

The brutal murders sent shockwaves through the gay community in North Wales and Moore was caught after the deputy editor of the Gay

Times persuaded police to open a confidential hotline. Among the names passed on anonymously was one that came up many times. It was Peter Moore, and one man who left a message said he had been taken back to Moore's place six months earlier, where he had been tortured for several hours. He said he kept quiet about the episode because he felt ashamed.

On 21 December 1995, police visited Moore at home. As detectives questioned him about the murders, others searched the house. In his bedroom they found many of the tools of sexual domination, including a black wooden truncheon, handcuffs and rubber gags. In the wardrobe there was a staff sergeant's uniform, leather trousers, long black boots and leather caps. On his bedside table was a book entitled The World's Most Evil Men. As well as his many suspicious belongings, police also found a number of items stolen from his victims, including the Nazi flag taken from Henry Roberts and several sets of keys.

He was arrested and taken to Llandudno police station where, during 14 hours of questioning spread over two days, he delighted in telling detectives about his crimes. His blood also matched that of a sample found on the beach where Anthony Davies had been slaughtered. He explained that he had cut himself on his knife as he stabbed the man. Police were aware of only three murders, so he then told them of the fourth: 'There's one you haven't found yet, a young man I picked up in Paco's club in Liverpool. I drove him to North Wales to a forest and I murdered him. The body is in the woods there; that was about 12 weeks ago.'

Relishing the attention, Moore said to shocked detectives: 'I used the same knife on them all.' Asked why he bought the knife, he said: 'To kill somebody. With the sole intent of killing somebody.' He added that killing 'relieved pressure on me, it was a relief from stress. I don't feel any remorse whatsoever for what I've done.'

As well as the murders, he confessed to many more crimes, informing police: 'I want to tell you that I have been responsible for a lot of things going back to the 70s, like attacks on men in the Conwy Valley, assaults, another on a tramp in a garage... In the 70s and 80s, mostly sexual.'

Despite his detailed confessions to police, Moore pleaded not guilty at his trial which began on 11 November 1996, claiming a gay lover of his called Alan, whom he nicknamed 'Jason', committed the murders. Eric Somerset-Jones, QC, defending, told the jury how Moore had met 'Jason' in the 'twilight world' of gay sado-masochist sex in the summer of 1995. On the 11th day of his trial, when asked how Jason had earned his nickname, Moore said: 'He was fascinated by knives, he always had a flick knife with him, so I called him Jason after the character in Friday the 13th.'

In court, Moore said it was Jason who had 'wielded the knife' while he remained at a distance. When questioned by Mr Somerset-Jones about the murder of Anthony Davies, he burst into tears as he described his death. He said that he cradled him as he bled after Jason had stabbed him six times. 'He said he loved his wife and that he had two children. Then he gave a sigh and he died on the beach; he died in my arms.'

Moore said he had been an unwilling bystander to all the murders and that he had argued with Jason to make him stop. The jury heard how on one occasion Moore was in fear for his life after Jason had forced him to drive at knifepoint to where Keith Randles was murdered. Moore had been 'heartbroken' by Tony Davies' killing and had fought with Jason, a waiter, who he had not seen again after his arrest. Asked how he felt about Jason now, he answered: 'I still love him.' Asked by prosecution counsel why he had confessed to the police about the killing, he replied: 'I led them up the garden path and back because I wanted Jason to get away.' Mr Carlile then asked Moore to look around the court. 'Do you see Jason here?' he asked. Moore replied: 'No.' 'He doesn't exist?' suggested Mr Carlile. Moore replied: 'He does exist; he's still out there – I don't think he will ever stop.'

At one point he referred to Jason in the past tense, but quickly corrected himself. 'Do you have reason to believe that he no longer exists?' Mr Carlile asked. 'I know he does still exist,' was his reply. 'Is Jason just your imagination, and how you would like yourself to be – but even more aggressive, even more cruel?' Mr Carlile asked. Moore replied: 'No, no, no!' But he agreed that he liked to dress in black because the clothes made him appear 'aggressive and dominating, and provoked fear in those he attacked.' He agreed that he was fascinated by knives and had twice stabbed men during homosexual assaults; he also admitted that he kept handcuffs and a truncheon in his car, 'on the off-chance of meeting a man who he could assault.' 'You're a bad man, aren't you, and you like other bad men?' Mr Carlile suggested. Moore replied: 'Yes.'

Mr Carlile revealed that Moore told police he saw yellow flashes in his eyes 'like zigzags' immediately prior to and during the murders. 'But there is no evidence at all of a psychiatric nature in this case,' the barrister said. 'There is no question of insanity; there is no question of diminished responsibility.' He told the jury: 'This most dangerous of men killed coldly – for fun, to relieve tension, to gratify his sadistic instincts.'

The jury of eight men and four women did not believe Moore's story about the mysterious Jason and after two hours and 35 minutes' deliberations, they found him guilty of all four murders. Sentencing him to four life terms, Mr Justice Kerr told Moore, who wore his trademark black shirt and tie: 'I consider you to be as dangerous a man as it is possible to find. You are responsible for four sadistic murders in the space of three months. Not one of the victims had done you the slightest bit of harm; it was killing for killing's sake.'

He added: 'As you had said to the police earlier, you told one of your victims as he was pleading for his life that you were doing it for fun. At no stage have you shown the slightest remorse or regret for the killings, or for the 20 years of killings which preceded them.' As to the possibility of release, the judge said: 'I don't want you or anyone else to be in the slightest doubt as to what I shall say – in a word, never.'

When the judge finished speaking, Moore nodded his head and smiled grimly. When he was led away to begin his sentence, there were shouts of 'Scum!' and 'I hope you rot in hell, boy!' from the packed public gallery, where the relatives of some of his victims were sitting.

Justine Ingrams, 26, whose father, Keith Randles, was stabbed to death outside in his caravan, said outside court: 'He is an evil man and I am delighted with the verdict. Justice has been done and the best place for this person to be is where he is going to be for the rest of his life and that is in prison. Nobody deserves to die in the way that my father and the other men died. It was a horrific death done by an evil, homicidal maniac. Only now can we let my dad rest in peace, knowing that his killer will never walk the streets at night ever again.'

Detective Superintendent Peter Ackerley, who led the investigation, told reporters: 'Evil, vile and depraved just doesn't seem adequate to describe a man who is so evil. He clearly took care and prepared to commit his offences, which made it a little more difficult for us as a police service to bring him into custody. But at the end of the day I am pleased for the families with the convictions because the families really have suffered.'

Moore's defence solicitor Dylan Jones read out a bizarre statement from his client. It went: 'I knew from the start that nobody could win in this matter – not the deceased, the relatives, nor myself – nobody.'

Detective Constable David Morris heard Moore confess to the murders. He said: 'What he said was quite shocking and horrific in places. If I had shown any emotion, be it anger or horror, it would have restricted him speaking to me. I tried throughout to remain professional and unmoved by what he was telling me, to keep him speaking; I believed everything he was telling me, but I couldn't believe how dispassionately he was talking. He was talking the way you or I would talk about going down to town to buy a newspaper or a pint of milk.'

18

'WE HAD A LITTLE ARGUMENT'

'What he did to my Mum was straight out of a horror film. I think he killed her in some kind of sick, satanic sacrifice.'

Daughter of victim

Name: Glyn Dix
Crime: Murder
Date of Conviction: 16 December 2005
Age at Conviction: 51

At around 5pm on 2 October 1979, Pia Overbury left work at a cake shop in Gloucester. She told her builder husband James that she was going straight to a friend's party and he did not expect her home until late that night. He never saw her alive again.

At some point shortly after leaving the shop, the 32-year-old mum-of-two met schizophrenic maniac Glyn Dix. Three weeks later a woman walking her dogs found Pia's body in an isolated copse in the nearby village of Hartbury. She had been tied to a tree, raped and shot in the head.

The police investigation eventually led to Dix, a 26-year-old hospital porter, and he was charged with murder. At his trial at Bristol Crown Court in July of the following year, the jury heard Dix's claim that prior to the night Pia Overbury died, she had approached him and offered him £2,000 to kill her violent husband. The pair had gone to a remote woodland area so they could discuss the killing in private and, Dix claimed, so he could fire a shotgun at a tree and thus show how he intended to assassinate Mr Overbury. In reality, there was no such murder plot. Dix forced Pia to the ground and tied her hands round the trunk of a tree. Once he'd raped her, he shot her in the back of the head and left her to rot in a shallow grave.

He denied murder, claiming Pia had broken down and told him that she would rather be dead than continue her unhappy marriage. He said she begged him to kill her and that he obliged.

On the third day of the trial, faced with overwhelming evidence of sexual assault, Dix changed his plea to guilty on the advice of his solicitor. He said he had been inspired to rape and kill by the 'change of the seasons' – suggesting a black-magic link. He was sentenced to life in prison.

Dix remained behind bars for 19 years, spending a significant part of his sentence in high-security psychiatric hospitals before a gradual process of release. As part of this process, he was moved for a while to low-security Gloucester Prison, where the more relaxed regime would ready him for life in the outside world. During his months at Gloucester, Dix shared a cell with Adam Langford, 21, who was serving six months for driving offences. The pair became close friends and when Dix was sent to nearby Bristol jail's psychotherapy ward to serve out the last stretch of his sentence, Adam – by now released – kept in touch. He was disqualified from driving so his mother Hazel drove him to prison visits. At 50, Hazel had plenty in common with Dix, who was by now 46, and the pair got along swimmingly.

After that first meeting Dix began writing to Hazel from prison and a romance started. He was warm, witty and charming in his letters and Hazel soon visited him on her own. The relationship developed at a pace and days after Dix's release on life licence in September 1999, they married at Redditch Register Office.

Dix moved into Hazel's home in Seymour Drive, Redditch, and for five years the couple seemed normal and happy. That situation changed on 19 June 2004, in a shocking, barbaric and bloody way that left Hazel's family destroyed and several policemen in need of counselling.

On the afternoon of that sunny Saturday, Hazel and Dix had an argument over what to watch on television and the convicted killer flipped, stabbing his wife to death and chopping her body into 16 pieces. Her son Adam came home at around 3.30pm to find his former cellmate standing naked, knife in hand, over his mother's mutilated body. He had used 15 different instruments on her, including a knife, hacksaw and scissors.

He had also daubed murals on walls, depicting a scantily-clad woman on her knees and a hooded knifeman standing over her. As a sickened Adam tried to take in the horror before him, Dix grinned and said: 'We had a little argument.' In deep shock, Adam ran across the road to his sister Rachel's house.

Rachel, 32, recalled: 'Suddenly Adam ran through the door and said that Glyn had stabbed my mum. My sister Vicky and I were in my kitchen. He was shouting: "He's killed Mum, he's chopped her up!" and then he flew out of the front door. "What's that about?" I thought. "What's he on?" We ran to Mum's conservatory and stood at the door. It was open and the kitchen door was open.

'Dix was there and he had nothing on, no clothes. He had put them in the wash because they were covered in blood. Mum was on the floor. I saw her hair; her body had gone yellow. Dix said calmly, "We had a little argument." The knife was still in his hand, but there was nothing on it. He was clean – he'd washed himself and the knife. He looked straight through us.'

She continued: 'Then he slowly beckoned at me with his finger to go to him. "Come here," he said. He'd cut Mum into 16 pieces. He dismembered her everywhere. He even took pieces of skin off her rib cage so you could see them as well. He stabbed her in the heart so at least we believe she died quite quickly. I swore at him at the top of my voice and ran back to my house, locked the front door and phoned the police.'

Adam said: 'When I went back, Dix looked at me with evil eyes and said, "Now we can be one." I grabbed him and punched his head – I wanted to kill him. He tried to stab me, but then the police burst in. My mum gave him everything. He took her life and ruined mine.'

Blaming himself for his mother's horrific death, Adam said: 'I have sleepless nights. If I'd never gone to jail, I'd never have met this animal and Mum would be alive today. I knew he was in for murder, but couldn't find out anything about his past.

'He told me he was ex-SAS and had been fitted up after a woman hired him to kill her violent ex-partner. He also conned my mum. By marrying her, he was able to get out of jail on licence – he repaid her by butchering her.'

When police arrived at the house, Dix told them: 'That's my wife Hazel, and I love her. We had an argument and it went too far.'

Because of the extreme nature of the murder, Hazel's remains had to be left in her house overnight, despite most of her children living nearby. 'I know the police have to do their job,' said Rachel. 'But whether she was dead or not, they should have taken her out. My poor mum had gone through that and they just left her there on a cold floor all night.

'I couldn't sleep at my house. I went to my sister Jodie's round the corner. Adam lived with Mum and Glyn. Adam and I can't bear to be in the house now.'

Dix admitted murder and was quickly diagnosed as suffering from extreme schizophrenia. Doctors found he displayed psychotic tendencies when he failed to take his medication. He was remanded at Ashworth Psychiatric Hospital on Merseyside until 16 December the following year, when he pleaded guilty to his wife's murder at Birmingham Crown Court.

Prosecutor Jonathan Gosling told the court that on the day of the murder, Dix, 51, said that he and Hazel were watching television naked in the living room after making love. They then rowed over which channel to watch. 'When the police arrived, moments later, the defendant was still kneeling astride his wife with a knife in his hand,' said Mr Gosling. He then quoted a statement Dix had made to police in which he said: 'Hazel had said, "Right, that's it!" and she got hold of a knife and I got hold of a knife and as we started facing each other, I stabbed her. She was going on and on, and I felt under pressure. I felt my anger rise, I said I had had enough of her.'

His defence counsel Andrew Fisher said: 'Mr Dix wants to put it on the record and acknowledge the gravest regret and deepest remorse for what occurred.' Mr Fisher continued: 'He is bitterly, bitterly regretful and remorseful for what happened. He loved her dearly. She was, in his words, his soulmate. He can't explain quite why he flipped that day.'

Sentencing Dix, Mr Justice Butterfield told him: 'You stabbed her to death and dismembered her body. It was brutal, horrific and abhorrent. You took the life of a woman who did much to help you and showed you much kindness. You have also deeply hurt the family, who welcomed you with open arms.' The judge added: 'Your risk has been described as extremely high. Your counsel has sensibly decided that I should not apply a set period and you will be detained on a whole life order. You will be detained either in a specialist hospital or a prison until you die. You are an extremely dangerous man.'

Outside court, Hazel's brother Wayne Denver, 67, said the family was pleased with the sentence and that they hoped Dix would never be released. He said: 'We have each lost a sister, a mother, a grandmother and a very dear friend, and no words can describe the devastation this family feels about a man who gave the persona of a loving, caring person. He must never be set free for any reason. This will stay with us for the rest of our lives.'

Rachel said that she was haunted by the thought that she might have prevented her mum's grisly death: 'I think, if I'd sat there on the Saturday afternoon with no telly or music on, I might have heard something. I could have done something.' She added: 'I dream that I'm looking at Mum when she was at the funeral home. I also dream that I'm looking at her in pieces. It's horrible.'

Of Dix, she said: 'He has never really said much to the police, just that it was a row about the TV programmes. That's all we know.'

Despite the horrific nature of Hazel's death, her children are determined not to let it destroy their lives completely. 'Mum wouldn't have wanted that,' insisted Rachel's twin sister Jodie. 'She would have wanted us to stay strong. We have children of our own and they keep us going.'

They suspect they will never understand how a man who seemed 'so in love' with their mother could put her through such an unimaginable ordeal. 'Him saying sorry wouldn't make a difference,' said Rachel. 'He will rot in jail for the rest of his life and we're glad.'

Another of Hazel's daughters, Tracie Gower, 34, told how she boycotted her mum's wedding to Dix. She fought back tears as she explained: 'I couldn't stand the idea of having a killer as a stepdad, but Mum wouldn't listen. I'd never met him, but felt it was a terrible mistake. The family asked questions, but got no answers – he convinced Mum he wasn't guilty.

'Despite our warnings, she married him believing he'd been wrongfully jailed. Yet it was clear he was a menace to society. I asked Mum just before the wedding, "Do you know what you're doing?" and she replied, "He's the man for me."' She added: 'I only met Dix after Mum married. At first he struck me as devoted to her. There were never any tell-tale signs of what he'd do. That's why we think it was a ritual killing, he'd planned it all. I'm convinced he was into the Occult. What he did to my mum was straight out of a horror film. I think he killed her in some kind of sick, satanic sacrifice.'

Rachel said: 'We put our trust in him to look after our mother for the rest of her life. I wish they could bring back hanging, but that would be too quick for him – he should be buried alive.'

Tracie told of the family's anger that someone as dangerous as Dix was ever allowed out of prison: 'Someone decided to let this man out to kill again. I've written to the Home Office asking why he was allowed out. I want to know why nobody warned us of his past. This man has destroyed the lives of two families. Unless action is taken, the same mistake will happen and other innocent lives will be taken by evil men like him.'

The Parole Board said the case would be referred to a Review Committee. A spokeswoman commented: 'Regrettably, no matter how much care we take, a few people will reoffend. When they do, we try to look at what lessons can be learned.'

Recalling the day he saw his mutilated mother, Adam Langford said simply: 'I wouldn't wish the pictures I have in my head on anyone else.'

19

'VIAGRA MAN'

'They called him "The Viagra Man" as they said he took that drug before helping himself.'

Culshaw's neighbour

Name: Paul Culshaw
Crime: Serial rape and murder
Date of Conviction: 10 February 2005
Age at Conviction: 37

Residents of Lancaster's deprived Ryelands estate might have been forgiven for thinking Paul Culshaw was a decent, charitable man. Unlike many of his neighbours, who shunned and loathed the estate's growing number of drug addicts, Culshaw, despite not being a user himself, gave them refuge at his rented flat. He kept an open house, where they could take heroin and crack cocaine in relative safety from the dangers that lurked for homeless people on the city's streets. Often he would supply the drugs himself if the desperate addicts had none and he thought nothing of letting them sleep over.

But what the casual eye couldn't see was that behind closed doors the vicious pervert would use the zombied girls – they were always female – to satisfy his insatiable lust for warped sex. One victim of this appetite was heroin user Clare Benson-Jowry. The 23-year-old mother-of-one was a regular visitor to Culshaw's home, where she would take heroin with fellow addicts. She and her friends were wary of visiting his place alone, knowing of his tendency to 'try it on' and conscious of the stories they had heard of what he did to girls when they were too out of it to resist. Clare knew Culshaw's flat was a dangerous place to visit alone, but that's exactly what she did on 20 June 2004 – and she paid the price. Three-and-a-half weeks later neighbours complained of a 'dreadful smell' coming from the property and police found her badly decomposed, half-naked body in Culshaw's bedroom the following day. She had been sexually assaulted and strangled with a shoelace, tightened with a fork.

One former addict who often visited Culshaw's flat, a girl who asked not to be identified, knew Clare and remembers the first time that she accepted Culshaw's offer of hospitality. She recalled: 'Paul was always really nice when you arrived, but he would often change once you'd had your gear and you didn't know – or care – what was going on. He made out that he was this really nice bloke who wanted to keep girls off the streets, but that was not why he let us stay there.' The 27-year-old, who is now beating her addiction through Lancaster's Inward House Projects rehabilitation initiative, added: 'I first met him just after Christmas in 2003. I had only just moved from Preston to live with a mate, after leaving my boyfriend. I was on a come-down so I was drinking cider to make it easier. I was drunk, but wanted some brown [heroin]. Paul came over and offered me a rolly [a cigarette] and we started chatting. He was really down-to-earth and charming. I told him I was dying for a fix and he invited me round to his and said he would give me the money for a tenner's worth as long as I paid him back.

'I went with him to his flat and he already had some gear there. I smoked some on the couch while he watched a porn DVD. I don't remember much about the rest of the night but when I woke up on the couch the next day I knew he'd done something. My blouse was buttoned up, but my bra was pulled down; my jeans were undone as well. It freaked me out and I left the place before he got up.' She continued: 'I told a few people about what happened and they said Paul was a creep, but handy to know. They said he was always sound if you wanted to go round, but you had to make sure you only went when other people were there; he never did nowt when people were around. I went to his place plenty of times after that, but never on my own.'

When Clare's body was found on 15 July, Culshaw was nowhere to be seen. Police ran checks on the flat and knew they needed to look no further than the tenant in their search for the man responsible for the murder. Records showed Culshaw was unemployed and had a history of violence against women. In 1985, aged 18, he broke into a woman's home in Up Holland, West Lancashire, in the early hours. Armed with a penknife and broom handle, he attacked the 43-year-old resident in her sleep, brutally raping her. He told her that he would return and kill her if she dared phone the police.

For that offence he was jailed for three-and-a-half years at a young offenders' institution but his time inside did little to subdue his deviant desires. Weeks after his release in 1988, he again forced his way into a lone woman's home, where he subjected the occupant to a vicious sexual assault. This time, however, he attempted to kill his victim to prevent her from identifying him. He was only stopped from doing so when disturbed by a neighbour during the final throes of strangulation. Culshaw was jailed for 10 years for attempted murder and indecent assault.

At his trial for Clare's murder at Preston Crown Court in February 2005, Culshaw, 37, denied any part in her sexually motivated killing. Giving evidence, he told defence counsel John Bromley-Davenport, QC, he had 'panicked' when he saw 'one of my best friends' dead on the sofa. He claimed that because of his police record he immediately thought he would be blamed for her death, regardless of his innocence. In mitigation, he said that he had admitted in court all his previous crimes and also assaults on his former wife. While he acknowledged that he was the obvious suspect, he insisted that in this case, the police had the wrong man. 'You pleaded guilty to those offences – are you guilty of this offence of murder?' asked his counsel Bromley-Davenport. Culshaw replied: 'No, I am not.' He then told the court how Clare would occasionally visit his flat to smoke heroin. 'She was very honest, a very open person,' Culshaw said. He added: 'She was very attractive. I fancied her, but I never did anything about it.'

He told the jury how, on the night she died, Clare had visited his flat, asking if she could come in and watch television: 'We watched telly for a while, watched videos and stuff, and talked about nothing, really. She asked me if she could smoke a bit of heroin on foil and stay the night. I said yes, rolled myself a joint and had a bath.' He added: 'When I came out, I automatically assumed she had got her head down on the sofa.' He told the court he had then left the flat to go to nearby bus stops in search of cigarette ends so that he could take the tobacco from them and roll his own at home. When he returned an hour later, he discovered Clare's body. He told the court: 'Her eyes were wide open and dry; her head did not look natural. She was fully clothed. I automatically assumed someone had killed her while I was out.' He insisted that at no stage did he touch the body. Asked why he did not phone 999, he said: 'She was too far past help; I was satisfied in my mind she was dead. I have no trust in the police. I knew as soon as I phoned them, I would just get blamed for it.' Standing emotionless in the dock, he added: 'I was physically sick and just panicked.' He said he then left the flat and made his way to Penrith, a picturesque town in the Lake District, making most of the 50-mile journey on foot and taking none of his belongings with him.

Days after the discovery of the body, police were led to Culshaw when a man fitting his description was reported stealing bread from a baker's shop in Penrith. They found him living rough in nearby woodland. He had been staying in a den made from dead tree branches covered by black plastic. When he was arrested, Culshaw said he knew the police would be looking for him but insisted he had nothing to do with Clare's death.

'VIAGRA MAN'

The circumstantial evidence against Culshaw, his damning criminal record and the fact that he fled the scene meant that it took the jury less than an hour to find him guilty of murder. Sentencing him, judge Mr Justice Hughes said: 'The evidence shows that for much of the time you are able to lead a normal, fairly solitary life. You suffer from a severe personality disorder: you are a person who is an enormous danger to other people, chiefly to women, and whose danger lies hidden most of the time.' The judge said that, prior to strangling his victim, Culshaw forced her to have sex. He went on: 'It was a violent and determined decision to kill. I regard it absolutely clear you forced yourself on her sexually, you stripped her largely naked. The overwhelming likelihood is that you killed her to stop her revealing the very serious sexual assault you carried out on her. This is a case for a life sentence without any recommendation for a minimum period - that is for a whole life order. Early release provision will not apply here. Life in your case must mean life.'

After the trial, Clare's family said in a statement released through police: 'The result can in no way compensate for the loss of our precious Clare. No words can describe our feelings at this time regarding the inexcusable and callous actions of this man, which left Clare's son without a mother shortly before his fourth birthday. Paul Culshaw has shown no remorse whatsoever and at no time has he attempted to ease the sufferings of the family during the case. The trauma has continued throughout the trial, where we have heard the graphic details of how Clare was killed. No sentence is long enough to make up for the actions of this evil man.'

One woman, who lived opposite Culshaw's flat, told how he would stand staring through his neighbours' windows for long periods of time. She said: 'He would hang around shelters for the homeless and lure vulnerable women to his home with heroin and then he would have his way with them. They called him "the Viagra Man" as they said he took that drug before helping himself. He wasn't one for talking to neighbours and he would walk straight past you on the street. But there were always people coming and going from his flat. He was a bit of a creep and I had to close our kitchen shutters at night as he could see through when he was staring out of his window.' The 50-year-old recalled that around a year before Clare's murder she saw a naked young woman screaming from a window of his flat. She said: 'The girl seemed to be off her head on drugs but you could tell he had beaten her up because she had black eyes and a bloody nose.'

Detective Chief Inspector Steve Brunskill, who led the investigation, said: 'Clare was a much-loved and popular girl. Sadly though, because of her addiction to heroin, she led a chaotic lifestyle that made her vulnerable. We cannot begin to imagine the horror of the attack he subjected her to.'

20

'A LOVING AND CARING FATHER'

*'You beat your wife to death in her bedroom and then
coldly and deliberately you brought your sleepy children
downstairs to meet their deaths.'*

Trial judge David Clarke

Name: Rahan Arshad
Crime: Quadruple murder
Date of Conviction: 13 March 2007
Age at Conviction: 37

Flies swarmed around the windows and doors of the Arshad family's
end-of-terrace on Turves Road, in Cheadle Hulme, Manchester. A
putrid smell leaked from inside the three-bedroom home to beyond
the driveway. One neighbour complained about the 'stomach-turning
stench' that worsened daily and on the swelteringly evening of Sunday,
22 August 2006, police smashed their way into the house.

In the living room were the bodies of the Arshad's three children –
sons Adam, 11, and Abbas, eight, and daughter Henne, six. Furniture,
walls and ceiling were spattered with blood. The body of their mother
Uzma Rahan, 32, lay in the marital bedroom, which was also a
bloodbath. All four victims had had their skulls smashed to pieces with
a rounders bat.

About a month earlier, late on 28 July, the man of the house, Rahan
Arshad, brutally murdered his family in a bid to protect his honour

after learning of his wife's three-year affair with another married Asian man. He killed Uzma, beating her about the head 27 times. Then the taxi driver – described by all as a doting dad, who worked 12-hour shifts to provide for his family – carried his sleeping children, one-by-one, downstairs and savagely killed each of them in turn. He covered the bodies with their duvets and bed sheets and left them to rot while he jetted off to holiday in Thailand.

DCI Tony Mole, one of the first officers at the house, described the scene that greeted the police as the worst any of them had ever come across. He said of the children: 'The bodies were so badly decomposed that the floor was soup because the bodies had basically melted. The forensic team that worked on this deserve a medal – they could hardly step anywhere.'

After the murders, Arshad, 36, drove to Heathrow Airport in his new BMW, caught a plane to Bangkok and travelled on to the resort of Phuket. He was stopped at the Thai-Malaysian border by an alert border official who was carrying out a routine visa check. 'Amazingly, he put Rahan's name in Google and found out that he was wanted in Manchester for the murders of his wife and three children,' said Detective Supt Martin Bottomley, who led the investigation. 'Up until that point all we knew for sure was that he had flown into Bangkok. Obviously he'd made his way down to the border.'

The Manchester police team did not have sufficient evidence to extradite Arshad but he agreed to fly back to England of his own accord. When he got off the plane at Heathrow, he told the policeman who met him: 'I don't regret killing that f**king bitch but my beautiful kids, killing my kids.' Moments later, when the detective formally arrested him, Arshad said, 'I confess to murder' and broke down in tears.

He was driven 200 miles up to Manchester for interrogation, but on advice from his solicitor, he clammed up, offering 'No comment' to every question. Police had only circumstantial evidence against him and were hoping forensic examination of his luggage would change that. They were in luck. A pair of shorts Arshad brought back with him from Thailand had microscopic traces of each of his children's blood on them. Police were able to tell from the distribution of the blood that whoever was wearing them was less than 90cm away from Adam, Abbas and Henne when they were murdered. Also, the trainers Arshad was wearing as he stepped off the plane had traces of Uzma's blood in the seams and on the laces.

Armed with this new forensic evidence, police charged him with four counts of murder and on 27 February 2007, six months after the bodies were found, his trial began at Manchester Crown Court.

One female member of the jury openly wept as Paul Reid, QC, outlined the case for the prosecution, giving details of the repeated blows suffered by the family. On the advice of the judge he moved on to a more general account of the appalling injuries suffered. Throughout, Arshad sat impassively in the dock as the court was told how he had been plotting to slaughter his family for several weeks.

The jury heard that he booked his flight from Manchester to Bangkok on 11 July, originally for travel on 31 July. He later transferred the booking to a 29 July flight from Heathrow, presumably because he'd decided to bring forward the day of the killings. In the days before the murders, Arshad showered his wife with presents, including jewellery, a TV and a sports car, and told his family that he had booked a holiday for them in Dubai.

Prosecutor Mr Reid told the jury that not long before she died, Uzma had revealed to her brother, Rahat Ali: 'He's planning something. Count the days until he kills me.' Arshad told the same brother that he'd bought a £30,000 BMW as an early birthday present for his wife. When Rahat expressed shock at such an expensive gift, his brother-in-law had replied: 'Well, just wait. There will be a much bigger surprise.'

Arshad and his wife were wed in an arranged marriage in 1992. For more than a decade, they seemed happily married but in late

2003 Uzma began an affair with a man called Nikki Iqbal. Chief Supt Bottomley explained: 'Mr Arshad found out about this affair and that resulted in their separation and we know that Uzma and the children only moved back in with Rahan around June, shortly before they were killed. Uzma didn't try to hide the affair – in fact she flaunted it, driving around Cheadle with Nikki, calling at his house. She had started dressing in a very Westernised way, wearing skimpy tops, showing her midriff, very tight jeans, boots, and people were talking. Perhaps this had been playing on Rahan Arshad's mind, perhaps he's thinking she's dressing and behaving like a prostitute. Perhaps he's thinking he's lost his honour, he's lost his respect and he's got to take the ultimate sanction and in this case the ultimate sanction is to kill her.'

The court heard how Arshad bought a £1.99 'Funsport' rounders bat on 27 July and on the following day – the day of the murders – took some, or all of the family to Blackpool for a day out. 'Wristbands were issued to at least two of the children at Blackpool Pleasure Beach,' said prosecution barrister Reid. 'The wristbands were still being worn by Henna and Abbas when their bodies were discovered.' When police found Arshad's car at Heathrow, the boot still contained the children's sandy buckets and spades.

In court, Arshad denied four charges of murder but admitted the manslaughter of his wife, claiming he killed her after finding that she had murdered their three children. He said that when he found the bodies lying in the living room, he went upstairs to confront his wife. She said to him in Urdu: 'Are you satisfied?' He then told the court that he had 'blanked out', claiming, 'I found myself in the shower – I mean in the bath. I found myself in the bath with the bat. That is the last thing I remember.'

Arshad described his wife as 'a beautiful, bad-tempered, materialistic spendaholic', who constantly put him down. 'But I adored her,' he said. 'I am the worm that turned.' Defending him, Ian Glen,

QC, asked Arshad to explain why he had bought the single plane ticket to Thailand two weeks prior to the deaths of his family. 'It would have been a holiday,' he said. 'Uzma had been to Pakistan in February on her own and I needed a break as well.' He explained that he did not tell his wife for fear that she might refuse to let him go. Mr Glen then asked his client what he had meant when he told the arresting police officer: 'I confess to the murder... but my kids, killing my kids.' Arshad explained that he meant that he had killed Uzma, but that she had killed their three children.

Before the accused gave evidence, the defence barrister turned to the jury and said: 'The question is: which one of them killed the children?' he said. 'If the defendant returned home to find his wife had killed his three children, you can't imagine a better case for provocation for killing her: it is an unusual case, it is a shocking case.

'You may debate the possibilities. What mother, no mother could possibly kill her children? Leaving the slightly greater possibility of the father. It is no more likely that a father would do it than a mother would do it.

'We would say this – we have a father, or a mother, who was mentally ill. Only one of these two was mentally ill unfortunately, and that was Uzma, and that tends towards concluding she did it.'

The barrister suggested Uzma was paranoid and suicidal. As evidence, he read out an extract from her diary: 'Allah, take me to yourself. If I could start again, I would not have any more lies in my life.' Mr Glen told the court: 'We suggest she was on that very slippery slope that is depressive illness.'

Arshad closed his eyes as the jury of eight women and four men delivered their unanimous guilty verdicts after deliberating for just over two hours. Uzma's brother Rahat shouted 'Yes!' as the first verdict was returned. Four members of the jury cried as judge David Clarke told Arshad that in his case life meant life and he would never be freed on licence. The judge said: 'The jury have convicted you on overwhelming evidence: you killed your entire family in circumstances of great brutality. You beat your wife to death in her bedroom and then coldly and deliberately, you brought your sleepy children downstairs to meet their deaths. You left the scene and fled the country. It was over three weeks before the bodies were discovered. There is no suggestion of mental illness on your part. Life imprisonment in your case means life.'

After the verdict, Detective Supt Bottomley said: 'Rahan Arshad's defence has been nothing of ridiculous. The only time he has ever shown any remorse was when he got off the plane from Thailand.'

In an impact statement read out to the court, Uzma's brother Rahat, who heard the verdict with his mother, Safia Hassnain, and brother, Mustajab Ali Haider, said that he had not slept between the discovery of the bodies and Arshad's return to Britain and told of his grief at seeing the four bodies on mortuary slabs. His sister had been his 'best mate' and the pain of losing her and her children was unbearable. He said: 'None of us could understand how a father could do such a thing to his children and his wife also. What must they have been thinking when it was happening to them, especially the children?'

Weeks later, in a BBC television interview, Rahat recalled seeing Arshad and the children just days before the killings. He said: 'The last time we saw all the family together was in McDonald's. I found his behaviour very strange – he just kept hugging me all the time, about eight to ten times in 45 minutes, and I was wondering why he was doing that. I was getting suspicious about his behaviour. I found out after three weeks why he was doing that: it's because he planned to kill them when they broke up from school for the holidays. He planned to leave them in the house in horrendous positions and leave this country forever, and that is what he did.'

Describing the grim task of identifying the bodies at the morgue, Rahat added: 'It was the worst moment of my life. I don't know where the love was that time when he was killing them – he had no

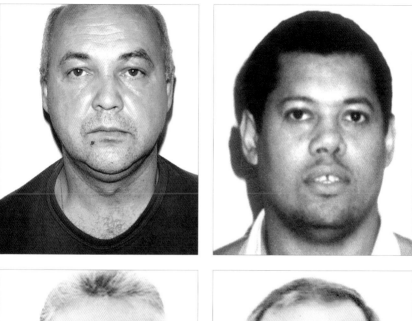

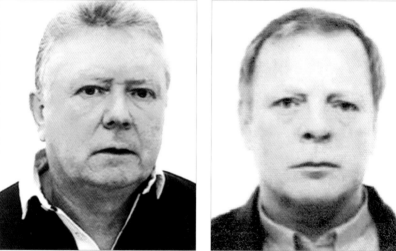

Top left: Prolific rapist Andrezej Kunowski who fled from his native Poland to London where he murdered schoolgirl Katerina Koneva in 1997.

Top right: Victor Miller, the 'Paperboy Predator' who terrorised young boys in the West Midlands, culminating in the 1988 murder of 14-year-old Stuart Gough.

Bottom: Drug smugglers Kenneth Regan (left) and William Horncy who, in 2003, murdered businessman Amarjit Chohan, his wife, two young children and mother-in-law in order to take over his export business.

Top: 'Bus Stop Killer' Levi Bellfield, who murdered Amelie Delagrange and Marsha McDonnell. He is suspected of other attacks including the murder of Milly Dowler.
© *Rex Features*

Bottom: Dennis Nilsen, who, between 1978 and 1983, murdered at least 15 young men in London, keeping his victims' bodies under the floorboards before dissecting them and flushing many of the parts down the lavatory.
© *Rex Features*

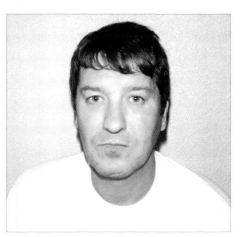

Top: A reconstruction of Dennis Nilsen's kitchen in his attic flat at 23, Cranley Gardens, Muswell Hill, north London, where he cut up and cooked body parts from his victims. He was caught when neighbours complained of a rotting smell from the drains.   © *Brian Harris/Alamy*

Bottom left: John McGrady, a serial rapist who murdered 15-year-old Rochelle Holness in 2005.   © *Rex Features*

Bottom right: A poster produced by the *Sheffield Star* asking for information on the whereabouts of Arthur Hutchinson, who murdered solicitor Basil Laitner, his GP wife Avril and their son Richard at their home near Sheffield in 1983.   © *Ross Parry Syndication*

Top left: Sadist Colin Ireland, dubbed 'The Gay Slayer' who, in 1993, murdered five gay men in London in a bid to become famous.
© *Rex Features*

Top right: Jeremy Bamber, who shot dead five members of his family in 1985 and tried to frame his mentally ill sister for the crime.   © *Rex Features*

Right: Psychopath Robert Maudsley as a child with his siblings. As an adult he was jailed for murder before killing four of his fellow prison inmates. He is believed to have eaten part of one victim's brain.

Top: Jeremy Bamber crying crocodile tears at the funerals of his murdered family. He later spent the night partying.

© *Trinity Mirror/Mirrorpix/Alamy*

Bottom left: Ian Brady, the notorious Moors Murderer.   © *PA Photos*

Bottom right: Peter Moore, a violent and sadistic predator who brutally murdered four gay men in North Wales in 1995.   © *PA Photos*

Top left: Rahan Arshad who, in 2006, beat his wife and three young children to death with a rounders bat at their home in Manchester.

© *Rex Features*

Top right: Trevor Hardy, 'The Beast of Manchester', who brutally murdered and mutilated Lesley Stewart, Wanda Skala and Sharon Mossoph between 1974 and 1976.   © *Manchester Evening News*

Bottom left: Serial rapist Viktors Dembovskis, from Latvia, who murdered 17-year-old Jeshma Raithatha near her home in London.   © *Rex Features*

Bottom right: Anthony Arkwright, who brutally murdered and mutilated three people in Wath, near Doncaster, in a bid to be as famous as Jack The Ripper.   © *Ross Parry Syndication*

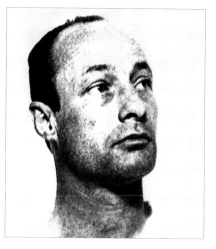

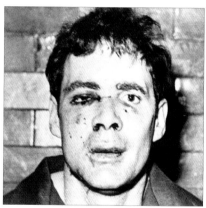

Top left: 'Body-in-the-Bags Killer' Malcolm Green, who murdered prostitute Glenys Johnson in 1989 and then killed for a second time within a year of his release from prison for that crime.   © *PA Photos*

Top right: John Duffy who, in partnership with fellow 'Railway Rapist' David Mulcahy, attacked countless women, killing three, in London in the 1980s.   © *Photo News Service/Rex Features*

Bottom left: Mark Hobson, who, in 2004, brutally murdered his girlfriend Claire Sanderson, her twin sister Diane and elderly couple James and Joan Britton in North Yorkshire.   © *Rex Features*

Bottom right: 'The Black Panther' Donald Neilson, who kidnapped and murdered 17-year-old Lesley Whittle and killed three postmasters in armed robberies throughout the North and Midlands in the mid 1970s.

© *Trinity Mirror/Mirrorpix/Alamy*

Top: Infamous serial killers Rose and Fred West, many of whose victims were buried in the gardens and cellar of 25, Cromwell Street, Gloucester, dubbed the 'House of Horrors'. © *South West News Service/Rex Features*

Bottom: A young Steve Wright, the 'Suffolk Strangler', who killed five prostitutes in a two-month killing spree in Ipswich in 2006.

© *Jason Bye/Rex Features*

mercy for them. The kids were sleeping; he picked them up, one by one, to bring them downstairs and kill them, like animals. I am never going to forgive what he did to his own kids, especially Henna. He used to love her more than anything in the world and the way he killed her was terrible.'

DCI Dave Law said: 'The fact that he volunteered to come back to this country is quite remarkable because clearly he knew what he would face. Obviously there will never ever be an excuse for what he did to Uzma, but in his mind there is a lot of hatred and venom there from the comments he made when he was arrested and there is perhaps an understanding that he was driven to that. But why kill the children? How can a man described by many people as a loving and caring father bring himself to end their lives? That is the biggest question of all.'

Of the trip to Blackpool in the hours before Arshad killed his children, Detective Supt Bottomley pondered: 'Was that evidence of pre-planning? Was that Rahan mentally saying goodbye to them, or was it more cynical? Was he tiring them out for the day with a view to getting them home, tired out, putting them to bed and then sleeping through what he had in mind for them, for killing them?'

Nikki Iqbal later told of the passionate three-year romance he had with the murdered wife. He said they hid the affair by meeting for sex at Nikki's brother's house. He revealed: 'I was at my brother's and she used to come there. I saw her and thought she was nice – I got her number and we took it from there. We would meet occasionally, anywhere, wherever.'

After Arshad was jailed, Iqbal told the *Manchester Evening News*: 'There's a million and one women out there having affairs. The murder is nothing to do with me.' He added: 'They should give him a lethal injection for what he's done. What he did to them kids was bang out of order.'

The delivery driver, 42, and his forgiving wife Musarat told the

Mirror how they heard Uzma and the children were dead. He said: 'We watched the news together and we were all crying. We were so upset. It's still a shock she and the kids have been murdered – they didn't deserve that. He has wiped out a whole generation. It will be on my mind till the day I die.'

21

'I WANT TO HURT SOMEBODY'

'If you've killed one, you might as well have killed 21. I'm going to be the city's first serial killer.'

Mark Martin (to a fellow prisoner while on remand)

Name: Mark Martin
Crime: Triple murder
Date of Conviction: 25 February 2006
Age at Conviction: 26

At 6.39pm on 1 November 2004, Mark Martin dialled 999 from a public phone box and told the operator: 'I'm getting thoughts in my head that I want to hurt somebody. I'm going to end up killing someone.' He added: 'I was locked up last night for trying to strangle my ex-wife.'

It later turned out that Martin had 'lost it' when his ex-wife told him that she no longer trusted him alone with their son because of his foul temper. Filled with anger and resentment, he moved from Ilkeston, Derbyshire, to Nottingham, eight miles away, where he slept rough on the city's streets.

Known as 'Reds' among Nottingham's homeless community because of a distinctive red birthmark on his face, he robbed others who were sleeping rough of their money or whatever possessions they had. When he was not bullying other homeless people, he was boasting about how he would one day be infamous. His behaviour did not win him any friends – and Nottingham's intensely loyal homeless community realised very quickly they had a dangerous man in their midst.

A community worker named Stephan, who had worked with Nottingham's homeless for six years, told the Nottingham Evening Post: 'Word soon got around from different organisations who work with the homeless that he was a psychopath. Here was a potentially dangerous character who should be watched closely. Homeless people have to give off a lot of bravado to survive, but Martin was talking about how he was going to make a name for himself, that he was dangerous and was going to hurt people. We got the sense that there was something else; that he was capable of serious violence and that it wasn't just bravado.'

On 29 December 2004, Katie Baxter, 18, vanished. She was last seen alive leaving her sister Charlene's house in West Bridgford. Katie had been living on the streets for about a year but managed to hide it from her family, with whom she regularly attended Nottingham Panthers ice hockey matches. When she failed to show up to the fifth game in a row, they reported her missing.

Two days after Kate vanished, Zoe Pennick, 26, disappeared. Her father had last seen her when she called at his home in Derby a fortnight earlier to collect some clothes. She had lived by herself in the city's suburb of Littleover and had taken to the streets after failing to hold down a job. Since becoming homeless, she was a regular sight in Nottingham city centre and was last seen alive on New Year's Eve. Zoe had a seven-year-old son, looked after by her father, who said she always got on well with people but had found it difficult to settle down. He said she had been homeless, on and off, for about six years.

A derelict warehouse off Great Northern Close, near London Road was a lonely spot by the railway tracks. But it was a favourite shelter among the city's homeless and rumours started to spread that there were bodies there.

'I WANT TO HURT SOMEBODY'

On the afternoon of Friday, 11 February 2005, a police cordon appeared around the warehouse. At 11am that day, a police dog discovered the decomposing remains of Katie Baxter near a wall heater, underneath 'carefully placed' pieces of soil, bricks and debris. Five days later, while searching the building for forensic evidence, police found Zoe Pennick's body. She was buried under rubble, less than two metres from where Katie was discovered.

Post-mortems revealed that both women had been beaten and strangled. Police linked the deaths to that of another homeless woman, Ellen Frith, who was found on 24 January in a burning squat in Marple Square, in the St Ann's area of the city. The 25-year-old mother-of-two had also been beaten and strangled.

After the discovery of Ellen's body, police interviewed scores of homeless people in Nottingham and kept hearing the same name, 'Reds', who had been staying at the Marple Square squat. One detective who worked on the investigation said: 'Martin had been boasting to people that he was a violent man, who was capable of killing. He was a bully with a short fuse and there was barely a homeless person in Nottingham who did not have a bad experience to tell about him. Nearly everyone we spoke to pointed the finger at him.'

Martin was arrested, along with his homeless associate John Ashley, 34, and within hours both men were charged with Ellen Frith's murder. When the crudely buried remains of Katie Baxter and Zoe Pennick were found, police set about building a case against Martin and Ashley for all three murders. Detectives learned that both women had links to the men, and that Katie had once had a relationship with Ashley.

Inquiries among the homeless community turned up the names of Martin and Ashley, time and time again. One homeless man, who was interviewed by police, later told reporters: 'If you heard Reds was on one side of town, you would go to the other. He used to draw on porno magazines to show what he was going to do to women.'

But it turned out the police did not need such testimonies to secure

Martin's conviction – he was doing a good job of that himself while on remand in prison. After his arrest for Ellen Frith's murder and before the discovery of the other dead women, he borrowed a book from the prison library called Rats and Reptiles. He told fellow inmates that he wanted to know how much meat rats could consume and therefore how quickly they could eat 'the other bodies'.

Of the witnesses who heard Martin's grisly boasts, an inmate who shared a cell with him proved to be the star witness when the case came to trial. Martin told the witness, who was allowed to remain anonymous for fear of reprisals inside: 'I'm going to be Nottingham's first serial killer. If you've killed one, you might as well have killed 21.' In a sworn statement, the witness said it was this boast and his repeated threats to 'kill his baby's mother' that compelled him to testify against the thug. But he was so scared of Martin that police spent two weeks persuading him to come to court. The witness said: 'Katie scratched him [Martin]. He burnt her fingers because he wanted to get rid of the evidence. He said he picked her up and took her down the factory [the warehouse] because she fancied him. They were chatting and went into his tent. Then he just snapped and strangled her. He dragged her out of the tent, into the factory and buried her with debris.'

Days later, Martin persuaded Zoe Pennick to go with him to his tent to pick up 2,000 cigarettes that he wanted her to sell for him. Once there, he grabbed her by the throat and strangled her. He then laid her body near to Katie's and buried her in the same way. Later, he bragged that he had killed Zoe because she left a hypodermic needle in his bed. The witness said: 'He said he'd sorted her out and he'd "smashed her legs up like biscuits" and "we weren't going to be seeing her for a while."' The prisoner added: 'He [Martin] said it was hard and she didn't want to die. He was punching her, kicking her; in the end, he stood on her throat.' He also revealed that Martin told him he had vomited over one of the girls because she had soiled and urinated herself while being strangled. He had removed the girl's top, scared that it had his DNA on it from his vomit.

The accused were joined by another homeless man, 31-year-old Dean Carr, who was also charged with Ellen Frith's murder. All three denied the charges when their trial began at Nottingham Crown Court on 16 January 2006. The court heard that Ellen went with the men to the squat to smoke drugs. Martin had told Ashley of his plan to kill Ellen and he grabbed her as she bit into an apple in the makeshift kitchen. He pressed his thumbs into her throat until she passed out, then Ashley finished her off. The witness testified: 'He [Martin] said him and John lifted her up and put her on the sofabed and set fire to the body. Reds was playing with her body, making it look like she was talking. Reds put a needle in her hand and stuck it in her leg.' Giving testimony, Ashley said the atmosphere in the room became cold when Martin began staring at Ellen. 'It was the way he was looking and the tension. He was looking at her in a horrible way – evil – it was just a horrible look, a cold look. He was being overpowering with her – really, really overpowering. He went over the line, way over the line.'

Ashley said: 'I know it sounds strange, but after Ellen's murder I went and made something to eat – that's the only thing I could think of.' He said he was so scared of Martin that he did nothing to stop him killing Ellen. 'At least I couldn't see it,' he told the court. 'I heard some weird noises; I think he was pushing down on her chest and it was making a horrible noise.'

One witness, a homeless man, testified that Martin said to him: 'You might as well finish her off – she's almost dead, anyway.' The witness said that Carr told him how he had walked up to Ellen while her body was still twitching and strangled her. Martin then wrapped up Ellen's body on the settee, covered her with newspaper and set fire to her. They then left the flat with Martin telling his friends: 'She'd cook like a bit of bacon.'

Another witness told the court that he was living at the flats where

Ellen's body was found and that following the fire, he was walking to a late-night garage when Martin called him over to speak to him in an alley. He said: 'He told me he'd strangled and killed her [Ellen] because she wouldn't lend him a tenner. He said she wouldn't die and her eyes kept twitching. He was joking about it, like it was funny.'

Peter Kelson, QC, prosecuting, asked a witness who spent time in prison with Martin while he was on remand if he had ever told him the number of girls he had killed. He replied: 'Oh, five.' The witness was not told the names of the other two victims, but said Martin told him that he had fed them to pigs at a farm in Leicester (a claim that was never substantiated). He also told the court that Martin complained that he did not have pictures of the bodies to prove he had done it.

Martin 'seemed to be glorying in his notoriety', said the prosecuting counsel. 'He was relishing the prospect of being known as Nottingham's first serial killer. He seems to have had a fascination with violence against women, and the crimes he committed and the suffering his victims endured.'

It took the jury almost a week to deliver its verdicts. As Martin stood impassively in the dock he was unanimously convicted of murdering the three women. Mr Justice Butterfield told him: 'These murders were committed by you because you positively enjoyed killing. You took the totally innocent lives of these women for your own perverted gratification. You have devastated the lives of those who loved them and have shown not a moment of remorse. You have revelled in the macabre details of each senseless, brutal, callous killing. The facts of the offences are so horrific and the seriousness of your offending is so exceptionally high, you are to be kept in prison for the rest of your life.'

Ashley, who had a previous conviction for wounding, was cleared of Zoe Pennick's murder, but was jailed for life and ordered to serve a minimum of 25 years for his part in the murders of Ellen Frith and Katie Baxter. Dean Carr was also jailed for life, to serve at least 14 years, for his involvement in Ellen's killing.

From a young age, Martin had been strange and twisted. His childhood heroes were serial killers and gangsters rather than footballers or pop stars. He idolised Moors Murderer Ian Brady and revered 'Black Panther' Donald Neilson, who slaughtered five people. His best friend at school, Gareth Moyes, remembers thinking something was deeply wrong with Martin. He said: 'I once saw him try to smother a baby because it was crying and I just shouted at him, "What are you doing?"'

Gareth added: 'When we were 15 or 16, we started doing cannabis and speed together and that made him worse. He became more and more aggressive towards the females. Mark would hit them and swear at them. He said his dad was in prison with Ian Brady; he would say he had respect for him and that he admired the Black Panther; he said we would be the next Kray Twins. He was deadly serious about it, so I would just humour him. Mark's dad died when we were younger, but when Mark told me he was laughing. I thought that was weird. When your dad dies, you don't laugh about it.'

Martin had also written a letter to a probation office, asking: 'How long till I kill someone?' In it, he complained that he would have liked a probation officer who wanted to help him and that he had a 'real bad temper'. He added: 'Everything that moves gets hurt — it could be a lady, it could be an animal. It was so sweet and nice until my dad died and now I'm evil.'

22

'THE BEAST OF MANCHESTER'

'He's one of the strangest, coldest men I've ever met. Physically, he's like a whippet – small, but tremendously tough, and completely unemotional.'

Detective Chief Inspector John Bennion

Name: Trevor Hardy
Crime: Triple murder
Date of Conviction: 2 May 1977
Age at Conviction: 31

On New Year's Eve 1974, 15-year-old Lesley Stewart set off to meet her boyfriend at the Phoenix Hotel in Moston, Manchester. She never made it. When Lesley – a former Rose Queen at her local church – failed to return home the next day, her frantic parents reported her missing. By 3 January 1975, hundreds of locals joined police with tracker dogs in the search, but no trace of the pretty, dark-haired schoolgirl was found.

Seven months later, shortly before midnight on Saturday, 20 July 1975, barmaid Wanda Skala, 18, went missing on her way home from work at the Lightbowne Hotel in Moston. The following day, police found her partially-naked body on waste ground. Wanda's clothes had been ripped off and her face was so badly beaten that her jaw hung loose. Her killer had tried to rape her, her right nipple had been bitten off and her socks were tied round her neck. Repeated blows from a paving stone had shattered her skull.

Local thug Trevor Hardy, 32, was drinking with his brother Colin as news of the brutal murder buzzed around the pub. Unable to resist, he drunkenly boasted to Colin that he was the man the police were after. Colin had no reason to disbelieve his deranged sibling, who had been jailed three years earlier for attacking a man named Stanley O'Brien with a pickaxe.

He recalled: 'We were having a few pints and the question of Wanda Skala came up. Then he suddenly said: "I did it! I didn't mean to kill her – I was going to mug her. I only wanted her handbag. I hit her with a brick; she must have had a thin or weak skull.' Colin replied: 'I don't believe you.' But Hardy insisted: 'It's true. But I didn't touch her sexually. I got £48 from her – I've still got the handbag.'

By the time the brothers got to Colin's flat, Hardy, by now sobering up, regretted his revelation and decided a beating would secure his brother's silence. Colin said: 'We went back to my flat and then the next thing I knew he was beating seven bells out of me. He ripped the clothes off me, battered me with a telephone and finally left me senseless and covered in blood on the stairs. There was blood everywhere – even on the ceiling. He wouldn't let my wife call for an ambulance, or help me in any way. Then he walked out... and returned ten minutes later, as calm as anything, and ordered her to cook him beans on toast.'

The attack left Colin and his wife petrified and they turned their home into a fortress using bolts, padlocks and bars. But Hardy still came round most nights, smashing windows and yelling threats through the door that he would kill them both if they breathed a word about Wanda's murder. Despite the threats, Colin decided he was safer with his brother off the streets and he told police about his confession.

Hardy was arrested and police demanded an impression of his teeth to compare to the bite mark found on Wanda's breast. Hardy agreed, but filed his teeth to points to change their shape. He later wrote: 'I had a file brought in on a visit to cells and used it to change teeth to beat check.' Hardy also convinced his girlfriend, Shelagh Farrow, to say they had been in bed together when Wanda was killed. Police had to release him without charge.

On 6 March 1976, Hardy attacked 20-year-old Christina Campbell in the ladies' of the King's Arms in Hollinwood, gripping her throat so tightly that she bit off part of her tongue. Before he could finish her off, he was disturbed and he fled the scene, later claiming that he 'throated' the girl because he caught her in a lesbian embrace with his girlfriend.

Three days later, on 9 March 1976, Sharon Mossoph, 17, left a work party at the Pack Horse Hotel in Bolton to catch the night bus home to Failsworth, 18 miles away. She called home at about 11pm and spoke to her stepmum, Jackie, to let her know she was on her way. Sharon caught the number 98 bus, which dropped her off less than half a mile from her home.

Early the next morning, dark-haired Sharon was found by a man taking a short cut to work across the Rochdale Canal. Her naked, strangled and mutilated body was floating face down among rubble and debris of the disused lock. Her tights were tied round her neck, she had been stabbed in the stomach with a screwdriver and her left nipple had been bitten off. Her attacker had tried to disguise his bite marks by slashing at the wound 64 times.

Police sealed off the area, just 30 yards from a discount wallpaper shop, where Sharon had just started work as a cashier. One of her workmates gathered at the scene said: 'The party had been fixed because we had all done so well. Sharon had worked with us for just three weeks... she was a lovely and very happy girl.' Later that day, the Manchester Evening News nicknamed her killer 'The Beast of Manchester'.

The similarities to the Wanda Skala murder meant Trevor Hardy was the only suspect. Police, already hunting Hardy over the incident in the

King's Arms, tracked him down to a hideaway flat in Stockport. He was arrested for both murders and held on remand in Manchester's Strangeways Prison awaiting trial.

On the night of Monday, 27 August 1975, while Hardy was in custody, Detective Chief Inspector John Bennion received a surprise call saying that the suspect wanted to meet with him. Hardy handed him a 40-page handwritten statement confessing to three killings – the two murders with which he was already charged, and also to the slaying of missing Lesley Stewart, about whose disappearance he had earlier been questioned. Of the confession, DCI Bennion said: 'It went into incredible detail, with carefully and precisely drawn maps of what had happened where; it told of his past, other crimes he'd committed, even about his childhood. Obviously he thought that if he was going to confess, he might as well do it properly.'

Hardy's statement said that while serving his prison sentence for the pickaxe attack on Stanley O'Brien, his young girlfriend Beverley Driver had written to him to end their relationship because she was now going out with a boy of her own age. She said in her letter: 'I don't want to waste my life on someone like you.' Hardy wrote in his statement: 'I sat there with the letter in my hands, shaking, with tears running down my cheeks. From that day I gave up the fight with my demons; no one gave a damn.' He was determined to see his former girlfriend dead. On his release, he revealed: 'The man they had protected society against was out, a bigger danger than when he went in. I had one reason to live: to kill her.'

Weeks later, on New Year's Eve 1974, Hardy went out drunk and armed with a kitchen knife to look for Beverley and her boyfriend. He saw Lesley Stewart getting out of a car in Ten Acre Lane in Harpurhey, Manchester. The driver said: 'Goodnight, Lesley' but in his drunken stupor, Hardy thought the driver had said 'Goodnight, Beverley'. He grabbed the girl and asked: 'Do you remember me, Beverley?' Lesley replied: 'What do you want?' and in response Hardy lashed out at her with a knife and cut her throat. Watching her die, he realised he had killed the wrong girl, but he wrote in his statement: 'I didn't give a damn after what I'd been through.'

He dragged Lesley's body to a hollow and partially covered it with grass. Afterwards, he went home to watch a Hogmanay TV show with his mother, then returned later to the corpse and buried it completely with soil and turf near to Moston Brook High School. In the weeks afterwards, he visited the shallow grave several times to mutilate the corpse. He cut off her head and threw it in a lake, then dismembered other limbs with his hands so the victim's identity could not be revealed. He wrote: 'The body on the canal got dissected to destroy the evidence. Kiddies from Moston Brook School have actually seen me at the grave.'

Hardy removed Lesley's watch and ring and gave them to Shelagh Farrow, who washed the ring before slipping it onto her engagement finger. He had told his girlfriend the whole story: 'I told her why I had knifed the girl. If ever a man should have been born dumb, it was me.'

Police launched a search for Lesley's skeleton after Hardy's statement and found her buried where he said. Though unable to identify the body, they had no reason to question his story.

Of Wanda Skala's murder, Hardy wrote in his statement: 'The murder started as a robbery, but the girl struggled. I hit her on the jaw. She collapsed and I carried her round behind some boards and left her. Then I went back, tried to strangle the girl, but couldn't, so I picked up a brick and hit her in the face four times. I had been reading a book from the library on murders and had read about the Heath case and decided to make it look like a sex attack.' (Neville Heath was hanged in 1946 for murdering two girls whom he sexually mutilated.) Hardy took Wanda's handbag and her bloodstained clothing as grisly mementoes, which he kept in a secret bolt-hole tunnelled into a wall. He was an early suspect for her killing, but his girlfriend Shelagh told detectives that on the night in question, he had not been out of her sight.

His third victim, Sharon Mossoph, disturbed him as he attempted to break into a shop while she was on her way home from her work party. Hardy promptly attacked Sharon, stabbing her with a screwdriver and strangling her. He then desecrated her body, making it look like a sex attack, and then threw it in the canal. Hardy wrote that he returned home to Shelagh Farrow, made love, then went on the run. Fearing he had left clues, he went back to Sharon's body and slashed the area where he had bitten off her nipple to disguise his teeth imprints.

DCI Bennion said of Hardy: 'He's one of the strangest, coldest men I've ever met. Physically, he's like a whippet – small, but tremendously tough, and completely unemotional. He's never ever shown any remorse or even emotion. No one really knows him. Why did he kill like this? There was no real reason.'

Hardy, who was 31 when he committed his final murder, struck fear into others even as a small boy. His mother, Edith Hardy, admitted: 'We always knew there was something wrong with Trevor. Even as a child he frightened me. It all stems from an accident he had when he was a child. Apparently a sliver of bone was dislodged in his head and sometimes it presses on part of his brain. It's when that happens that he erupts.'

His brother Colin said of Hardy's brain condition: 'When you get excited, or when you've drunk a lot of alcohol, your brain expands slightly. It is then that the bone touches the brain and so triggers the violence.'

Hardy's long criminal record began with a housebreaking conviction at the age of eight. The archetypal school bully, he underwent almost every category of punishment in the judicial system. Approved schools (from which he escaped 14 times), remand homes and borstals could not control him. He was convicted of robbery with violence when he was just 14. A relative said: 'He was always thieving – and even when they put him away he would be out again and on the run within days.' Hardy's crimes became increasingly violent and soon he had a criminal record of 147 convictions. His only previous sex offence was in 1968, when he was sent to jail for one month for indecent exposure.

Former schoolmates from St Mary's Road Secondary School, Newton Heath, recall that Hardy would try to impress or intimidate pupils and teachers. Once, when a woman teacher slapped his face after a four-letter torrent of abuse, he retaliated by trying to grab her throat. 'Everyone was frightened of him,' one ex-pupil recalled. 'He was a nasty boy who became an evil young man. His mere presence was enough to put people on edge.' Another said: 'Trevor was small, but incredibly strong. He was impossible to put down in a fight.'

Despite his written confession, Hardy pleaded not guilty when he appeared before Mr Justice Caulfield at Manchester Crown Court in April 1977. Three days into his trial he admitted manslaughter on the grounds of diminished responsibility, a plea not accepted by the Crown and the trial continued.

During the trial, a leading psychiatrist told the court that Hardy was 'a woman-hater who could kill again.' He was capable of murder, 'undoubtedly at any time, and for many years,' said Dr Michael Tarsh, Consultant Psychiatrist to Hope and Prestwich Hospitals. The expert said the accused derived 'aggressive sexual satisfaction' from mutilating the bodies of his victims. He remarked on 'the lack of care, the callousness or remorselessness in the way he [Hardy] talked about what he had done.' This, together with other evidence, led him to the conclusion that his patient was 'so psychopathic that his responsibility for these crimes must be seriously diminished.'

On the ninth day of the trial, the jury had to decide whether Hardy suffered any abnormality of the mind which might have impaired responsibility for his acts. In his summing-up, the judge said: 'The defendant drank heavily. He fought, and he has beaten up members of his family. He is very strong and is proud of his good physique. How, and why, Lesley Stewart was killed, only he himself knows. Indeed, it is only the defendant's admission that fixes the killing on him. Did he murder her, or have the defence proved an abnormality of mind that substantially impairs his mental responsibility?'

On 3 May 1977, Hardy was found guilty and given life for the murders of Lesley Stewart, Wanda Skala and Sharon Mossoph. The courtroom echoed with claps and cheers when the verdicts were delivered. The judge told him: 'This is a happy place but it will be happier without you.'

Shelagh Farrow received no punishment for covering for Hardy, much to the disgust of the victims' families.

In 1995, Sharon's father, Ralph Mossoph, asked for a reassurance from Home Secretary Michael Howard that Hardy would never be allowed out of prison, after hearing of a leaked list of whole life sentence killers. He was horrified that Sharon's killer did not appear among them and wanted to know why.

Mr Mossoph said: 'If such a list exists, then it should be made public so everyone knows whose names are on it. All people talk about are Hindley and Brady and people like the Ripper, but Hardy was a vicious and sadistic killer, who had a criminal record from the age of eight. It is coming up to the time when he might just be considered for parole and we need to have an assurance that he will die in jail. He is a menace to society and must never be allowed out.'

Finally in 1997, after years of inquiries, Mr Mossoph received a letter from the Home Office, giving him the news that the killer of his 17-year-old daughter would never be released. He said at the time: 'I feel like I've won the Lottery – I am just so happy. I don't know why it has taken all this time.'

23

'LOCAL HARD MAN'

'The reasons I did it – well, I'll be keeping to myself.'

Vinter (to police)

Name: Gary Vinter
Crime: Double murder
Date of Conviction: 21 April 2008
Age at Conviction: 37

On 2 August 1995 Railtrack signalman Gary Vinter entered a cabin near his signal box at Grangetown, Middlesbrough, to 'pass some time' with his colleague Carl Edon. Carl, 22, who was working as a relief train repairer, ended up stabbed to death and the cabin awash with his blood.

After the killing, Vinter, then 26, went back to his signal box to ensure everything was in order for the passage of trains on his stretch of line. Next, he drove to the police station at nearby South Bank, where he admitted the attack.

Vinter, a well known local hardman, who stands at 6ft 7in tall, was anxious the police should contact Railtrack's control room to inform them his signal box was unmanned. He was worried his absence might cause trains to crash. Vinter also drew police a map, directing them to the remote stretch of track where the cabin was located.

When interviewed by detectives, Vinter denied murdering his colleague, claiming manslaughter on the grounds of provocation. The case went to trial the following May.

Teesside Crown Court heard from pathologist Dr James Sunter, who said knife wounds were found over a wide area of Carl's body, suggesting a violent struggle. He had been stabbed 13 times with two knives. When the first knife broke, a second one was used to continue the attack. The last knife was still in the body when police arrived, with the broken one laid on the floor nearby.

Martin Bethel QC, defending Vinter, said there was no evidence of premeditation in the attack and that the killing arose out of a 'short-lived incident'. Giving evidence, Vinter said he and Carl had had an argument and that he had laughed at Carl when he shouted at him because he had never seen him lose his temper before. He said Carl then threatened to kill him and grabbed a knife from the sink. Vinter claimed he wrestled the knife from his colleague's hand and stabbed him in the struggle.

For the prosecution, Guy Whitburn, QC, argued that stabbing someone so ferociously that a knife breaks, then fetching another knife to continue the attack, were the actions of a very dangerous man. The jury agreed and found him guilty of murder. On 21 May 1996, he was sentenced to life in prison.

The judge reserved his decision on the exact length of sentence until September of that year when he recommended a minimum term of 12 years. Carl's girlfriend, Michelle Robertson, received notification of the killer's sentence in a letter from the Prison Service.

Michelle, 20, and Carl had two daughters together. When she learnt of Vinter's sentence, their eldest, Sophie, was nearly three, while Karla, who was born after her dad died and named in his memory, was about to turn one. Michelle, who lived with Edon in Middlesbrough, was angry that Vinter could kill her boyfriend in such a frenzied manner and receive 'such a low sentence.' She said at the time: 'It's not only an insult to me and his two children, but it doesn't dignify his name. I'm also scared that he'll be out sooner than 12 years, with good behaviour. I couldn't cope with it being so soon.' She added: 'I won't stand for it. I'm writing to the parole board, my MP and the Home Office about this.'

Her worst fears were realised when, with favourable reports indicating he was a model prisoner, the Parole Board chose to release Vinter early and he was back on the streets in August 2005. When he was jailed for the murder of Carl Edon, Vinter was already an intimidating sight. During his 10 years in prison he became an obsessive bodybuilder, using anabolic steroids to pump up his physique. On his release, Vinter was a giant of a man with an already-bad temper made worse by steroid use.

In a series of home visits from prison between 2003 and his release, Vinter met and courted Anne White, a pretty mum-of-four from Middlesbrough. They moved in together in the town's Eston area and married in July 2006. But friends and family were concerned about the relationship from the start. Those fears would later prove to be well-founded.

On New Year's Eve 2006, Vinter was involved in a brutal fight outside the Miners Arms pub near his home in Eston. He found himself back in the dock at Teesside Crown Court in July 2007, along with fellow brawlers Thomas Hoe, 22, Geoffrey Ewart, 40, and Carl Ewart, 19. CCTV footage played to the court showed the men piling out of the pub. There followed a lengthy fight between Hoe and the Ewarts. Vinter – who the court heard had earlier been hit across the back of the head with a glass – was seen delivering a 'mighty blow' to Geoffrey Ewart, knocking him to the ground and bringing the fight to an end.

Judge George Moorhouse said it was a 'horrific scene, enough to terrify any passer-by.' For his part in the fracas, Vinter – out on life licence – was sent back to jail for six months. Again, he was released early from prison after behaving 'impeccably' inside. He was back on the streets in December of that year. Two months later, in the early hours of 11 February 2008, he murdered again. This time the victim was his wife.

When the case came to Teesside Crown Court on 21 April 2008, prosecution counsel Jamie Hill told how in the fortnight leading up to her death, Anne, 40, had told friends that she wanted to leave her violent bully of a husband, but she was afraid he would come after her. Then, five days before the murder, Vinter went berserk during a row and smashed up a TV set. He moved out, taking Anne's passport with him.

She did not see or hear from Vinter again until he spotted her out drinking with friends on the night she died. He stalked his wife round pubs in Eston and nearby Normanby. Fuelled by alcohol, cocaine and the anabolic steroids he took for bodybuilding, Vinter became paranoid and jealous, wrongly believing Anne was exchanging text messages with another man.

Trouble flared at the Miners Arms – the pub where Vinter had the New Year's Eve brawl – when he argued with Anne and her 16-year-old daughter Paige. The argument spilled outside and Vinter ordered Anne into the back seat of his friend's car, where onlookers saw him screaming at his cowering wife. The two men with Vinter, Phillip James and Andrew Drury, both 22, grew nervous of the muscle-bound older man, of whom they had previously been 'in awe'. Before they dropped the pair off at Vinter's mother's home in Normanby, Anne said to them: 'You don't know what you're getting yourselves into, being with him.'

Alerted by Anne's friends, police began looking for the couple. But when they called Anne on her mobile, she said she was out drinking in town and having fun, apparently in a bid to appease her maniacal husband. The court heard that later that night Vinter called the police, trying to convince them she was safe and well at home. Less than half an hour later, she was dead.

After killing his wife, a breathless Vinter phoned for the young men who had earlier dropped them both off to come and collect him from his mother's. When they arrived, the agitated, sweating hulk climbed into the back seat and yelled: 'Go, go!' Minutes later, Vinter – his hands and T-shirt covered in his wife's blood – used Anne's mobile to ring the police and report her murder. He said: 'Right, my name's Gary Vinter. I'm solely responsible for the death of my wife. There's nobody else involved, just me. I killed my wife. That's all I'm prepared to say.'

Vinter's mother, who had been asleep upstairs during the killing, found her daughter-in-law's body on her kitchen floor. In a chilling echo of his first murder 13 years earlier, two knives – one of them broken in half – were laid next to her. Anne, who weighed less than half Vinter's 20 stone, had been strangled and then stabbed four times, with a single wound to her heart.

When police found Vinter at around 2am, they had to subdue him with baton rounds. Finally handcuffed, he said: 'I'm a convicted murderer. Nobody's going to take a blind bit of notice of what I've got to say. I'll be pleading guilty at the earliest opportunity; I will not be running a trial.'

Later interviewed, he said that he and his wife were trying to patch up their differences, but other people had interfered, making him lose his temper. He told detectives that he 'felt bad about it' but said he could not help himself, that he was 'beyond angry' and that he 'knew it was going to happen.' He added: 'The reasons I did it – well, I'll be keeping to myself.' He directed his lawyer, Brian Russell, to offer no mitigation whatsoever on his behalf.

Vinter, wearing a tight white T-shirt that showed off his pumped-up physique, smirked when Judge Peter Fox, QC, the Recorder of Middlesbrough, told him: 'Regrettably you are incapable of self-control. Your extreme violence to others cannot be viewed as other than continuing for as far as can be seen. You therefore fall into that relatively small category of people who should be deprived permanently of their liberty in a civilised society. It is a whole life sentence.'

The public gallery, filled with friends and family of both his murder victims, rose to its feet as Vinter was led away, with shouts of 'Rot in hell!'

Once Vinter was caged, Anne's father Jim White, 71, wondered why he was allowed back out of prison after the pub brawl. He said: 'When a man's got life and gets parole after 10 years, surely if he breaks that parole, he goes back and finishes the life sentence?

'All we want to know is why he didn't finish his sentence when he went in. He was only out two months when he murdered her. It's unbelievable. It's broke us all, the whole family. She was our only girl and she's gone.'

Anne's mother Peggy, 62, said: 'He's never given any reason, nothing. She was a beautiful woman. She did everything for him. She was terrified of him.'

Val Edon, the mother of Vinter's first victim, said: 'When we heard he had killed again, it traumatised us. If he hadn't been let out, it wouldn't have happened. Ten years was not a life sentence – it is the ones left behind who are serving a life sentence.'

Mrs Edon told reporters that it was 'marvellous news' that her son's killer would die in prison. She said: 'He is not going to get out again. I feel so sorry for the other family that they have had to go through what we have been through; we know exactly how they are feeling at this present time. It takes an awful long time to recover. Your life is never the same again; you never get over it. My son had two small children.'

Detective Superintendent Gordon Lang, who ran the investigation into Anne White's death, said outside court: 'Gary Vinter is clearly a dangerous man with a history of extreme violence. He inflicted horrific injuries on Anne White and I hope that her family and friends can now take some comfort from today's events.'

Edwige Robertson, mother of Carl Edon's girlfriend Michelle, said: 'At the end of the day he shouldn't have been let out in the first place. I blame the system. He is supposed to have got life when he killed Carl. For murderers, when they say life, it should mean life.'

24

'AN EXTREMELY DANGEROUS MAN'

'He was so cool after the murder – he even invited me to his flat and sat me down on the settee where Derek had been killed.'

Victim's girlfriend

Name: Phillip Heggarty
Crime: Murder
Date of Conviction: 23 July 2004
Age at Conviction: 49

Small-time drug dealer Derek Bennett could not resist boasting to pals that he was, for once, flush. The 41-year-old was at an all-night party in Rumney, Cardiff, with his best friend Phillip Heggarty. That night, the inseparable pair – both 'mad keen' Cardiff City fans – drunkenly hugged as Derek told anyone who'd listen that he'd landed a lucrative cannabis and cocaine deal that had made him thousands. He had more than £3,000 in cash in his money belt and £11,000 of drugs in his car.

Three days later, on Monday, 14 April 2003, Derek's grey Renault Laguna was set on fire in the car park of the Earl Haig British Legion Club in the city's Whitchurch area. Firefighters considered it the work of joyriders until they spotted a charred arm protruding from a rolled-up carpet on the backseat. The body was burnt beyond recognition, but was identified from dental records as Derek Bennett.

A post-mortem examination found no soot in Derek's lungs, meaning he was almost certainly dead before the fire was started. He had been battered round the head at least six times with a hammer-like object. Such was the ferocity of the attack that his skull was broken into 23 pieces. Home Office pathologist Andrew Davidson said it was 'highly likely' the deceased would have been unconscious after the beating, though he probably lived for at least 90 minutes afterwards. There were no defence wounds to his arms and hands, indicating he did not resist the beating.

Detectives learned that the dead man left the all-night party the previous Friday with a man who was already well known to them: Philip Heggarty. The 48-year-old call centre manager had a long record of violent crime and police were soon knocking at his door. When they searched his flat in Clare Road, Grangetown, Cardiff, they found Derek's blood on the walls and he was arrested for the murder of his life-long best mate.

At the opening of Heggarty's trial at Swansea Crown Court on 16 June of the following year, prosecuting counsel Gregory Bull, QC, told the jury that the defendant's sole motive for killing his friend was greed. He murdered him for the large quantity of cash and drugs that he made no secret of having in his possession, said Mr Bull. Then, with a callous indifference to the man who called him 'Bruv', he rolled his body up in carpet, bundled him into his car and set fire to it 'in a deliberate and calculated attempt to destroy evidence he may have left on the body.'

Mr Bull told the court that on Friday, 11 April 2003, Heggarty and the deceased had been out with friends on 'an all-nighter'. Derek left his car at the Cardiff International Arena, where he had a parking arrangement with staff, and then he and Heggarty met up with his brother Paul and nephew Matthew in a city centre pub. The prosecution said Derek made it clear he was flush with money by peeling off notes from his wad of cash every time he bought a round of drinks. Later, at the party in Rumney, he boasted of having a large stash of drugs in his car.

Afterwards, Heggarty drove some of their group of friends home and took Derek to collect his car. Mr Bull said: 'It was decided Mr Bennett should collect his car and follow Heggarty's car to Clare Road and there, the two men would get their heads down. Mr Bennett did retrieve his Laguna and made his way back to Clare Road, where later that day he was murdered.'

The prosecutor added: 'Following Mr Bennett's death, Heggarty – who was known to be normally strapped for cash – was found to be flush with it. A large quantity of drugs taken from Derek Bennett were found at the home of Heggarty's girlfriend, Ann Kerslake.'

The accused made no effort to hide his newfound wealth and paid off a number of debts in the days immediately after his friend's death. Mr Bull said Heggarty paid £750, plus £50 interest to a colleague who had lent him money. He also paid off £500 of a £1,000 loan from Robert Nash, the owner of the telesales business that he had managed. Mr Nash told the court he was surprised when Heggarty phoned him on 12 April to tell him that he was going to repay half the loan.

Mr Nash said he learned of Derek's death when he phoned Heggarty with a query about work. The witness told the court: 'I began the call by asking him how he was and he said he was not very well. He said, "Derek has been found dead in the back of his car."' Mr Nash described the accused as 'shocked and shaken' with a 'completely different demeanour' from Saturday, when he handed over the money. He said: 'I asked him if the police had been to see him and he said, "My God, yes!" He told me that apparently he had been the last person to see Mr Bennett.'

Cross-examined by defence barrister Francis Aubrey, Mr Nash agreed that at the time of the murder his company had been making record profits from selling a weekly newspaper in the North of England. He said it was 'like shooting fish in a barrel' and that his staff were expecting large commission bonuses and had good reason to feel flush.

Prosecutor Mr Bull said the fire was extinguished in time for police to collect damning evidence that would prove Heggarty's guilt. He told the court that Derek's body had been wrapped in a carpet that was covered in hairs matching those of Heggarty's dogs. A pink-and-white towel wrapped round the deceased's head and a pillowcase covering his feet both matched others found at the Clare Road address. But when Heggarty was arrested, he told police that he did not own the carpet used to wrap up the body and that he'd never seen the pillowcase and towel.

Heggarty told police that after the party he took Derek to his car before they went their separate ways. He said Derek had told him he was going to get some breakfast and 'had a few things to do'; that he had watched his friend drive off, and then went to his girlfriend's house to pick up his dogs. But Mr Bull said witnesses, including a gas worker and two neighbours, said Derek was at the flat on that Saturday morning. The defendant agreed that he must have 'forgotten' his friend was with him that morning, after all.

Mr Bull said Heggarty would 'say anything to get away with murder.' He turned to the dock and told him: 'Not only have you told many lies to the police, you have told many lies to the jury.' He asked Heggarty how he could give a detailed description of the all-night party, but could not recall seeing the father-of-two at his flat the following morning.

In the dock, Heggarty agreed that his friend was 'probably attacked' at his flat and suggested it must have happened when he was out between 10am and 3pm. Mr Bull said that if this 'ludicrous' possibility was true and his attackers had killed him for his drugs and money, they had missed out on the 'jackpot' – around £10,000 of cannabis and cocaine stashed away in a kitchen drawer.

The barrister also wondered how the 'murderers' knew Derek was staying at Clare Road and that he would be alone when they went round. He added that it would have taken at least two people to carry a 12-and-a-half stone man out of the flat and into his car. Asked who his accomplice was, Heggarty replied: 'I did not have one because I did not do the murder.'

Mr Bull said that in the hours after the murder, Heggarty set about faking himself an alibi. He went to a Tesco store and made a point of being caught several times on the CCTV; he also met a friend in a pub. 'He was making attempts to be sure he was seen out and about,' said Mr Bull.

The jury also heard that Derek Bennett's blood was found inside Heggarty's flat and on clothes he was wearing on the night of the killing. The accused's fingerprints were discovered in blood on a wall in the cellar of the flat, said Mr Bull. He told the court: 'In order to leave a fingerprint in blood you must put your finger in it while the blood is still wet.' The prosecutor said splashes of blood on Heggarty's settee were consistent with the attack occurring while the victim lay on it. Derek may have been 'asleep or dozing with his back to his attacker' at the time, Mr Bull explained. He also told how police found blood sprayed on the walls close to where he was attacked. Derek's blood was also found on walls leading to the basement of Heggarty's flat, underneath a handrail along the basement stairway and on a phone bill in the defendant's name.

Asked why the flat had been thoroughly cleaned in the hours after the killing, Heggarty said he was cleaning up vomit from one of his dogs. He said he noticed no signs that Derek had been attacked at his home, adding: 'The police sat in front of the blood splashes on the wall when they were interviewing me. They didn't see anything either.'

Mr Bull also referred to Derek's blood found on Heggarty's shoes and jeans: 'Can I suggest it could have only got there while you were moving the body or while you were attacking him?' Heggarty answered, 'No, that's not right.'

His defence counsel asked Heggarty: 'Did you kill your friend, Derek Bennett?' He answered: 'No, I definitely did not. He was like the brother I never had.' He went on to describe Derek as a man who lived a dangerous life as a drug dealer, and said that he juggled money he owed to various dealers to 'keep the wolves from the door'. Heggarty told the court: 'He was robbing Peter to pay Paul. He would have a number of suppliers and would get his drugs on credit – he would get some drugs from dealer one and pay for drugs from dealers two and three from the profits.' He said that about a month before his death, Derek had, in his own words, 'dropped the balls'. Heggarty went on: 'He'd lost the use of his car – which he used to do all his business in – and could not pay the people he owed.' Defender Mr Aubrey asked: 'How much was he owing?' Heggarty answered: 'I knew it was a thousand pounds-plus.' The accused said he agreed to lend his friend £1,000 so that he could give his dealers 'a gesture of goodwill in part payment.' Mr Aubrey asked: 'What did you think might happen to him?' Heggarty replied: 'He was in fear of his life.'

Mr Audrey then called Derek's girlfriend, Colleen Jacobs, to the witness box. Ms Jacobs, who had lived with the victim for five years, agreed that he had been worried about his debts to drug dealers 'higher up the chain'. She said the 'lay-on' system was common practice in the drugs underworld, where suppliers would hand over large amounts of drugs to local dealers without charge, but the money would have to be paid as soon as the drugs had been sold. Mr Aubrey asked: 'He was not a man who was easily frightened, but he was frightened this time?' She replied, 'Yes.' The barrister continued: 'One of the men he referred to as a "heavy" lived in nearby Whitchurch, is that right?' She answered, 'Yes.'

The jury deliberated its verdict for 36 hours before finding Heggarty guilty of his best friend's murder. They then sat shocked as the killer's 79 previous convictions were read out before the court. Heggarty's long criminal career began when he was 10 and he stole from neighbours. He spent most of his childhood in approved schools and borstals for theft and assault.

By his 20s he was beating up old ladies for their handbags, then in

'AN EXTREMELY DANGEROUS MAN'

1988, aged 33, he was sentenced to 15 years in prison for torturing a 60-year-old man in his own home. He slashed the terrified victim's face until he told him where he kept his savings. After 10 years, he was released.

During his trial, Heggarty argued that he could not have dumped his friend's body in the Whitchurch area because he was completely unfamiliar with the place, but his criminal record showed that he had committed at least eight burglaries there.

Sentencing Heggarty, 49, judge Mr Justice Roderick Evans said: 'You are a resourceful and manipulative liar. This was a brutal and very violent killing and you are an extremely dangerous man. There is no doubt he enjoyed your company that night, drinking, taking drugs and going to an all-night party.

'Within hours of that coming to an end, you bludgeoned him to death, hitting him about the head with a blunt object, shattering his skull into 23 pieces. He took one-and-a-half hours to die. I have no doubt your motive was robbery.'

The judge added: 'Thirty years is not enough. The sentence is whole life: you will spend the rest of your life in prison.'

Outside court, the victim's girlfriend, who was bringing up their children Josh, three, and six-month-old Kian, who was conceived shortly before Derek died, said: 'Phil could be charming and likeable, but I suspected he did it from the outset. He was so cool after the murder – he even invited me to his flat and sat me down on the settee where Derek had been killed.'

Derek's brother Paul, 45, welcomed the sentence, saying: 'Justice has been served and it has given me faith again in the justice system. There is no jubilation for me in this. At the end of the day that man should never be on the streets. He should have been locked up a long time ago.' He added: 'Derek was a lovable rogue, well-liked in the community and always put a smile on people's faces with his wit and personality. It hasn't been easy listening to the evidence or reports that Derek was the best friend of his murderer.'

25

'THE ENFORCER'

*'I find it almost impossible to understand the workings of a
mind as twisted and evil as yours.'*

Trial judge Mr Justice Rougier

Name: Victor Castigador
Crime: Double murder
Date of Conviction: 28 February 1990
Age at Conviction: 35

At around midnight on 2 April 1989, staff at an amusement arcade
on Wardour Street in London's Soho were cashing up when one
of their former employees burst through the door. Victor Castigador –
a former hit man for President Marcos of the Philippines – had
recently been overlooked for promotion at the arcade and he held a
very bitter grudge.

Standing at only 5ft tall but as broad as a heavyweight boxer,
Castigador stormed the arcade with four young accomplices: Calvin
Nelson, 19, Paul Clinton, 17, and their respective girlfriends, Karen
Dunn, 17, and Allison Woodside, 20. After flooring a security guard,
he rounded up the four staff and marched them down to the basement
with his gang in tow.

Downstairs, Nelson held a gun to the neck of relief manager Yurev
Gomez and forced him to unlock a steel strong-room, where the

money was kept. Once the terrified employee had done so, Castigador stormed in, hitting him to the floor with an elbow to his back. He then emptied the day's takings, totalling £8,685, into a rucksack.

Yurev and cashier Debbie Alvarez were then herded into the vault, along with Sri Lankan security guards Ambikaipahan Apapayan and Kandiahkanapathy Vinayagamoorthy. All four were made to kneel down while their captor tied their hands behind their backs.

Castigador, 34, then fetched a bottle of white spirit from a nearby store cupboard and squirted it over them. As they knelt, cowering, the vengeful maniac emptied a wastepaper basket around the cage.

Yurev told the Old Bailey murder trial in March the following year: 'Victor threw bits of paper from the dustbins into the cage. I saw him emptying a fire extinguisher. He went off and reappeared with what looked like a jiffy bottle. He came into the cage and started squirting the liquid over our heads. He made sure everyone was soaked. He slammed the cage door shut and secured it with a coat hanger.'

Castigador – whose name translates to 'the enforcer' in Spanish – laughed and yelled abuse in his native tongue as he and Nelson threw lit matches into the cage like darts.

One of the guards managed to get to his feet and stamp the matches out, but Castigador was already packing newspaper along the bottom of the cage door, taunting his former colleagues by teasingly stroking a match across the lighting strip of its box. The petrified manager yelled at him: 'How can you do this? These are people just like you.' One of the guards begged: 'Don't light it – I would rather you shoot me.' Ignoring his pleas, Castigador used every remaining match to light the paper, threw the empty box at his victims and led his accessories up the stairs, locking the basement door behind them.

At 7.55 the following morning, two members of staff arrived for the early shift and smelled burning. As they opened the basement door, they were consumed by smoke and immediately dialled 999. When fire fighters arrived shortly afterwards they found four bodies lying on the floor of the cage. The two security guards were dead from asphyxia and inhalation of fire fumes.

Two of the victims were alive, but the fire damage to their bodies was so extensive that only afterwards, when they arrived at the Burns Unit at Queen Mary's Hospital, Roehampton, West London, was one of them identified as a woman. Yurev suffered 30 per cent full thickness body surface burns, including the whole of his left arm from shoulder to fingers, patches on the face, right arm, back and chest. He had severe internal burns from breathing in the scorching hot smoke.

Debbie, the cashier, sustained 28 per cent burns. Her face was essentially burnt off and she had severe injuries to both arms and hands, her back, buttocks and thighs. She also suffered severe internal burns to her upper airways and lungs.

In court, Yurev, 25, told how he and his colleague had survived the fire. He said he had managed to untie his hands and drag himself and 27-year-old Debbie across the scorching steel floor to the air supply coming from beneath the strong-room door. Once there, they took turns in breathing from a keyhole, where the airflow was stronger. He told the jury: 'There was a ball of fire. It was like an oven. My skin was on fire and I could feel myself disintegrating, but there was nowhere to go. I undid my hands and rolled myself on the floor and the wall and put myself out. I managed to get my mouth near the keyhole. I kept going down for 10 minutes and coming up again.'

Yurev noticed Debbie's leg was still alight. 'She was unconscious and there were little bits of blue flame over her body,' he said. 'I stretched over and put my hand on her leg and put the fire out. I caught alight again and that is how I burned all over. I put myself out again and pulled her over.' Wearing a leather glove on his left hand, he told the court how he heard the two guards die. He said Mr Vinayagamoorthy took one deep breath, then breathed out and died. Controlling his emotions, Yurev recalled: 'The other one said something in his own language — I believe he was praying. About 20 minutes later, he went exactly the same way.'

The survivors told police: 'Victor did it.' When they arrested him, detectives were shocked by Castigador's callous indifference. 'He couldn't understand what all the fuss was about,' one senior officer recalled.

At the trial, prosecuting counsel Jean Southworth, QC, said the victims died as a result of 'murder most foul'. She added: 'What happened on this dreadful night can be put down in two words – grudge and greed. Castigador is the main villain. He obviously sees himself as a tough guy. He often bragged of his life in the Philippines, saying he had been in the commandos and the secret police. He said he was used to guns, and had killed and could not return to the Philippines.'

Miss Southworth explained that Castigador had worked as a security guard at both the Wardour Street arcade and another owned by the Leisure Group Company in Oxford Street, but he was angry because he thought he should have been promoted to assistant manager.

'The reason for not promoting him was absenteeism and because of arguments with other staff,' the prosecutor said. 'Although he bragged he could cope with trouble, his employers found that when he was off duty there was not much trouble because he seemed to be creating it, rather than cooling it.'

When he turned up for work on 31 March 1989 he was already seething at his failed promotion bid days earlier. Insult added to injury when he was told that he no longer had a job at all. It was the last straw and Castigador was not a man to be messed with.

The court heard that, on the night of the killings, Yurev was forced to unlock the safe. He had a gun – albeit a plastic one – pushed into his neck by Nelson. Then Yurev, Debbie and the two guards were pushed into the wire cage while Castigador fetched the white spirit.

Miss Southworth told the jury: 'Castigador poured it over the victims and onto the floor, and with Woodside and Clinton watching him, he and Nelson lit matches and threw them in. The two guards, who were at the back of the cage, were asphyxiated after sustaining dreadful burns, but miraculously Yurev and Debbie survived.'

Castigador denied any part in the crimes until the start of his trial when he admitted murder, attempted murder and robbery. His male accomplices, Nelson and Clinton, denied the charges but were found guilty of murder and attempted murder. Nelson was sentenced to life in a young offenders' institution and Clinton ordered to detention during Her Majesty's pleasure. The females were found not guilty of the murder and attempted murder charges, but guilty of robbery. Karen Dunn was given three years' youth custody and Allison Woodside received three-and-a-half years' imprisonment.

Prior to Castigador's sentencing, his own counsel, James Mulcahy, conceded: 'It would be very surprising if you had not come to the conclusion, having heard the evidence and seen the witnesses, that Castigador was a ruthless, callous and inhuman monster.' Mulcahy told how Castigador had worked as a driver in the Philippines before being recruited, aged 21, into 'the Philippines constabulary', a quasi-military organisation combining military and police duties. 'It is clear from what he has said to those instructing me, that in that body he was called upon to perform duties involving the loss of human life in circumstances which would not have even been contemplated in any of the Western democracies.'

Sentencing him, Mr Justice Rougier told Castigador: 'I find it almost impossible to understand the workings of a mind as twisted and evil as yours.' Referring to the Soho murders, he told him: 'You were the man who planned this and recruited for it, and with evil determination saw it through. You have forfeited the right to walk free for a very long time. Some might say you have forfeited the right to live at all, but unlike you, we do not go to that length in this country.' The judge said Castigador had condemned his victims to an agonising death without 'one shred of pity or mercy.' Debbie Alvarez, terribly disfigured by burns, was at the Old Bailey to see her attackers punished. She said: 'I wanted to be here so that Victor could see what he had done to me.'

Castigador boasted to detectives that he had killed 'around' 20 people, indicating his proud tally with his fingers. He said he had been a member of an official assassination squad under the Marcos regime. His squad leader in the Philippines was called Colonel Lagman. Castigador chose burning to despatch some of his victims – they were wrapped in chicken wire, set on fire and once dead, dumped in water. But in the majority of cases, he was happy to simply shoot them in the head.

In the Philippines, Castigador met Englishwoman Jacqueline Haddon, who had moved there with her husband, a diver. Castigador told her he was 'a sort of policeman' and befriended her after her marriage broke up. The couple began an affair. Mrs Haddon returned to England in 1984, setting up home at Middleton-on-Sea, near Bognor in Sussex. The following year, Castigador followed her to get married and obtain UK citizenship, but after moving in he began to beat her up and started ill-treating her two children. She told him to leave and he moved to London, where he found accommodation with a distant relative, whom he referred to as 'Auntie' in a council flat in Bow, East London.

He went to work at the Leisure Investment arcades, where he enjoyed strutting about in his uniform, asserting his authority on customers. He considered himself excellent at the job and was angry when after four years he had still not been promoted. And so the grudge built up that was to lead to murder.

After the arcade raid, Castigator's young accomplices – Nelson, Clinton, Dunn and Woodside – used their share of the stolen money to go on a spending spree in Torquay, Devon, where they laughed and joked about the horrific fate of their victims. As they were being driven from a pub in a taxi, one of the women complained of being cold and the driver offered to turn on the heater. One of the youths joked, 'We don't want to burn', and another started singing a pop song, 'Burn It Up'. All four passengers collapsed in laughter.

On 12 November 2003, solicitors for Paul Clinton appeared at London's Royal Courts of Justice to appeal for a reduction in the minimum 20-year tariff set by the trial judge. During the appeal, representations were heard on behalf of the surviving victims, who both wanted Clinton to serve his full sentence. The court heard how relief manager, Yurev Gomez, was left disabled from his ordeal 14 years earlier. Inhaling fumes during the eight hours trapped in the vault caused serious injury to his one remaining lung, putting him at risk of pneumonia for the rest of his life. He was dependent on oxygen and his skin remained terribly scarred.

Cashier Debbie Alvarez still suffered from damage to her windpipe and had trouble speaking. The court was told that she was severely disfigured and only left the house once or twice a week. She was constantly falling over because of injuries to her legs and continued to suffer fractures to her feet because of those falls.

The Lord Chief Justice was quick to deny the appeal.

26

'THE FRANKENSTEIN KILLER'

'Don't scream – there's nobody around, nobody will help you.'

Dembovskis (to victim)

Name: Viktors Dembovskis
Crime: Serial rape and murder
Date of Conviction: 29 March 2006
Age at Conviction: 42

Jeshma Raithatha was last seen alive on Monday, 16 May 2005, at Claremont High School in Kenton, West London, where she had been revising for her upcoming A-levels. She was a talented musician and hoped to become a professional singer after studying at university. After being accepted onto an arts degree course, Jeshma was excited and, eager to make her predicted grades in English, Computer Studies and Music, she had attended a revision class at school that day.

The 17-year-old left just after 1pm, dressed in a blue sweater and navy blue jeans. She was carrying a black school bag with red hearts on it. Jeshma also wore three silver bangles and had a nose stud.

She caught a bus and went shopping on Wembley High Road, visiting a branch of Primark, where she was captured on CCTV buying a top at about 2.20pm. Next, she bought a candle from a discount store called Pound City. She then caught a 92 bus, getting off at Sudbury Hill tube station. But Jeshma, described by her head teacher as a 'delightful, sensitive, caring and creative young woman', did not complete the 10-minute walk from the bus stop to her home in Greenford, West London. It was three days before her 18th birthday.

Her mum Manula recalled: 'She usually leaves a note for me, saying something like, "I have gone to the gym", but there was nothing. At four or five o'clock it started raining. I called her mobile phone and left a message; it was getting a bit late. I texted her – she always replies to a text message. At about six o'clock, I started to get worried. I called the police at 10pm. I got the impression that it was not that unusual for a 17- or 18-year-old to be gone for a few hours. I was calling all her friends; they were all linked with each other. Her friends came round at night – we knew something had happened.'

Manula said her daughter had no problems at home, that she was happy and ambitious, and that 'her life was about to take off.' She added: 'Jeshma was in a happy state and was looking forward to her life. She had planned a holiday with her friends to the Canary Islands. Her birthday was on a weekday and she was not sure if her friends would come, with the exams – I think they were planning to go out for a meal. We did a puja [a Hindu invocation] at home on her birthday to give her strength.'

By her birthday, Jeshma had already been dead for three days. Her partially-clothed body was found on Tuesday, 24 May, eight days after she went missing, in thick undergrowth near the David Lloyd Racquet and Fitness Club in Sudbury, a mere 500 yards from her home.

As she took a shortcut through an overgrown path, Jeshma was attacked and dragged 20 metres to a secluded woodland den. A post-mortem later revealed that her attacker had throttled her unconscious before repeatedly raping her. He then stabbed her twice in the neck and three times in the heart.

Police quickly had a prime suspect in the form of Viktors Dembovskis, a Latvian, whom the tabloid press would soon label 'The

Frankenstein Killer' on account of his large rectangular head, vacant eyes and lumbering gait. Dembovskis, who worked at a local carwash, became a suspect when he vanished from a nearby house that he shared with a dozen or so fellow immigrants around the time of Jeshma's disappearance. His roommate at the property – located just five minutes' walk from the murder scene – said that on the day Jeshma went missing, Dembovskis had come back to the address with scratches on his face. He also told police that the Latvian had stolen £370 from him before leaving in a hurry. Police searched Dembovskis' scattered belongings and found his passport missing. Colleagues told detectives he had not turned up to work on the day of Jeshma's disappearance and had not been at the carwash since.

Police were convinced he had fled to his homeland and examined passenger lists for planes, ferries, coaches and Eurostar trains. Four days after the murder, the suspect was caught on CCTV, queuing at the ticket office at Victoria Coach Station. Records showed he had bought a one-way ticket to Latvia.

On the evening of 2 June, police swooped on Dembovskis at his mother's home in poverty-stricken Livani, 120 miles east of Latvia's thriving capital Riga. His 77-year-old mother, Varvara Danilova, told how police called for her son as she watched a soap opera on TV. 'Viktors opened the door,' she said from her dilapidated concrete flat. 'They were in the kitchen, discussing his trip to London. Then they said he must go with them. They took his clothes, T-shirts, underpants and a sweater – I guessed it was something to do with England. Maybe now I will never see him again. Photographs will be the only memory of my boy.'

When told why her son was a wanted man in England, Mrs Danilova said: 'The horror, the horror! I thought he could do bad things but he could never kill anyone.'

On 5 June, Dembovskis made his first court appearance in the town of Preili, 150 miles from Riga. When reporters asked him through the bars of the dock if he had killed Jeshma, he said: 'I have no idea what happened to the girl – I did nothing wrong.' He showed no emotion throughout the 15-minute hearing, but when the judge allowed cameras into the court, he smiled and posed for photographs. At one point he lent over to his lawyer and whispered: 'Do I look good?' He was remanded to custody in Riga, where the prosecutor-general had 80 days to decide whether or not to extradite him. Within three weeks, he was back on British soil.

His trial began on 14 March of the following year at the Old Bailey, where he denied raping, sexually assaulting and murdering Jeshma Raithatha. The court heard how the 42-year-old, who had twice been jailed for rape in his homeland, lay in wait in an undergrowth den before pouncing on the teenager as she made her way home.

Jonathan Laidlaw, prosecuting, said: 'Her murder occurred in the most brutal and horrific of ways. Jeshma was abducted as she was walking through an area of woods and a field to her family home. The defendant had planned this attack with some care. He took up a position that gave him a view down the road and also gave him access to undergrowth nearby. He was armed with a knife.

'The defendant abducted Jeshma at about 3pm. By 4pm she was dead. Nobody saw her taken from the road, but she was led into his den. There, the defendant removed some of her clothing before he strangled her. Jeshma managed only to scratch the defendant before she lost consciousness. While she was unconscious the defendant raped her. When the sexual attack was over, he stabbed her to death, no doubt motivated by his intention that Jeshma should be in no position to identify him.'

The court heard how Dembovskis had come to Britain looking for work in November 2004. After a while he found himself living in a house rented by East Europeans in Dimmock Drive, just a street away from Jeshma's family home. The prosecution told how shortly after Jeshma's murder, officers met his Russian roommate Vladimir Ivanov.

'He told the police that after Jeshma's disappearance the defendant had come back to the address bearing scratches to his face,' said Mr Laidlaw. 'He also told the police the defendant carried a knife.'

Police found a blue zip-up fleece that the defendant had left behind when he fled to Latvia. 'In one of the pockets were two necklaces that belonged to Jeshma. Her blood was found upon them', said Mr Laidlaw. When police spoke to the defendant's mother in Latvia, she gave them tourist photos that he had taken of his stay in London, in which he was wearing an identical blue fleece to that in which Jeshma's jewellery was found.

Outlining the accused's record of sex crimes in his native Latvia, Mr Laidlaw told the jury: 'It would be an affront to common sense to deny you evidence that the defendant has a propensity to commit sexual attacks on women. In June 1990 the defendant followed Anastasia Skadinya as she was crossing a bridge. He put a knife to her throat, and said: "I want you, or I'll cut you. Don't scream, there's nobody around, nobody will help you." He then dragged her to the riverbank, put the knife to her neck and raped her.

The prosecutor went on: 'In November 1997 he telephoned Ineta Maliseva and asked her to go to a flat, where he was drinking with friends. At about 5am she walked home accompanied by the defendant. At the stairwell to her flat, he grabbed her, put a penknife to her throat and told her to keep quiet or he would "cut her up." He then dragged her to a cellar and raped her.'

The court also learned how Dembovskis' house keys were found at the scene of Jeshma's murder. All this damning evidence, said the barrister, made it clear that the defendant was the man responsible for her death.

When Mr Laidlaw concluded his summary of the case against Dembovskis, Jeshma's father Suresh let out a wail of anguish before sobbing with his head in his hands. And as the shattered parent did so, Dembovskis was laughing in the dock with his female interpreter.

'I'm suffering all my life for these awful allegations,' said Dembovskis from the dock. He could not account for his keys being at the scene of the crime and claimed the blue jacket in which Jeshma's jewellery was found was not his, saying he 'had one similar.'

After less than three hours' deliberation on 29 March 2006, the jury unanimously found him guilty on all counts. Judge Peter Beaumont told him: 'From the first to the last you have not displayed one jot of remorse for the appalling crimes you committed that day against that girl, or for the consequences to her family, who have to live with the loss of their child for the rest of their lives.

'They have had, thanks to you, the added trauma of having to endure a two-week trial, in which you have twisted, lied and cast about for any excuse you could think of to avoid your responsibility for the abduction of a 17-year-old girl as she made her way home in broad daylight on an afternoon in suburban London. She had nothing to defend herself with – and why should she? All she had done that day was go to school, dropped off by her mother, and do a little shopping.

'You killed her so you could get away, and you very nearly did. For behaviour as appalling as that there is only one sentence – a life sentence from which you will never, ever be released.'

After his trial, three women raped by Dembovskis in his home town of Livani spoke of their ordeals. In June 1990, kindergarten teacher Anastasia Skadina, 31, was walking across a bridge when Dembovskis leapt out at her, brandishing a knife. The mother-of-two recalled: 'He shoved me into a bush near the river. It was horrible, he was saying, "Just relax like you are with your husband." He had a tattoo of two eyes on his abdomen; it was very weird. The whole thing was horrible.' The terrified woman reported the attack to police, who recognised her attacker from his distinctive tattoo. Dembovskis was caught the next day and was jailed for seven years.

From prison, he took twisted pleasure in taunting his victim further. Anastasia said: 'He wrote a letter to me from his cell. It was filthy, really filthy. He drew a picture of a baby's dummy as if to suggest maybe I was pregnant from what he did. When I read his letter, it was like being raped again.' Of Jeshma's murder, Anastasia, by then aged 47, said: 'I am so sorry for the poor girl's family. I was so lucky to escape with my life. I still don't like to leave the house without my husband and I worry all the time about my own daughter. She is now living in England and if I had known he was there, I would never have let her go.'

Dembovskis served his full sentence for the attack on Anastasia, but he was far from rehabilitated and within weeks of his release in 1997 he viciously attacked another woman. Svetlana Dolbikova, 19, was three months pregnant when he raped her in September of that year. She said: 'He held a knife to me while he raped me. I screamed at him, "I'm pregnant, I'm pregnant!" but he did not care.' Svetlana lived on the same estate as Dembovskis and, with a group of friends, went to a party that he was holding at his mother's flat. When she went to use the toilet, he seized his moment and dragged her into the kitchen at knifepoint, whispering: 'If you want to live, keep quiet or you will die before the morning.' He then repeatedly raped the teenager, only letting her go the following day. Svetlana was so traumatised that she was too afraid to report the incident, terrified her attacker would come after her and her baby. When she heard that he had been jailed for the rest of his life, Svetlana, whose daughter was by then aged seven, said: 'I look at her beautiful face and shudder to think that monster could have hurt her. I am glad he will rot in jail.'

Two months after the attack on Svetlana, Dembovskis claimed his next known victim. He dragged Ineta Maloseva into a filthy basement as they walked home together from a party. She said: 'He pushed me to the wall and put a kitchen knife to my neck, drawing blood. He said: "If you start crying, I will kill you immediately." I will never forget the foul smell in that basement. His body was covered with a skin infection and he had medication all over him. He smelled of sweat and he was unwashed.'

Dembovskis was jailed for a further seven years for the attack but incredibly, at a bungled appeal in 2000, he was released early when it was decided that because Ineta was friends with his previous victim, Svetlana, she must have known what he had done to her and had been 'foolish' to go near him. He was back on the streets after serving less than half his time.

Latvia joined the EU in 2004 and Dembovskis automatically acquired EU citizenship, giving him the chance to start afresh abroad, where the authorities were ignorant of his past. He seized the opportunity to wipe the slate clean and bought a one-way ticket to London. In November of that year, he strolled through British immigration without any checks.

When he arrived in London, he slept rough on the streets and drank heavily. A Russian-based Christian charity realised his plight and put him in a hostel in Harrow, North-West London, and paid for dental treatment as he had already lost most of his teeth.

He was befriended by fellow Russian immigrant Datsyuk Ramonovich, who helped him get work at the Car Valet UK car wash in Harrow town centre, where he earned up to £400 a week, paid in cash. But he soon tired of the hostel's rules and moved into the eight-bedroom house, close to where he killed Jeshma. One colleague at the car wash recalled: 'He had spent more than half his life in prison and sometimes he told me he missed it. He would tell stories about it, how they would fight each other. It was cold and damp, but he said he got used to it. Outside, he was alone and he said he felt lonely; there was no one to help him. When he was waiting around at work, he would walk from one side to the other with his hands behind his back, like he was in the exercise yard.'

According to his roommate, Vladimir Ivanov, Dembovskis would often skip work through being drunk or hungover. 'He always kept a bottle of brandy in his bedside cabinet,' he said.

After the trial, Jeshma's mother, Manjula, and father, Suresh, said in a statement: 'The man had a violent past, yet he was easily allowed into this country. We have to ask how and why this came about and what checks were made about his background before he was allowed to set foot on British soil.'

Roberts Snepits, the Police Chief in Dembovskis' hometown Livani, said: 'He is a maniac. Jeshma would be alive today if only the Latvian appeal court and everyone else had listened to us.'

His mother was not at the Old Bailey to see him caged, but from her crumbling apartment in Livani she said he had been a happy schoolboy, who always wanted to be a lorry driver. She said the family had been torn apart by the deaths of his brother Ivans and his father Vladislav in the space of just three years. She remembered: 'When he was a boy at home he was very clean and never swore, but he got in with a bad crowd and changed; he became bad. What he got up to, I can only guess: it was horrible. His father drank alcohol very rarely, but Viktors drank a lot, usually at the homes of his friends. He had parties here, but I did not like them – I used to tell his friends to get out.'

When Latvia found independence in 1991, Dembovskis moved to Rija and joined the Seventh Day Adventist Church, where he earned certificates for bible reading. His mother, sitting beside a picture of Jesus, said solemnly: 'He found God. I thought he was going to make something of his life.'

27

'A MADMAN ON THE LOOSE'

'He is the sanest man in the building.'

Psychologist at Ashworth Hospital.

Name: Anthony Arkwright
Crime: Triple murder
Date of Conviction: 12 July 1989
Age at Conviction: 22

Skinny survival fanatic Anthony Arkwright had only one ambition in life – to be an infamous killer. He even boasted to friends that one day he would be as well known as Jack the Ripper.

In August 1988, aged 21, he murdered three defenseless people in such a sadistic and gruesome manner that even hardened police were physically sick when they saw the slaughter. But despite the horrific nature of his crimes, Arkwright never won the notoriety he craved.

In the weeks leading up to the 56-hour killing spree, the 6ft 4in, spikey-haired loner was working at a scrapyard near his home in Wath, near Rotherham, South Yorkshire. He spent his nights constructing hideouts by railway tracks, assuming the role of an SAS-style survivalist. For hours on end, he sat crouched watching from his camouflaged dens, a hunting knife tucked down his boots. In summer he preferred sleeping there to his council flat.

During the long periods of time he spent alone, Arkwright fantasised about the people he would kill. In the months leading up to the murders, he became obsessed with the mistaken belief that he was born out of an incestuous relationship between his mother and her Lithuanian-born father, his grandfather Stasys Puidokis.

On Friday, 26 August, Arkwright was sacked from his job for poor attendance. He took his severance pay and got drunk at the nearest pub. Then the carnage began. At around 4.15 that afternoon he walked to his grandfather's home in Ruskin Drive. He was not there, so Arkwright went to the nearby allotments where the old man spent much of his time. As he looked up from his weeding to greet his grandson, Arkwright stabbed the 68-year-old in the neck. The knife cut through the pensioner's spinal cord, paralysing him. As Mr Puidokis lay still and bleeding on the ground, he grabbed his feet and dragged him into his shed. There, he grabbed an axe and buried it in his grandfather's chest. He then smashed his skull to pieces with a 14lb lump hammer.

After locking his grandfather in his shed, he went back to the dead man's house and stole his life savings of £3,000. His grandfather's housekeeper, Elsa Konradite, 72, was later found dead in the kitchen. Both she and Mr Puidokis lay undiscovered for six days.

That night, Arkwright went on a pub crawl round Mexborough and dropped hints to people he met of the brutal murder he had committed. One barman remembered the 'wild-eyed weirdo' ordering a drink and saying: 'It's been murder on the allotment today.' Several more witnesses recalled similar remarks from him that night, demonstrating his need for public recognition. As he walked home at the end of the evening, Arkwright tried to pick a fight with a group of nightclub doormen. The wannabe SAS hard case suffered the humiliation of being picked up by his trouser-belt and hurled across the pavement by one of the burly bouncers.

By 3am the following day, Arkwright, angered by the bouncer incident, was back at his flat on Denman Road in Wath. He got changed and entered the flat of his next-door neighbour, Raymond Ford, who Arkwright enjoyed bullying. Raymond, 45, was a depressed ex-teacher, who spent his days drinking cheap cider and completing the Guardian crossword. He was tormented by his sadistic young neighbour who regularly smashed his windows and shoved excrement through his letterbox. Earlier that week, Arkwright had burgled Raymond's flat, stealing a clock and a microwave. Raymond reported the harassment and burglary to the police, naming Arkwright as the offender. The sadist was aware of this and he wanted revenge.

Naked apart from a Prince of Darkness devil-mask covering his face, Arkwright entered the flat through a window he'd smashed with a brick a few days earlier and he attacked Raymond as he sat slumped in an armchair in front of the television. He stabbed him more than 500 times, thrusting the knife deep into every part of his victim's body. The maniac then gutted and disembowelled the corpse, using a technique similar to that used by Jack the Ripper on his victims in Victorian London. Raymond's body was discovered three days later, his entrails draped around the room. Describing the scene that greeted police, one seasoned detective said: 'It was the most brutal act of slaughter I have ever seen. It is all the more chilling when you realise he must have spent at least half an hour inflicting those terrible wounds.'

Next, Arkwright went home and showered to remove the blood from his body. Four hours later, two policemen knocked at his door. Unaware of the horrors next door, the officers arrested him for the burglary at Raymond Ford's flat. He was detained for three hours before being released on bail to appear in court the following week.

Amused at being a murderer allowed to walk free from a police station, Arkwright spent Saturday evening in high spirits, drinking in pubs around Mexborough. In the early hours of Sunday, 28 August, he murdered another of his neighbours on Denman Road. He entered the specially adapted bungalow where wheelchair-bound Marcus Law lived after a motorcycling accident. Marcus was stabbed at least 70 times. Arkwright then tried to gut his victim, but failed. Instead, he rammed his victim's crutch into a gash in his stomach.

In what he would later describe as punishment for all the cigarettes Marcus had scrounged off him, Arkwright gouged out the 25-year-old's eyes and placed unlit cigarettes in the sockets, as well as in his ears, up his nostrils and in his mouth.

The following morning, the killer bumped into Marcus' mother and smirked as he told her how sorry he was to hear of the suicide of 'poor old Marcus'. She hurried to her son's bungalow, where she made the horrific discovery.

By 1pm Arkwright was arrested for his disabled neighbour's murder. While being interviewed, he took a pack of cards from the table and shuffled through them. He picked out the Four of Hearts, laid it down in front of the two detectives and said: 'This is the master card – it means you have four bodies and a madman on the loose.' As if interpreting the card like a Tarot reader, he added: 'I can see Marcus Law, but the others are indescribable. They are just too horrible to describe.'

An urgent search was made for the three missing bodies and, one by one, they were discovered by sickened police. But after being charged with the four murders Arkwright felt out of the limelight – that he was no longer the one calling the shots. So he invented a fifth victim, which led to police frogmen searching a lake while another team of officers worked their way through a drainage ditch.

Arkwright's attention seeking continued while awaiting trial at Hull Prison: he was offended at the lack of respect and recognition afforded him and staged a 'dirty protest' by smearing his excrement over the walls of his cell. He managed to convince prison doctors that he was insane and he was transferred to Rampton Psychiatric Hospital on Merseyside. But after detailed examination, he was declared fit to plead. 'He is the sanest man in the building,' reported one Rampton psychiatrist.

At his trial in July 1989, prosecution counsel Steven Williamson, QC, described the murders in chronological order, ending with the death of Marcus Law. Of that dreadful final crime, Mr Williamson said: 'The mother of Marcus Law was to find her own son dead. Even before the discovery, Arkwright spoke to her about the death of Marcus, thus betraying his knowledge.'

After an adjournment requested by his lawyers, Arkwright changed his plea to guilty of the murders of the three men, but not guilty to that of his grandfather's housekeeper, Elsa Konradite. The judge ordered that particular charge to lie on file.

Before sentencing, Arkwright's barrister, James Chadwin, QC, stated: 'Arkwright is a young man who suffers from severe personality damage and disorder. He has shown signs of disturbance since the time his mother left him when he was four years old.' Recommending he serve at least 25 years, judge Mr Justice Boreham said the murders '...can only be described as horrible offences of sadistic cruelty. Cruelty for its own sake.' He added: 'I accept you have had a deprived and disturbed childhood, but that cannot be any excuse for the appalling cruelty and apparent sadistic pleasure with which you carried out these offences. There is nothing in the medical evidence to suggest anything to mitigate what you have done. I have no doubt, having read the reports of three eminent psychiatrists and others, that you constitute a serious danger to the public and will remain so for a very long time to come, and the horror of this case leaves me no option but to pass life sentences.' Home Secretary Jack Straw declared the 25-year minimum sentence too lenient and ordered Arkwright to serve a whole life term.

A retired senior detective who worked on the Arkwright case said: 'From the day we brought him in for the Marcus Law murder to the day he was jailed, Arkwright seemed genuinely proud of what he had done. He expected everyone to revere him, to be fascinated by him. He was a messed-up kid, desperate for attention. In his defected mind he chose murder to get the attention he craved. He's the most dangerous person I ever met in 25 years on the job – he should never get out.'

The son of a miner, Arkwright was born and bred in the small mining town of Wath. He was the middle child of five and took it very badly when his mother walked out on him and his siblings. Throughout his formative years and into his teens, the young Arkwright displayed the traits of a boy who felt rejected and unwanted. He was in frequent trouble for fighting, stealing and vandalism. Eventually he was expelled from school and served time in a borstal. Child psychiatrists were unable to get through to him and he ended up spending several stints in prison.

During his last jail stretch for burglary, he boasted to fellow inmates that he would one day become a famous murderer. He used the prison library to read up on Jack the Ripper and Yorkshire Ripper, Peter Sutcliffe. He expressed his admiration for Sutcliffe and told friends he planned to enjoy the same notoriety.

But the name Anthony Arkwright has never made it into the public consciousness and his sadistic actions failed to achieve the public impact he desired. However, for those whose loved ones were killed by him, the memories remain raw and strong, and he has wrecked their lives. In 2002, 14 years after the murders, Marcus Law's father Tony committed suicide because he was haunted by his son's hideous death. The 62-year-old poisoned himself with car exhaust fumes. His wife Norma, Marcus's mother, said: 'No parent could ever come to terms with something as traumatic as that. What happened to Marcus preyed on Tony's mind. He kept having nightmares Marcus was screaming for his dad, but he just couldn't get to him. We moved for a fresh start, but Tony couldn't escape the memories.'

The inquest into Tony Law's death revealed that Marcus was the couple's only surviving son after their firstborn killed himself in 1973, aged 13. Coroner Peter Brunton said: 'This man was badly affected by the violent deaths of his two children. This is the most tragic set of circumstances I have ever come across.'

28

'THE BODY-IN-THE-BAGS KILLER'

'Have you found the body yet? There will be four more. This is
The Ripper.'

Green (to 999 operator)

Name: Malcolm Green
Crime: Murder
Date of Conviction: 31 October 1991
Age at Conviction: 44

In the early hours of 21 June 1971, crane driver Malcolm Green left a nightclub in the docks area of Cardiff and came across street prostitute Glenys Johnson. Only Green knows whether she went willingly with him to waste ground at Wharf Street in the area's Butetown, but once there, he killed her by slashing her throat with a broken bottle.

He then tore her clothes open and frenziedly slashed away at her body. When Green had finished with Glenys, she had more than 20 gaping wounds to her neck, chest and abdomen. Such was the ferocity of the attack that her head was almost severed from her body.

Hours after the murder, police received a phone call from a man who asked the operator: 'Have you found the body yet? There will be four more. This is The Ripper.'

Glenys Johnson's mutilated corpse was found shortly after dawn, by which time police had traced the call to a nearby steel factory where Green was working the early morning shift. Detectives were quick to arrest the 24-year-old, who colleagues described as a 'weird loner'. He had turned up, sweating and shaking, shortly before the time of the call.

When arrested, Green denied any involvement in the prostitute's murder, but there was much forensic evidence linking him to the crime. Spots of the prostitute's rare blood group were found on his boots. He also had several cuts to the palms of his hands, which he put down to falling over on his way to work. In reality, Green had cut his palms on the shards of glass that he used to hack at his victim and his blood – also a rare grouping – was found on her body.

When police searched his flat, they found a crude dummy of a man that he had made from a rolled-up carpet, dressed in a buttoned-up shirt and suit jacket. A knife was stabbed through the left pocket of the jacket.

Despite the evidence against him, Green denied the murder and after a seven-day trial at Glamorgan Assizes, Cardiff, he was jailed for life in November 1971.

After 18 years in prison, psychiatrists were convinced that Green, by now apparently a placid and affable 42-year-old, was fit for release into the community. In October 1989 he walked free from Leyhill Open Prison, near Bristol. During his time at Leyhill, Green took several academic courses aimed at improving his chances of getting a job on the outside. He was allowed to leave the prison to attend classes at Bristol's nearby Filton Technical College, where he excelled in A-level Human Biology. The knowledge he learned on that course enabled him to commit his final gruesome crime.

On his release, Green moved into lodgings at 11 Luxton Street, Bristol, where travelling New Zealander Clive Tully also rented a room. Green took the 24-year-old under his wing and they became close friends. He allowed Clive to spend Christmas with him and his girlfriend Helen Barnes, whom he had met in his biology classes.

Green would later say of Tully: 'He was lonely. I was possibly his best mate while he lived over here.'

Three months into their friendship, Clive got itchy feet and decided to visit Spain for a few weeks of winter sun. Green drove him to catch the ferry from Plymouth and waved him off. According to Green, Clive returned 'penniless' one night in mid-March and asked if he could stay at his place for a few days. He said he agreed to let Clive sleep on his sofa while he went to stay at his girlfriend's house in Bristol's Fishponds area. He claimed he never saw his friend again.

Police believe that at some point that night, Green smashed his friend's skull to pieces with a hammer. He then neatly sawed up Clive's body – dismembering his head, arms and legs. Green also removed his victim's hands.

Two days later, two sports holdalls were found in a lay-by of the A467 bypass near Newport. One contained Clive's torso, the other his arms and legs. The head and hands were missing. Three days later, a farmer found the missing remains in a nearby field. They were wrapped in a bloodied sheet and the farmer at first thought the package was a red and white football.

Because of the state of Clive's remains, it took police weeks to identify him as the victim of what the tabloid press called 'The Body in the Bags Killer'. Once he was identified, detectives established that Clive was a friend of recently-released killer Malcolm Green and were soon knocking on the door of the ground-floor flat at 11 Luxton Street. After his arrest, Green told police: 'I know nothing about Clive Tully's murder, although I do know Clive Tully.'

As with his previous murder, Green left more then enough forensic evidence for police to charge him. As he awaited trial, psychiatrist Dr Arden Tomison, from the Fromeside Clinic, near Bristol, interviewed him. He found him to be: '…a cold, sadistic killer, who has killed for a second time, but is nevertheless capable of forming relationships'. Dr Tomison added: 'He has a high tolerance of stress and frustrations, which means he is not a psychopath. He is a very dangerous man.'

Opening the case against Green at Bristol Crown Court in October 1991, prosecution barrister Paul Chadd, QC, said: 'In March of 1990 in the sitting room of a ground-floor flat at 11 Luxton Street in Easton, the accused struck Clive William Tully on the head about a dozen times with something like a hammer, killing him.

'Whether on the floor of that room, or whether in a bathroom on the first floor, the Crown says that this man dismembered the body. He cut it up into pieces. It is a fact that up the stairs was found a trail of bloody drips. It is a fact that pieces of the body were parcelled in plastic bags and deposited where they would quickly be found alongside two highways in Wales.'

As Cardiff-born Green sat in the dock making notes, counsel continued: 'This particular dismemberment was neatly done. It was a dismemberment that had to deal, as you will appreciate for a moment if you reflect on the human body, with joints, with muscle. One of the holdalls left by the roadside in Wales belonged to the accused. The accused and the deceased appear to have been friends. Perhaps I have said enough to show that ordinary motive does not arise in this particular case. It is a case with unusual features. I emphasise that when interviewed by police, the accused denied any involvement. The Crown says that the evidence leads inescapably to him.'

Home Office pathologist Dr Stephen Leadbetter told the court: 'The cause of death was multiple blunt head injuries caused by something like a hammer.' He said the head was 'removed neatly by cutting through the soft tissue of the neck and through a part of the voice box.' He added that the separation of the lower arms, legs, hands and torso was similarly 'neat' with little damage or tearing to soft tissue.

Mr Chadd introduced the prosecution's chief witness, florist Robert Clarke. Mr Clarke told the jury of seven men and five women that he was '100 per cent' sure that he had seen the accused in the lay-by where the torso and dismembered limbs were found. The florist said he was driving along the A467 bypass from Newport to Risca on 21 March 1990 when he noticed a man standing beside a small 'light-coloured car'.

He thought the man had broken down, but reckoned the large holdall beside the car was a strange way to carry tools. Mr Clarke later picked Green out at an identity parade. He said: 'When I first went in, I was pretty certain I recognised him, but when I asked him to turn to the left, I was 100 per cent sure. I had a mental picture in my mind of this chap.'

Summing up the evidence against Green, Mr Chadd said that although the case was an 'oddity', the jury simply had to apply common sense to convict him. Turning to the testimony of florist Robert Clarke, he told the court: 'Firstly, he happens to have identified a man with regular access to a light-coloured Metro. Secondly, he happens to have identified a man who admits to have been using a light-coloured Metro that very day, 21 March 1990.

'Thirdly, he happens to have identified a man who admits to the police he was at Avonmouth on the motorway that very day. Fourthly, he happens to have identified a man in whose house the victim Clive Tully was battered and butchered. Just think about that when you consider the validity of Mr Clarke's evidence.

'Fifth, Mr Clarke happens to have identified a man who, as far as we know, is the last person to have seen Mr Tully alive. Sixth, he happens to have identified a man whose fingerprints appear on a white plastic bag used by the killer to contain the two forearms left in a maroon holdall by that very lay-by. Seventh, Mr Clarke happens to have identified a man whose fingerprint was on a black carrier bag, which contained a head left in a ditch. Credulity is now being stretched beyond common sense and beyond possibility.

'Eighth, he happens to have identified a man who owns one of the holdalls in which parts of the victim's body were found in a lay-by.

These eight matters not only support Mr Clarke, they combine in each other to form an overwhelming case.'

The jury reached a unanimous guilty verdict at the end of the trial which had lasted – like Green's first – seven days. Passing sentence, Mr Justice Rose told him: 'You are intelligent, cold-blooded, sadistic and a liar. It is impossible for anyone but you to know why you killed him and why afterwards you behaved as you did. What is clear from the horrific circumstances of this offence, from your attitude to it and from a psychiatrist's report on you is that you are a very dangerous man.' Twice during the judge's speech, Green interrupted, stating calmly: 'I did not kill Clive Tully.'

Mr Justice Rose said he would recommend to the Home Secretary that he should serve at least 25 years. As he was led away from the dock, Green turned and yelled at the jury: 'You are wrong!' But the Home Office thought the judge's 25 years minimum sentence was too lenient and ruled he must die behind bars.

Exactly when and why Clive Tully met his death, only Green can say. Indeed, the experts can only speculate on the reason for Green's bloodlust. Some psychiatrists have suggested his obsession with death and mutilation stemmed from seeing his younger brother decapitated under the wheels of a train when he was only 12.

In both murders, Green made it so easy for the police to find him that it appeared he wanted to be caught. In the Clive Tully case, police were baffled by an anomaly in the evidence in that although Green meticulously cleaned the bathroom, he left a large area of bloodstained carpet in the sitting room. He also dumped bags containing the body pieces in a lay-by on a busy bypass in the Newport area, close to where the victim had relatives.

One detective close to the investigation commented: 'It is almost as if he wanted to be caught in both murder cases. In the Cardiff murder, there was the telephone call leading to his workplace. It seems inevitable that he would be traced and the dummy would be discovered in his flat.' He added: 'In the Bristol case, it was strange he dumped the bags at a spot where they would certainly be found quickly and lead back to him.' Yet in both cases, Green strongly protested his innocence and claimed he was 'fitted up' as the suspect.

Kevin Hall shared a cell with Green at Leyhill Open Prison, where he served the last few years of his first murder sentence. He remarked: 'To me, he seemed quite normal. I honestly thought the Home Office had got it right and he was alright.' He said Green was due to be released in 1983, but was handed an extra six years for going on the run. Hall added: 'If he was released in 1983, God knows how many people he might have killed. It makes my skin crawl to think I shared a cell with him.'

29
'THE RAILWAY RAPIST'

*'We considered it a bit of a game. We were playing games with
the police and generally making it fun.'*

John Duffy

Name: John Duffy
Crime: Serial rape and triple murder
Date of Conviction: 28 February 1988
Age at Conviction: 29

In September 1970, one of the most despicable partnerships in
British criminal history began when two awkward, friendless boys
met on their first day at secondary school in North London.

Among the scores of children starting at Haverstock Hill
Comprehensive that day, something drew John Duffy and David
Mulcahy together. Mulcahy, a gangly youngster who counted the
neighbourhood dogs as his only friends, had been a particular target of
cruelty. At junior school, he was nicknamed 'Slaphead' because of his
unusually large forehead. Alone with his thoughts, the oddball would
roam the neighbourhood's streets and parks.

Duffy was a very short kid, with an ugly, impish face that gave a bad
first impression. If that was not enough, he had curly red hair that
made him a target for ridicule. He perpetually wore a Parka with the
hood up to hide his locks and keep taunts to a minimum.

An ex-schoolmate of the pair recalled: 'I can remember Duffy as a short, ginger kid – I don't think there was anything else about him. He was in the same class as me, but it was only the colour of his hair that made an impression. As for Mulcahy, I can't remember him at all, not a thing.'

Bonded by loneliness and bullying, the pair became inseparable. They increasingly played truant from school, spending their time daydreaming about beating up their tormentors. Afternoons were often spent watching kung-fu films and practising the moves on each other. Violence became their mutual interest.

At the age of 13, Mulcahy was suspended from Haverstock for playing cricket, using a hedgehog as a ball and a wooden plank as a bat. As other children looked on horrified, he killed the defenceless creature by stamping on its head. In a taste of things to come, his friend and soul mate Duffy was laughing at his side as he did so.

Together they took up martial arts and practised survival techniques from underground manuals, which gave advice on how to silence, incapacitate and kill opponents. Calling themselves 'Warriors', they armed themselves with kung-fu flails and knives, and used the techniques they'd learned to stalk courting couples around Hampstead Heath. Sometimes they would masturbate together as they watched people have sex.

Soon they realised that it became even more fun when they donned Halloween masks and jumped out on the couples, scaring them half to death. After their escapades, they revelled in the feeling of control that their dangerous games gave them, then fed off each other's excitement.

Duffy and Mulcahy had their first brush with the law in 1976 – the year after they left school without a qualification between them. They were caught shooting a powerful airgun at petrified passers-by and were arrested for actual bodily harm. Far from being deterred by their encounter with police, they were soon planning their first rape.

Mulcahy had been decorating a house in West London, but he fell out with the woman who owned it over the quality of his work. He wanted to teach her a lesson and told Duffy they were going to break in and rape her. They entered the house and lay in wait for her, but she did not return home that night.

Weeks later, they targeted another woman because Mulcahy thought she 'looked stuck up' and 'needed to be taught a lesson'. They broke into her house in Notting Hill and hid in her bedroom, but fled when they heard her enter through the front door with a man. As they scrambled out of the window and down the street, they were howling with laughter. The excitement was addictive, like a drug.

On 24 October 1982, they raped their first known victim. The 21-year-old was walking home from a party in West Hampstead, carrying a teddy bear she had been given by a friend. Duffy and Mulcahy, both wearing balaclavas, grabbed her by the neck, put a plaster over her mouth and told her: 'Don't worry, all we want is your teddy bear.' She was then bundled over a wall and raped by each of her attackers in turn. Duffy later described how they felt afterwards: 'We were both very excited and said we should do it again.'

And so they did, many times, developing an obsession with savage violence and callous lust that would lead to a reign of terror, during which they raped and killed a string of victims, aged between 15 and 32. 'We used to call it "hunting,"' Duffy recalled to detectives. 'We considered it a bit of a game. We were playing games with the police and generally making it fun.'

By the time of the first rape, both men were working for Westminster City Council, where Duffy was a carpenter and Mulcahy a plumber. They were both married and leading outwardly normal domestic lives. Mulcahy had married Sandra Carr, an Anglo-Indian shop assistant, in 1978. Duffy wed nursery nurse Margaret Byrne in 1980, three years after they met at an ice rink. But both men had sexual shortcomings that led them to rape strangers. Mulcahy was impotent unless violence was involved. Furthermore, his arousal depended on having sex against the woman's will. Duffy had no such problems getting an erection but he had a low sperm count, meaning he was unable to father children. In his deranged mind, this fed his bitter resentment of women.

Their 'hunting' expeditions were planned with care. They carried a rape kit of balaclavas, knives and tape, and they stuffed matchboxes with tissue paper so that the matches would not rattle as they crept up on their victims. The tissue was also used for wiping away bodily fluids, the matches to set fire to the tissues. Mulcahy stuck strips of tape to the inside of his jacket to blindfold and gag the terrified women. The pair were also careful never to go out hunting without the 50p coin they always tossed to decide who would rape the victim first.

After the first attack Mulcahy broke into a car and stole a tape of Michael Jackson's album Thriller. It became the soundtrack to their crimes and they cruised around with it, playing on the stereo, hyping themselves up to the lyrics of the title track. Duffy would later tell police: 'We normally travelled by car. We called them "hunting parties". Part of it was looking for a victim, part of it was tracking her, and part of it was having her. We used to put Thriller on and sing along to it as part of the build-up.'

With each attack, the violence increased. On 27 March 1983, they grabbed a 29-year-old French woman from behind as she walked home from work at a restaurant in West Hampstead. But she fought for her life and bit Mulcahy hard on the hand, drawing blood. This sent him into a frenzy and he repeatedly kicked her as she lay curled in a ball on the floor.

On 20 January 1984, a 32-year-old American social worker was walking across Barnes Common, South-West London, when the masked pair jumped on her. 'At some point he instructed the shorter man [Duffy] to gouge out my eyes, slice off my ears and slice off my nipples,' the woman later said in evidence. 'I believed I was going to be murdered, disembowelled, tortured.' She was stripped and raped on the freezing cold ground.

Four months later, on 3 June, they cornered a 23-year-old woman in the waiting room of West Hampstead train station. With a knife at her back, she was marched to a dark spot under a railway bridge and raped: 'There was a knife at my throat. They were very threatening. All I could say was, "Please don't rape me."'

The following month, a 22-year-old woman was dragged into the back garden of a house in Highgate, North London, but she was saved when the couple living there turned on the garden lights, forcing the rapists to flee.

On 15 July 1984, they dragged two Danish au pairs, both 18, into bushes on Hampstead Heath. The terrified girls were stripped and raped.

Their eighth victim was a German au pair, who they raped in Brent Cross, North-West London, on 26 January 1985. Just five days later, the rapists were back on Hampstead Heath, where Mulcahy grabbed a 16-year-old and asked her if she was a virgin. She said afterwards: 'The short man [Duffy] looked up and said something to the effect of, "Come on, I told you, none of that. Let's forget it."'

Next, they attacked a 23-year-old in South Hampstead, but she somehow used her wits to escape. She recalled: 'My mind was frantically searching for something which would put him off, so I told him I had AIDS.'

On 2 February 1985, they tried to rape another 23-year-old in South Hampstead, but she scared them away. The French au pair recalled: 'I had screamed so hard I couldn't speak any more.'

The following night, they stalked a solicitor's clerk as she walked on Hampstead Heath. She was blindfolded and raped by both men on a park bench. She later said: 'I kept begging them to stop – I couldn't stop crying and this seemed to annoy them.' She said the taller man told her not to look at him, 'or I will tear your eyes out.'

Duffy and Mulcahy had become an efficient partnership, working in unison like a pair of wild animals, stalking their prey. One victim described them as 'Two bodies with one brain – they didn't tell each other anything.' She added: 'They seemed to be able to communicate without words, just by nodding their heads.'

On Sunday, 29 December 1985, the prolific rapists graduated to murder. Alison Day, 19, was the only passenger to alight from her train at Hackney Wick, East London. She was going to meet her fiancé nearby, but Duffy and Mulcahy pounced from the darkness and dragged her at knifepoint to the banks of the River Lea. Duffy raped her first, then his friend. After her ordeal, Alison got to her feet and staggered around in the darkness, falling into the ice-cold river. Duffy hauled her out and laid her on the floor. Then she got back to her feet and tried to run away, but Duffy stopped her. Mulcahy, angered at the victim for trying to escape, pulled off her trousers and raped her again. At some point, Alison saw the men's faces and Mulcahy decided it was too risky to let her live. Duffy later said in court that Alison pleaded for her life: 'Please, it's only the moustache I have seen. I will not tell anyone, don't hurt me.' Her pleas ignored, Mulcahy tore a strip from her blouse and twisted it round her neck. He then ordered his friend to tighten it further and hold it until she died. Two weeks later, her body was found in the river, weighed down with blocks of granite. The friends were now killers together, their bond stronger than ever. Furthermore, after the buzz of killing, rape alone was no longer enough.

Maartje Tamboezer, 15, was on her way to buy sweets when she was snatched from her bike on a path through woods parallel to the railway line in Horsley, Surrey, on 17 April 1986. Duffy won the coin toss and was the first to rape the Dutch girl in a nearby copse. Her hands were tied behind her back; she was beaten about the head with a stone and finally strangled with her own belt. Her neck was broken after death, possibly by a karate blow. Maartje's body, partially burned to destroy evidence of rape, was found the following morning.

Newly-wed Anne Lock, 29, became Duffy and Mulcahy's 15th known victim on 18 May 1986. Anne, a secretary with London

Weekend Television, had parked her bike in the railway station shed at Brookmans Park, Hertfordshire. She was frogmarched with a knife held at her side to a field and raped. Duffy went first and when he had finished, Mulcahy took his turn while his accomplice went and sat in the car. When Mulcahy arrived at the car, he laughed as he told his friend that the latest victim would not be identifying them. Two months later, her body was found in thick undergrowth on a railway embankment, a few hundred yards from her home.

Early into Duffy and Mulcahy's violent crime spree, police set up Operation Hart, the largest investigation in the UK since the hunt for the Yorkshire Ripper. The pair, like hundreds of suspects, were brought in for questioning several times but because the investigation did not have the facility to collate information from different police teams, they were always released.

In August 1986, Duffy was arrested for beating up his wife. He was interviewed and his name added to the Hart computer system, along with his fingerprints and details of his rare blood group. As detectives caught up with the huge volume of evidence gathered over three years of investigation, they found that blood matching Duffy's group was found at several crime scenes. He was arrested and two rape victims identified him. When officers searched his home they found his rape kit of tape, knives and a matchbox containing tissue paper and eight matches.

Mulcahy was also brought in, but because of a quirk in his biological make-up, it was impossible to link him forensically with any of the crimes. Criminologist Professor David Cánter, who helped with the investigation, said: 'It was before DNA and Mulcahy was what is called a non-secretor. Even if he left tell-tale bodily fluids these couldn't be distinguished in the blood typing process, then used. Effectively Mulcahy was invisible.'

Furthermore, seven victims were unable to pick him out at identity parades and when they searched his home, police found nothing that linked him to the crimes. Although the obvious suspect as Duffy's accomplice, there was insufficient evidence to charge him. The only person who could bring Mulcahy down was Duffy, his best friend, but the playground pact made as schoolboys that they would never 'grass each other up' was strong. As one investigating officer said: 'Duffy was terrified of Mulcahy. They had this pact and he was scared. He didn't trust anyone. He stayed quiet.'

At his trial in February 1988, Duffy denied any involvement in the rapes or murders, claiming amnesia in his defence. But the weight of evidence against him meant that he was convicted of five rapes and two murders. On the judge's direction he was acquitted of Anne Lock's murder due to insufficient evidence. Handing Duffy seven life sentences with a recommendation that he serve at least 30 years, Mr Justice Farquharson told him: 'You are obviously little more than a predatory animal. The horrific nature of your crimes means 30 years is not necessarily the total you will serve. It may well be more.' Home Secretary Douglas Hurd increased the sentence to a whole life term. When Duffy was convicted, Mulcahy told the *Daily Mail*: 'I don't believe John was capable of doing all these things. He has always been a mummy's boy.' Holding his wife's hand, Mulcahy said that he planned to sue police for wrongful arrest, adding, 'and also for destroying my reputation.'

In November 1997, after more than 10 years in custody, Duffy told prison psychologists of intense nightmares he was having, in which he chased a girl down a canal towpath. Dr Jenny Cutler, a therapist at top-security Whitemoor Prison, Cambridgeshire, was called in and over the months that followed, she coaxed details of his crimes from him. After many hours of therapy, he gave her the name of his accomplice, David Mulcahy. Duffy told her he felt 'self-hate inside' and that he 'wanted to get things off my chest.' He said: 'I've been in custody for many years and have had a hard time coming to terms with what I'm in for – rapes and murders. I feel a lot of guilt for what I've done and want to make a clean slate.'

Detective Superintendent Andy Murphy, who re-opened the case, remarked: 'Duffy had been in jail for 11 years and had had plenty of time to think things over. He'd decided it was time to do the right thing and put the record straight. We spent weeks debriefing him – he'd never spoken about his crimes before.

'We took him back to all the murder scenes. They were very moving moments. Some of the places had changed since the murders, but he described them exactly how they'd been. When we checked against original maps and plans, we could see every word was true.' Duffy also confessed to the murder of Anne Lock, for which he had been cleared. In all he confessed to 25 sex attacks, telling officers: 'We considered it a bit of a joke, a game.'

Because of advances in forensic science, police were able to match Mulcahy's DNA to samples found on underwear belonging to one of the Danish au pairs who was raped on Hampstead Heath in 1984. Experts also identified a fingerprint on tape used to gag and blindfold another victim as Mulcahy's.

The smirking killer who thought he could not be caught had been proven wrong.

After painstaking work to build up a case against Mulcahy, police were finally able to arrest him. In the early hours of Saturday, 6 February 1999 the sex killer was dragged from his bed by police as his sons slept upstairs.

For 14 days, in January 2001, Duffy gave evidence against his friend at the Old Bailey, giving grim details of the crimes that sent shivers down the spines of all who heard them. On 2 February Mulcahy, 41, received life for three murders and a total of 258 years for seven rapes and five charges of plotting to rape.

The Recorder of London, Judge Michael Hyam, told him that the killings were 'acts of desolating wickedness in which you descended to the depth of depravity in carrying them out.'

Detective Superintendent Les Bolland, who visited Duffy in jail, said: 'Mulcahy is now in prison simply because Duffy became very annoyed that he was going to die inside while Mulcahy remained a free man.'

30

'MY CHINA DOLL'

'I still can't talk about what I saw in that room – it was worse than any Stephen King film or book.'

Boyfriend of victim

Name: Mark Hobson
Crime: Quadruple murder
Date of Conviction: 27 May 2005
Age at Conviction: 36

Early on Sunday, 18 July 2004, George Sanderson drove to his daughter Claire's home to check that she and her twin sister Diane were all right after they'd failed to get in touch, as planned, the night before. Together with Diane's boyfriend, Ian Harrison, Mr Sanderson arrived at the flat in Camblesforth, near Selby, North Yorkshire, at 8am to find the front door unlocked and an overpowering smell emanating from the property. When they entered the flat they found the 27-year-old twins' naked corpses on the bedroom floor. Claire had been dead for a week, her decomposing body wrapped in bin-liners. Her head had been hit 17 times with a hammer and a plastic carrier bag was placed over it. Forensic examination of the flat, which had been partly washed and cleaned with bleach, would later show that Claire had been beaten in the living room before being dragged, bleeding, into the bedroom.

Diane was lying nearby. Her naked body was on top of a large plastic bag and she had been subjected to a violent sexual attack. Tests later revealed that she had been subjected to a sustained assault and had received several blows to the head. Like her sister, she had been beaten with a hammer and a plastic bag covered her head. She had been killed the previous night.

Describing the shocking discovery Diane's boyfriend Ian said: 'I still can't talk about what I saw in that room. It was worse than any Stephen King film or book; it was absolute horror. I was physically sick and was shaking like a leaf. The scene was so appalling that the policeman who first attended had to go off work sick because of the stress of seeing what he saw.' Describing the moment when he spotted the bags, the twins' dad George said: 'I knew Claire was inside. I looked at Diane and wanted to cuddle her.'

There was no sign of the man responsible for the scene of horror – Claire's boyfriend Mark Hobson, an alcoholic drug addict, who beat her up so often he nicknamed her 'Eight Ball' because she was always black and blue. Hobson had been with Claire for 18 months, but weeks earlier he had told a work colleague that he'd picked the wrong sister, that he fancied Diane and was intent on having her. Hobson – who often drank 20 pints of lager a day while smoking strong cannabis – started plotting to kill Claire a week before her murder on 11 July. Later, he told police that he talked to her body as it lay rotting, calling her 'My china doll'. By the time Claire's father and boyfriend found her body, it was so decomposed that it was impossible to tell whether the hammer attack had killed her, or if she had been asphyxiated from the bag over her head.

After killing Claire, ex-binman Hobson, 35, washed her blood from the walls and set about luring Diane to the flat. A chilling note headed '2 do list' found at the flat said: 'Text Di, use Claire's phone. Tell Di to come down. Disable all. Use and abuse at will.' He intended to tempt Diane to the flat and kill her, using Claire as bait. A misspelt shopping list found alongside his to-do list revealed his preparations: 'Big bin liners, tape, tie wraps, fly spray, Nutrodol.'

A week after killing Claire, Hobson rang Diane at her parents' house in nearby Snaith village and asked her to come round to visit Claire, who he said was ill. Minutes later, Diane left the house, telling her parents that she was going to call in to see her sister before meeting Ian in the Cricketers Arms pub in Selby. She left at 7.15pm on 17 July and was not seen alive again.

Within moments of her arrival at the flat, Hobson brutally attacked her. For 10 minutes, neighbours heard screams but they thought little of it because violence was so commonplace there. Hobson rained blows on Diane and then trussed her up, tying her feet to her hands behind her back. As she lay dying, he methodically cut off her clothes and carried out a sadistic sexual attack. She had ligature marks on her neck and died of strangulation.

When Diane failed to arrive at the pub, her boyfriend became concerned. At 9pm he rang her and Hobson answered the phone, explaining that Diane was not available to talk to him. 'With a cool, collected voice he told me he needed to see me urgently as Diane's dad had died of a heart attack,' said Ian. Hobson and Ian met in the Cricketers Arms, where Hobson claimed that the twins had gone to the family home for the night after the news of their dad's 'death'.

Hobson handed Ian a ring that he had ripped from Diane's finger and told him that she had sent it. 'He then invited me back to the flat after closing time at the pub,' Ian recalled. When Ian commented on the stench inside the flat, Hobson said they had problems with the drains and that the toilet was blocked. 'He actually followed me upstairs to the toilet. He stood right behind me, explaining why it stank – little did I know that in the next room were the bodies of Claire and Diane. We'd already had quite a few drinks and we had a few more at his place. He kept pestering me to stay the night and was desperate for me to crash on the settee; he had even rolled a sleeping bag out for me. At one point I put my feet on the settee and then as I got up, I noticed there was blood all over the back of my jeans. He said, "Sorry about that mate, Claire's been having women's problems."' A hammer and a knife were found under the settee the following day. Police later told Ian that had he stayed the night, he would not have left the place alive.

Ian left the flat at around 1am. Six hours later, he woke and immediately went to see his supposedly grieving girlfriend. He said: 'I rushed round to see Diane, but I was stunned when her dad George answered the door. I said, "I thought you were dead."' With Hobson's lies exposed, the frantic pair drove to the flat, where their worst fears were realised.

When Ian went home the previous evening, Hobson had made his way to the nearby house of his mother, Sandra, where he came up with more elaborate lies. He told her that Diane and Claire had been run over and were in York District Hospital, 20 miles away.

Sandra agreed to drive him there. When they arrived, Hobson went in the hospital – he was caught on security camera at 2am – before returning to tell his mother that he was going to stay with the girls. The next day, he made his way to Strensall, near York, where he walked into the home of former World War Two Spitfire pilot James Britton, 80, and his wife Joan, 82. At 8.15am that day, a neighbour of the frail couple left them safe and well. Three hours later, the neighbour's wife went to check on the Brittons and found them dead.

Mr Britton had been attacked first. He had been beaten about the head several times with his walking stick and then stabbed in the chest with a 12-inch kitchen knife. Hobson casually wiped the blade clean and then plunged it into Mrs Britton's back as she hobbled into the room on her walking frame. She died from a stab wound, which entered her back and went through several organs, including her stomach and liver. The attack was so ferocious that the handle of the knife snapped off, leaving the blade still in her body. She too had been beaten about the head with a walking stick. According to their GP, both Mr and Mrs Britton would have fallen over 'if they were hit with a feather duster.' Hobson took another knife from the couple's kitchen and went on the run.

By 11.45 that morning, local police knew they had two double murders on their patch, but it was some time later before they were able to make a link after fingerprints matching Hobson's were found on shoeboxes in the Brittons' bedroom and on a door. The quadruple murders led to one of the biggest police manhunts in British history.

The killer was on the run for eight days before he was arrested after being recognised at a garage shop on the A19 at Shipton-by-Beningbrough, 10 miles from Strensall, where he bought water, cigarette papers and matches. The owner of the garage recognised him from his picture in newspapers and on TV, and within eight minutes the area was surrounded by armed police with tracker dogs. Hobson, with the scent of a man who had not washed for more than a week, was found cowering between a septic tank and a hedge in a nearby field. On his arrest, he told police: 'I'm a f**king murderer, aren't I? Then I'll take my punishment.'

In a police interview, he told detectives that he had taken cannabis, cocaine, ecstasy and alcohol, and could not remember anything about his girlfriend's death. He claimed to have 'lost a day and a half' and come round with a bloodstained hammer in his hand. By that stage, more than 500 police officers from 12 forces had taken part in the hunt at a cost of £690,000.

At Leeds Crown Court on 27 May of the following year, Hobson muttered pleas of guilty to four counts of murder. Wearing a dark grey suit, he sat with his head bowed and looked close to tears. At one point he started rocking backwards and forwards. The judge, Mr Justice Grigson, ordered him to die in prison. To cries of 'Yes!' from the victims' families, the judge added: 'You not only destroyed the lives of your victims, but you devastated the lives of those who loved them. The damage you have done is incalculable; the enormity of what you have done is beyond words.'

As he was led to the cells, the twins' mother Jacqueline Sanderson shouted: 'You bastard! Rot in there! Rot in hell!'

In a joint statement after the sentencing, the parents said: 'How could anyone be such an animal? Claire and Diane did not deserve to die such horrid violent deaths, both ending up naked, with a plastic bag over Diane's head and Claire inside a black bag. They didn't deserve to end up like that. Though we were advised not to go and see them because of the state they were in, we did get to see them for the last time at the mortuary. You can imagine what they looked like, but to us they were our beautiful daughters, Claire and Diane. We will never forget that Sunday morning – George and Ian finding Claire and Diane, and George coming home to break the news of their horrid and cruel deaths. It was so unreal and still is. We are both full of hate and we will never get over what that animal did to our Claire and Diane. We will never get over it and will never see things in the same way. He not only took Claire and Diane away from us, he took our future happiness away from us. He took the hope of us ever becoming grandparents and having a normal family life.'

It emerged in the course of the investigation that two years prior to Hobson's killing spree he stabbed a love rival five times, leaving him for dead. William Brace, 30, needed emergency surgery for a punctured lung. In court the following year, Hobson admitted wounding with intent to cause grievous bodily harm, but claimed he acted in self-defence. His victim's family expected a lengthy prison term, but instead, in what turned out to be a fatal error of judgment, he was sentenced to 100 hours' community work and two years' probation.

In November 2005, Hobson's lawyers asked for permission to appeal against his whole life order at London's Court of Appeal. His counsel, Jeremy Richardson, QC, said that however barbaric his crimes, he deserved some credit for admitting the murders. But the nation's most senior judge, Lord Chief Justice Lord Phillips, said: 'The facts of these four murders are so horrific that a whole life order was inevitable, guilty plea or no.' He added: 'The damage that he had done was incalculable and the enormity of what he had done was beyond words. No one knowing the facts of this case could be in any doubt as to why the judge had given no effect to the guilty plea. The application for permission to appeal is refused.'

By pleading guilty to the killings, Hobson avoided a trial and so the need to account for his actions. After the verdict, Detective Superintendent Javad Ali, who led the investigation, said: 'We do not know what Mark Hobson's motives were, or why he carried out the four killings. He has never given the slightest indication of what possessed him.'

The closest Hobson has come to any explanation was in prison visit conversations and letters to former neighbour Donna Kemp, one of the few people still willing to speak to him. 'When the booze took hold, I couldn't control myself,' he said from Wakefield Jail. 'Claire stirred something within me. There's something evil inside me that comes out when I've had a drink. When I was sober everything was fine between me and Claire but after a few drinks the arguments and violence would start. All her friends hated me – they wanted her to stop seeing me, but I quite enjoyed defying everything; that's the bad side lurking in me.'

Donna told the *News of the World*: 'He doesn't like to dwell on the past, but he said that he and Claire rowed on the day he killed her, and he flipped and went on to murder them all. It was the booze more than drugs that sent him over the edge, Mark says so in his letters.' Hobson made no apology for killing Claire and Diane, or for slaughtering the frail Mr and Mrs Britton. He concedes only that: 'As I try to sleep, I remember what I did. I get nightmares; it haunts me.'

When on remand awaiting sentence for the murders, Hobson wrote to Donna, saying: 'I wish I'd done more thinking and less drinking.' He said the educational facilities inside were excellent, that he'd gained a

B-grade in A-Level English and hoped to achieve a similar grade in GCSE maths. He boasted: 'I'll have more qualifications than Stephen f**king Hawking when I get out.' But, of course, he's going nowhere.

31

'THE BLACK PANTHER'

'The enormity of the crimes you have been convicted of puts you in a class apart from all other murderers in recent years.'

Mr Justice Mars-Jones

Name: Donald Neilson
Crime: Quadruple murder
Date of Conviction: 1 July 1976
Age at Conviction: 38

On the evening of Monday, 13 January 1975, 17-year-old Lesley Whittle climbed into bed after a hard day studying for her A-level exams. Her widowed mother, Dorothy, was out, but returned to their palatial home in the isolated village of Highley, Shropshire, at 1.30am and looked in on Lesley to find her fast asleep.

Dorothy Whittle rose at 7.30 the next morning and went to wake her daughter for college. But the bed was empty. Lesley's clothes for that morning were still lying neatly folded by her bed, untouched. At first she thought her daughter might have gone for a walk – she had taken sleeping tablets that night and so she would not have heard Lesley go out. After an hour, she became increasingly anxious and went to phone her son, Ron, and his wife Gaynor. Finding the phone line dead, she drove half a mile away, panic-stricken, to their home and banged on the door. Ron had the day off from the family coach business and was expecting to drive Lesley to college that morning.

The three of them raced back and found Lesley's college books still lying on the table in the lounge. Then Dorothy noticed that a vase usually sitting in the fireplace had been moved to the middle of the carpet. On top of it was a Turkish Delight box and inside were strips of black Dymo-tape embossed with capital letters. Ronald read the note out loud:

> NO POLICE £50000 RANSOM TO DELIVER FIRST EVENING WAIT FOR TELEPHONE CALL AT SWAN SHOPPING CENTRE TELEPHONE BOX 64711 64611 63111 6PM TO 1AM IF NO CALL RETURN FOLLOWING EVENING WHEN YOU ANSWER CALL GIVE YOUR NAME ONLY AND LISTEN YOU MUST FOLLOW INSTRUCTIONS WITHOUT ARGUMENT FROM THE TIME YOU ANSWER THE TELEPHONE YOU ARE ON A TIME LIMIT IF POLICE OR TRICKS DEATH.

A second strip read:

> £50000 ALL IN USED NOTES £25000 £1 £25000 £5 THERE WILL BE NO EXCHANGE ONLY AFTER £50000 HAS BEEN CLEARED WILL VICTIM BE RELEASED.

The notes sent their minds racing. Why had this happened to them? They were a wealthy family, well-known in the area for their successful coach and bus company, Whittle's Coaches. In May 1972, a local newspaper reported a dispute about Lesley's father George Whittle's will, citing the family as being worth over £250,000. It was also known that Lesley had been left £82,500 by her father.

Despite the chilling warning not to involve the police, Ron went to do just that, but quickly learned that the phone line outside the house had been cut. Instead, he drove home to make the call.

Detective Chief Superintendent Bob Booth, Head of the West Mercia CID, later said: 'I have never seen a mother so distraught in all my life.' He added: 'It was clear that this was a genuine ransom demand by people who had forced Lesley, possibly at gunpoint, into the night, naked apart from her mother's dressing gown. We can only imagine the terror and embarrassment she must have felt.'

It was arranged for Ron Whittle to go to the phone box in Kidderminster with the £50,000 ransom. Undercover officers were watching closely nearby, poised to record the telephone call, but the kidnapper's call was never answered. As Ron was preparing to set off, the operation was aborted because the police learnt that the story had been leaked to the media. A journalist in Kidderminster had been tipped off about the kidnapping and leaked the details to the BBC, who broke the story on *The 9 O'Clock News*. On learning this, the police were certain the kidnapper would abandon his plans to call the phone box, but they were wrong. This was the start of a catalogue of communication mix-ups and police blunders that were to blight the case.

On day three of the investigation the kidnapper got in touch again. Len Rudd, a family friend who worked for the Whittles' coach business, took the call. On the other end, he heard Lesley's voice. As he frantically asked her how she was and where she was, Lesley's voice talked over him: it was a tape recording. The message repeated explicit instructions. 'Mum, you are to go to Kidsgrove Post Office telephone box. The instructions are inside, behind the backboard. I'm OK, but there's to be no police and no tricks, OK?' The tape played twice to ensure instructions were fully understood.

Ron Whittle, fitted with a police radio transmitter, was to make the journey to the phone box. He travelled the 75 miles to Kidsgrove and found the booth easily, but it took almost an hour of searching to find the new message tucked right behind the backboard. It read:

LIFE MEANS LIFE

GO TO THE TOP OF THE LANE AND TURN INTO NO ENTRY GO TO THE
WALL AND FLASH LIGHTS LOOK FOR TORCH RUN TO TORCH FURTHER
INSTRUCTIONS ON.

Ronald followed the instructions, which led him to a Staffordshire
beauty spot called Bathpool. He turned into the lane marked 'No
Entry' and drove slowly, looking for the wall. There, he flashed his
lights as instructed and looked out for the signal. After an hour, he got
out of his car and cried: 'This is Ron Whittle, is anybody there?' There
was a deathly silence. Devastated, he made his way home.

Little did they know that Lesley had been within walking distance of
his car, concealed in a 60-ft damp sewer shaft, screaming for help,
tethered like a dog, naked and cold.

The police were confused as to why the kidnapper had not shown
up. Ron Whittle had been alone with no sign of police involvement and
had followed the instructions to the letter. Bob Booth and his team
regrouped to make their next move. After a brief, discreet surveillance
of the park, police decided against a full-scale search, believing such a
high-profile operation would make the kidnapper aware of their
involvement. That decision would later prove to be a tragic mistake.

In desperation, the Whittles made a direct appeal to the kidnapper
through the media, urging him to get back in touch. This attracted
huge press attention and inevitable calls from hoaxers and frauds,
wanting to collect the ransom money. Days passed and they were no
nearer to finding Lesley. Then police attention was diverted to an
abandoned stolen green Morris 1300, standing in a car park near the
Freightliner depot at Dudley. It had been dumped there two nights
after Lesley went missing. The security guard at the depot, 44-year-old
Gerald Smith, had been shot six times when he confronted the driver
of the car, who then fled the scene. Miraculously, the guard survived.
The car had been left eight days after the shooting before police went
to examine it and this delay may well have cost Lesley her life.

Inside, police officers found several suspicious items linking the driver to Lesley Whittle's disappearance. They discovered a gun, heavy-duty black plastic sheets, a torch, a foam mattress, a cassette tape-recorder with microphone and cassette tape and a number of Dymo tapes embossed with ransom demands. They also found details of a ransom run involving telephone boxes all over the West Midlands.

With an overwhelming sense of dread, Bob Booth put the cassette into the machine and pressed 'Play'. Lesley's voice was heard saying: 'Please, Mum, go onto the M6 North to Junction 10... and onto the A454 towards Walsall. Instructions are taped under the shelf of a telephone box. There is no need to worry, Mum. I'm OK, I got a bit wet, but I'm quite dry now. I'm being treated very well. OK?'

Booth quickly realised this was the car used to kidnap Lesley and the shooting of the security guard meant that they were dealing with a man who was not afraid to kill. Details of the ransom run showed the route Ronald Whittle would have taken, had he not missed that vital phone call made to the telephone kiosk at the Swan Centre on the first night of the kidnapping. When Ron had been waiting in the phone box hoping for a call on the second night of the kidnap, the abductor had been laying ransom notes to lead to a drop-off point at Dudley Zoo. It was a well-hatched plan. A worse discovery was to come. As police questioned the wounded security guard, a picture of the kidnapper emerged. Forensic examination of the bullets found in Mr Smith's body proved to be a direct match to those used in murders carried out by Britain's most wanted man, The Black Panther. This left Booth in little doubt that Lesley Whittle's life was in grave danger, if she was alive at all.

The Black Panther was wanted for many armed robberies, mainly of sub-post offices in the North and the Midlands. He had shot dead three sub-postmasters within nine months. Donald Skepper, 54, was killed when a hooded gunman broke into his Harrogate post office in February 1974. Six months later, Derek Astin, 44, was met by a hooded intruder in his post office, near Accrington and after a struggle he was murdered. Then Sidney Grayland, 55, sub-postmaster in Langley, Worcestershire, was shot as he confronted the man in black. His wife, Peggy, was ferociously battered with a pistol and left for dead. The killer earned his nickname by always wearing a black hood.

Before Lesley's kidnapping, Detective Chief Superintendent Bill Dolby, leading the investigation into the postmaster killings, made clear at a press conference the brutality of the man-at-large: 'My impression of this man is a person who is quite cold, utterly ruthless if he meets the slightest opposition at all. He is a man with no compunction about taking human life. Any member of the public who has any thoughts at all about having a go with this man, my advice to them is: DON'T. I REPEAT: DON'T.'

It was now more urgent than ever that Lesley Whittle was found. Bob Booth was becoming increasingly anxious for her welfare: 'In my heart I was convinced Lesley was living on borrowed time.' There had been no contact from the Panther and so they decided to use the media again. Ron Whittle and Bob Booth agreed to be interviewed together on TV about the kidnapping: Ron began to describe his visit to Bathpool Park and Booth acted surprised, saying he knew nothing of the ransom run. The intention was to deceive the kidnapper into thinking that the police had not been involved until now. It gave them a legitimate reason to launch a thorough search of the area.

The new search yielded many clues missed during the first inspection. Officers found tape near to a drain that read: 'Drop suitcase into hole'. Then a torch that the message had been attached to was discovered, as well as a spanner used to unscrew bars on a drain. DC Philip Maskery was brought in to search the network of underground shafts at the park. A bolt had been loosened on one of the manhole covers and so colleagues lowered him into the dark shaft below. Descending the 60-ft ladder and using a torch to survey his surroundings, DC Maskery saw a notepad, pens, batteries and a tape recorder. Dropping down onto a platform, he found a sleeping bag and a foam mattress. Then he spotted a piece of clothing hanging off an iron girder. It was Lesley's dressing gown. On the platform he saw a wire trail lead over the edge. He followed the wire, leant over to see where it went and came face-to-face with Lesley Whittle, dead and naked. She was hanging by a noose made from the wire and appeared to have been dead for a while.

If the stolen car and Bathpool Park had been searched earlier, she might still have been found alive. Bob Booth was distraught: 'I think she must have been absolutely terrified. Anyone would be, man or woman, let alone a teenager. To think that she could hear people walking above and she screamed with all her might for help and mercy, and nobody came to her rescue. It must have been a horrifying ordeal.'

Around this time, a young couple contacted the police to say they were at Bathpool Park on the same night that Ron Whittle was there and they had seen a flashing light in front of their car and what they thought was a police vehicle. After hearing about the ransom run in the press, they quickly realised they had been caught in the middle of the operation. The abductor must have thought the couple's car was Ron Whittle's and then having seen the 'police' car, he panicked and quickly left. In his panic, he had returned to the shaft, where Lesley was hidden and pushed her over the platform edge to her death.

Commander John Morrison was put in charge of the investigation. For months after Lesley's body was found, the hunt went on and yet the Black Panther continued to elude the police. Then, on the bitterly cold winter's night of 12 December 1975, two police officers, PC Tony White and PC Stuart McKenzie, were in their panda car in Mansfield, Nottinghamshire, and spotted a man acting suspiciously outside a sub-post office and stopped to question him. As they quizzed the man, he drew out a double-barrelled shotgun and pointed it at them, snarling: 'Don't move! Any tricks and you're dead.' He demanded they get back into the car, whereupon he sat in the passenger seat with the gun pressing into PC McKenzie's ribs. The policeman was told to drive through deserted countryside to Blidworth, a village eight miles away.

As they sped along the winding country roads, the gunman asked if they had any rope. PC White pretended to look and noticed that the shotgun was no longer pointing at his colleague. He seized his opportunity and pushed the gun upwards. As he did so, PC McKenzie slammed on the brakes, causing the car to swerve, and the gun to be fired through the roof of the car. PC McKenzie was thrown out of the driver door onto the road, while PC White grappled with the gunman.

They were outside The Junction Chip Shop in Rainworth and four miners ran from the queue to assist. Locals attacked the suspect so ferociously that the police ended up having to protect him. The two constables handcuffed the battered and bruised gunman to railings.

Once in police custody, the suspect refused to speak for two days until eventually he revealed that he was Donald Neilson, a 39-year-old joiner, who lived with his wife and teenage daughter in Bradford. He had been christened Donald Nappey, but changed his name by deed poll to Neilson after years of taunts. During a search of his house, officers found eight black hoods and more proof that he was the Black Panther.

Neilson confessed to the post office murders and kidnapping of Lesley Whittle, but insisted he never meant to kill her. Instead, he maintained that he accidentally knocked her off the ledge as he rushed to gather his belongings. He told police that the wire was round her neck to prevent her escaping.

On 14 June 1976, he appeared before Oxford Crown Court charged with 13 violent crimes, including the three postmaster killings and the murder of Lesley Whittle. By pleading not guilty to Lesley's murder, he put her family through the trauma of a trial that lasted five weeks.

Defending him, Gilbert Gray, QC, said to the jury: 'This was not murder. This was an unlooked-for misadventure.' But prosecutor Philip

Cox, QC, insisted Neilson killed his captive because his plans had failed and she would be able to identify him: 'Donald Neilson put his own safety above everything else. This cold, logical, military approach to the problem was paramount. It was safer and more logical to kill her than to release her and run the risk of subsequent investigation.'

It took the jury two hours to find him guilty. Handing him a life term for each of the four killings, Mr Justice Mars-Jones told him: 'The enormity of the crimes you have been convicted of puts you in a class apart from all other convicted murderers in recent years.'

In June last year, it was revealed that Neilson has Motor Neurone Disease. He is on the hospital wing of Full Sutton Prison, near York, crippled by the condition, which has no cure. He is dying a slow, painful death and doctors say he could go at any time. But few will grieve for the man who left a young girl to die slowly, hanging from a wire at the bottom of a filthy storm drain.

32

'GOTCHA!'

'He covered her body with a duvet, turned on a fan and sprayed
deodorant to mask the smell of decomposition.'

Prosecutor Nick Hawkins

Name: David Tiley
Crime: Serial rape and double murder
Date of Conviction: 14 July 2007
Age at Conviction: 47

When he was released from prison after six years inside for a brutal rape, the Probation Service said there was a 'low-to-medium risk' of David Tiley harming any more members of the public. That was 2001, and for a further six years he managed, as far as the police know, to resist his violent sexual urges. But by the afternoon of 16 March 2007, the official classification of Tiley had changed from low-to-medium risk to 'exceptionally dangerous' as police announced he was wanted in connection with the barbaric murders of two women.

Earlier that day, police forced their way into the home Tiley shared with his disabled fiancée Sue Hale, where they were greeted with a scene that one policeman described as being 'like something from a Hannibal Lecter film.' Inside their one-bedroom flat in Townhill Park, Southampton, were the bodies of Sue, 49, and her care worker, Sarah Merritt, 39.

LIFE MEANS LIFE

Sue suffered from cerebellar ataxia – a rare, but progressive disorder that affects the nervous system and causes unsteadiness and a lack of co-ordination. The crippling condition meant she relied on walking sticks and a mobility scooter to get around. Despite her illness, the mother-of-five 'would do anything for anybody' and kept herself active with a part-time job in a nearby Scope charity shop. It was this kind, frail woman who, according to Tiley, teased him about his past on the evening of 7 March – and paid the price. To this day Tiley, a petty thief and habitual liar since his teens, says he cannot remember exactly what it was that she said, but it was enough for him to explode into a fit of rage that would leave his former partner dead and the walls and ceiling of their bedroom covered with her blood. Tiley, at just under 6ft tall, with broad shoulders and thick, tattooed arms, hit his weak, vulnerable wife-to-be hard across the head with a hammer he'd grabbed from a toolbox in the kitchen.

He then dragged her into the bedroom, where he bound her ankles and wrists before stabbing her four times: twice in the chest and twice in the head. At some point during the vicious assault, he sexually assaulted her with a table lamp. When he was sure she was dead, he wrapped the body in her blood-soaked duvet. Then, with a meticulousness of mind, the former cleaner turned on a cooling fan in the room and sprayed deodorant over the bed, floor and around the door in a grisly bid to hide the smell of decay.

After the murder, Tiley went about his usual business, visiting local bookmakers and playing fruit machines on Southampton's seafront. For eight days he lived in Sue's flat as she lay rotting in the bedroom. He slept on the living room sofa and cooked meals in the kitchen, all the time ignoring the overpowering stench.

When Sue's friends and family rang or texted her mobile phone, he texted back saying she was poorly and that he was looking after her until she was better. In view of her condition, they had no reason not to believe him.

On 15 March, eight days after the murder, Sue's 'dedicated and committed' carer Sarah Merritt arrived at the flat, as planned, to help bathe her and to check that she was OK. She missed the remainder of her appointments that day and failed to return home. The following morning, her husband Peter and her employers – the Carewatch Agency – informed police that she was missing and Peter set about finding his wife.

Peter, 41, drove round Sarah's list of clients with one of her colleagues and found his wife's car parked outside Sue's home. He panicked. Graham McStay, who lived two doors away, recalled: 'A friend came round and said there had been a guy banging on the door of the flat down the hall. He said the man had been holding a concrete block and had been shouting and demanding to be let in.' Minutes later, police forced the front door to the flat and found the horrors inside. Sarah lay dead in the hallway. Like Sue, she had been tied up and stabbed. On the front door, Tiley had scrawled the word 'GOTCHA' in her blood.

Police launched a nationwide manhunt for Tiley, taking the rare step of naming him as the man they were after, calling him 'an exceptionally dangerous risk to the public'. DCI Richard John, of Hampshire Police, called on him to hand himself into a police station with a solicitor. He said: 'We are trying to locate Mr Tiley, who we believe is a threat and is wanted in connection with the double murder in Southampton. We advise members of the public not to approach him under any circumstances and report any sightings or information to the police as soon as possible.'

Two days later, on 17 March, detectives received a tip-off that Tiley had made his way along the coast to the seaside town of Swanage, Dorset – 55 miles away from the murder scene. Immediately they set up checkpoints on all exits from the resort and by 2pm that day, they found him walking on the seafront.

With overwhelming evidence against him, Tiley admitted the

murders and on 14 June that year he appeared at Winchester Crown Court, where he pleaded guilty. Prosecution counsel Nick Hawkins told the court that after his arrest, Tiley told police that he killed Sue following a taunt about his violent past. He hit her with a hammer, bound her ankles and wrists, and then stabbed her four times.

The court heard that when her carer arrived, she asked Tiley where Sue was. He said she was dead and told her to co-operate with him before tying her up and gagging her. Tiley then took her bank card and withdrew £150 from a nearby cash machine. The prosecutor said: 'He returned to the flat, smoked two cigarettes, then removed the gag and had a conversation with her. She started crying, so he got angry, removed her clothing and raped her.' Tiley told police that he then bound her ankles and stabbed her twice in the neck.

The killer then fled and withdrew another £100 before catching a train to Weymouth, where he booked into a bed and breakfast.

The court heard that Tiley had been convicted at Winchester in 1995 of two counts of rape and was jailed for six years. He had broken into the woman's home and threatened her with a knife. Then, during the brutal rape, he repeatedly punched her in the face as her children slept in the room next door. Mr Hawkins also told how, between 2004 and 2006, Tiley breached court orders three times and was jailed on each occasion.

The prosecution said Tiley had met Sue in the summer of 2006 – 14 months before her gruesome death – and moved into her flat soon afterwards. This put him in breach of court orders because he failed to register his address. For this, the third breach of his sex offender conditions, he was jailed for 10 months and released in January 2007.

The barrister explained that on his release Tiley moved back in with Sue – who was told by police that he was a sex offender – and registered her address with the authorities while applying to be her full-time carer.

When Mr Hawkins finished outlining the crimes, Tiley sat

impassively dressed in black trousers and a burgundy jumper as the families of his victims described the impact the murders had had on their lives.

In a statement, Sarah Merritt's husband said his children were devastated by the loss of their mother, who he said would do anything for anybody: 'When I arrived at the flat, I knew something was dreadfully wrong. There was no answer and the curtains were closed. I wanted to kick the door down, but the police arrived soon after and stopped me. From that moment onwards I felt utterly helpless, just standing there, watching events as they unfolded. Once I knew two bodies were in there, I knew Sarah was going to be one of them. I felt so alone; I was just waiting for them to tell me she was dead. I was truly robbed by this man that day. I pray to God that she didn't suffer long.'

He added: 'What is this world coming to when a kind, loving and caring person such as Sarah loses her life doing the job that she did, and being killed in such a wicked way while caring for others? I cannot get the thoughts out of my mind of how scared and so very afraid she must have been that day and that I could do nothing to help her in her hour of need. I am going to have to live with that for the rest of my life. Sarah didn't do anything to deserve such an end to her life.'

On behalf of Sue Hale's family of five grown-up children, her son David Chopra said the 'horrific details' of what had happened to his mother and her carer had 'shocked them to the core.'

Before sentencing, Tiley's defence barrister Lisa Matthews read out a short note from the accused: 'I want to express to you all my regret. No words that I can say will replace Susan and Sarah. I am so sorry for what I have done. I deeply regret what has happened. But no amount of justice would compensate for what I have done. I hope that when I am sentenced you will be able to find some closure and get on with your lives. I am totally to blame for what has happened.'

Offering no mitigation for her client's crimes, Ms Matthews said:

'There is nothing I can say that is going to change the outcome of the sentence. He knows that, and everyone in court knows that. He knows life is going to mean life.'

Jailing Tiley, Mr Justice Irwin told him: 'David Tiley, I will speak to you about what you have done, but your case is such I'm quite unsure if you will ever grasp the real enormity of your own acts. You have been convicted of offences of dishonesty from your early teens. In March 1995, at this court, you were sentenced for rape and buggery. You were sent to prison for six years and placed on the Sex Offenders' Register.

'After release from prison you failed repeatedly to notify your name and address to police. You breached sex offender orders and served prison sentences for these offences. Eventually, you complied with the obligations to notify police of your addresses. They knew you were living with Susan Hale at a flat in Southampton. As we have heard, she was disabled with cerebellar ataxia, making her vulnerable and needing care. You applied to the Department of Work and Pensions to become her registered carer. Instead of caring for her, you killed her.

'Mrs Sarah Merritt was a dedicated community carer, who did look after Susan Hale. You raped her and you killed her.

'The brutality and evil defies adequate description. The pain and grief of the victims' families left in the wake of the deaths is profound. We have heard it expressed poignantly and with dignity today. One's heart goes out to them; nothing can repair the damage done to them.

'On each count you will go to prison for life. These offences are quite exceptionally serious and the only appropriate sentence should be a whole life order. The only proper punishment for you is that you must never be released.'

Tiley's brother Ian – one of his five siblings – spoke on behalf of the family when he said after the sentence: 'We were disgusted when he committed the previous offence and raped a woman, and in my opinion he should never have been let out. They said there had been a murder and they were looking for David. I was, we were, shocked.

'I am just glad that this whole ordeal is now over and that the court case is complete. The fact that he pleaded guilty and he didn't go through a whole trial meant he didn't drag it out for both of the families. Someone had to be in court to see him sentenced for these crimes; I felt that one of us had to be here. I stood upstairs in the public gallery of the court, close to both families who had lost a loved one. I couldn't see David, but I could hear him. I want him to know we are there and we are thinking of him, because he is my brother, but he has done wrong and we don't agree with that. I am just so sorry for both families and hope that they will be able to try and move on with their lives, knowing that he won't be coming back out.'

Tiley's case raised concerns about the public protection mechanisms for dealing with dangerous offenders. Defending the police monitoring, Assistant Chief Constable Simon Cole, said he, 'was the subject of visits in accordance with national standards.'

He added: 'This type of offender is very difficult to manage within the community. This is a significant problem for society in terms of balancing the need to protect the community whilst at the same time managing offenders within the justice system. Short of 24-hour surveillance or locking an offender up for life, there can be no guarantees, and it is just not possible for agencies involved to do that. The professionals involved in monitoring this man did their best working within the system.'

33

'THE HOUSE OF HORRORS'

'Relax and enjoy!'

Rose West (to one of her 10 victims)

Name: Rosemary West
Crime: Serial killing
Date of Conviction: 22 November 1995
Age at Conviction: 42

Rosemary Letts, as she was born in Barnstaple, Devon, on 29 November 1953, was never going to be a normal person. Her mother was manic-depressive and young Rose only escaped her schizophrenic father's beatings by succumbing to his sexual perversions. In fact, the crime of incest was so ingrained into her that she often slept with her own younger brother, Gordon.

Fred West was born in the Gloucestershire village of Much Marcle. By the age of 12, he had been seduced by his mother, Daisy. He was encouraged into incest and even bestiality by his farm labourer father, Walter. In 1962 he married an old girlfriend, Catherine Costello – a former prostitute known as Rena. She was already pregnant by a bus driver, but when the child – Charmaine – was born, Fred took her as his own. Rena was soon pregnant again with a second daughter. This time it was Fred's and she was named Anne Marie.

The family fled from Glasgow to Fred's home county of Gloucestershire after he accidentally ran over and killed a four-year-old boy with his ice-cream van. In Gloucestershire, in August 1967, he murdered Ann McFall, who had come 'Down South' with the family, believing herself in love with Fred after a brief fling while he was working in Scotland. Fred and Rena's marriage ran into difficulties and Rena went back to Scotland. Ann McFall fell pregnant by Fred and begged him to divorce Rena and marry her. Instead, he murdered her.

Fred was about to meet Rose Letts, who was officially working as a 'seamstress' but was in reality a child prostitute in Gloucestershire. The fateful meeting took place at a bus stop near Cheltenham, where the curly-haired labourer chatted up the pretty 15-year-old. The two became besotted and by the autumn, Fred, Rose, his daughter Anne Marie and stepdaughter Charmaine had moved into 25 Midland Road, Gloucester.

Rose hated her stepdaughters and would regularly beat them with little or no provocation. To the outside world, she looked like the perfect stepmother – taking the children picking flowers from the grass verges, while telling them stories. She was, in fact, a tyrant.

Her chance for killing came in November 1970 when Fred was jailed for petty theft and tax evasion. When he came out on 24 June 1971, Charmaine had gone. Rose told friends and neighbours that the child had been taken back to Scotland with the former whore Rena, her natural mother. In fact, Rose had killed the child and the corpse of the little eight-year-old was roughly buried under the garden at Midland Road. Jobbing builder and devoted partner Fred made a better job of hiding the crime when he came out of jail. The remains would not be found until 5 May 1994, during the notorious 'House of Horrors' investigation.

In August 1971, Fred's wife Rena came looking for her children. He killed her, dismembered her and buried her in the countryside.

On 29 January 1972, Fred made Rose his wife at Gloucester

Register Office. The bride was already five months pregnant with their first child. Neither husband nor wife was deterred from their infatuation with kinky sex by Rose's pregnancy. They moved to bigger premises – 25 Cromwell Street, Gloucester – so more people could take part in their depraved antics. Fred quickly set to turning upper rooms into bedsits and improving the cellar. Meanwhile, Rose paid for the improvements by taking in a stream of what they termed 'gentlemen callers' – to the delight of Fred. He was especially glad if they were black, and even more so if he was able to watch through one of the peepholes he had bored into the walls.

When Anne-Marie was just eight years old, she was led down to the cellar of Cromwell Street by her father and stepmother. Rose removed the child's clothes and gagged her, all the while groping and touching her sexually. Fred then raped the child, while Rose looked on, 'laughing and giggling.'

Upstairs, lodger Caroline Roberts could not believe her luck. Days before, while hitchhiking, she had been picked up by the Wests in their Ford Popular. She was urged to 'pop in' by a friendly-seeming Rose. The 16-year-old was astonished by the freedom she was allowed at 25 Cromwell Street: she could invite boys back, smoke dope and was even given pin money to babysit the Wests' daughters.

But in the weeks that followed, Caroline became perturbed by increasingly graphic talk of sex, incest and abortions – and the lesbian advances of Rose, so she fled home. A month later, the same Ford Popular that first snared her appeared as she walked alone along a quiet road. She was bundled inside by the thick-set builder and sexually assaulted by a sneering Rose. After being knocked unconscious, she woke to find herself being raped by Fred while his wife chuckled. 'Relax and enjoy!' said Rose. Meanwhile, her male tormentor threatened: 'We are going to keep you in the cellar and let our black friends use you. Then we will kill you and bury you under the paving stones of Gloucester.' After demanding the terrified teenager's silence, the Wests let Caroline go. She reported the sadistic pair to police, but found herself unable to press ahead with a rape prosecution. They received a fine for sexual assault. Understandably, Caroline remained traumatised at the hands of the evil couple, though later she founded a charity for troubled youngsters. Not all were so lucky.

Over the next six years, between 1973 and 1979, Fred and Rose West abducted or enticed eight girls into their perverted web:

- Lynda Gough, aged 19, was a lodger at 25 Cromwell Street. She is said to have slept with several of Rose's 'gentleman callers'. Her body was found under the bathroom floor of the House of Horrors.
- Carol Anne Cooper vanished from a children's home in Worcester, aged 15. The Wests enticed her into the back of their car after a visit to the cinema – and her remains were found on 8 March 1994.
- Lucy Partington, a 21-year-old student, and author Martin Amis's cousin, was unusual among the Wests' abductees in that she was not a drifter or runaway. Her disappearance sparked a national search and her remains were eventually found on 6 March 1994, in the Cromwell Street cellar.
- Therese Siegenthaler, 21, from Switzerland, was hitchhiking when the Wests picked her up. She was never seen again until 5 March 1995 when her bones were uncovered by forensic archaeologists.
- Shirley Hubbard was in care and travelling back to her parents' house in Droitwich. She never made it, after accepting a lift from the Wests.
- Juanita Mott, aged 18, was a lodger at 25 Cromwell Street. Her bones were found on 6 March 1994.
- Shirley Ann Robinson was another lodger of the Wests. A

runaway who had found herself lured into prostitution, she was last seen alive in May 1978.

- Alison Chambers, 16, was last seen alive in August 1979. She ended up in the Wests' garden.

Fred and Rose's final killing, at least the last-known, was their daughter. Heather was beaten if she ever refused demands for sex. At school she was withdrawn and quiet, refusing to remove her clothes for games for fear of showing the bruises that covered her body. In June 1987, she, too, disappeared.

It was in 1992 when Fred was arrested on accusation of rape and Rose of child abuse that the net began to tighten on the wicked couple. Even though the case did not proceed, the remaining West children were placed in care. After a tip-off, detectives began asking about Heather. On 26 February 1994, they found her, buried at a spot where Stephen West had dug a fishpond on the order of his parents. The lad had unwittingly dug his own sister's grave.

Faced with the mass of evidence against him, Fred West confessed in detail to his crimes, though insisted his wife had nothing to do with them. For her part, a smirking Rose coldly replied 'No comment' to all police questions. In the summer of 1994, Fred was charged with 12 counts of murder. Despite his pleas, Rose was charged with nine counts at first, then the 10th – Charmaine.

Fred's insistence that his wife was innocent was the last favour he did her. On New Year's Day, 1995, he was found dead in his cell at Winson Green Prison in Birmingham, having suffocated himself with torn bedclothes.

The trial of Rose West began at Winchester Crown Court on 3 October 1995. Winchester was chosen rather than the Wests' hometown of Gloucester, as it was thought feelings were running too high there. As it was, feelings ran high across the world, with camera crews and reporters from every country clamouring for a place in the courtroom.

Opening for the prosecution, Brian Leveson, QC, said police had found scenes 'more terrible than words can express... young girls dumped without dignity or respect.'

A defence bid to block evidence from Caroline Roberts and Anne Marie West was overturned. The judge ruled it vital for the jury to hear evidence of the most horrific crimes committed against vulnerable girls and young women.

West's defence counsel, Richard Ferguson QC, argued that Rose had never known about the killings, let along taken part in them. A weeping West took to the witness box, insisting she had been raped as a child and was a victim at the hands of Fred, who was described as 'a sadistic monster.' But her tears fooled no one. In all, Rose West was found guilty of the murders of 10 girls and young women: Charmaine West in 1971, Lynda Gough in 1973, Carol Ann Cooper in 1973, Lucy Partington in 1973, Therese Siegenthaler in 1974, Shirley Hubbard in 1974, Juantia Mott in 1975, Shirley Ann Robinson in 1978, Alison Chambers in 1979 and Heather West in 1987.

Sentencing her to life for the murders, judge Mr Justice Charles Mantell said: 'If attention is paid to what I think, you will never be released.' He also praised the jurors for their conduct during the trial: 'You will never have had a more important job to do in your life – I am aware of the great stress it must have placed you under.'

Detective Superintendent John Bennett led the investigations in the House of Horrors case. He is insistent Rose's sexual perversion led to the deaths of the young women in Cromwell Street and beyond. He spent 19 months bringing the Wests to justice and said: 'It is sexual motivation that makes people become serial murderers. I don't think we can begin to comprehend the minds of these two – they were constantly reaching out for further experience and to extend their appetite for sexual thrills.

'The whole case was about Rose being sexually insatiable. There were huge amounts of pornographic material and sex objects in the house. I firmly believe that Rose murdered the girls and Fred disposed of the bodies.'

And he scoffed at her claims during the trial that she had been a victim of her husband: 'She could have egged him on. Within the household at least, Fred was certainly subservient.' The detective added that during questioning, Fred was co-operative, chatty, joking even. Rose answered only 'No' or 'No comment' during 50 hours of questioning.

Rose West spent 10 years in Durham Jail, until 2005. Today, she is a prisoner at the all-female Bronzefield Jail at Ashford, Middlesex. Conditions there are comfortable. Her cell boasts a TV, DVD player and a stereo. The windows are curtained and the walls covered with pictures, photos and – remarkably – cards and letters from well-wishers. She also has access to a sewing machine and embroidery kit, and works in the prison laundry room, loading and unloading washing. Considered one of the jail's 35 'most well-behaved' prisoners, inside she is allowed her own kettle and cutlery. She chooses her own bedspread and duvet from catalogues.

Known institutionally as Prisoner GJ 0017, Rose was pictured in the *Daily Mirror* last year, enjoying a Bank Holiday fair, munching barbecued chicken, listening to a steel band and spending the money earned at her laundry duties on fairground games.

Many people have struck up a correspondence with her. She wrote to one pen friend, Stephen Potts: 'Do you know they have a rabbit and a guinea pig here? Quite a big garden too, which is always a positive. Anyway, we have got three guinea pigs now. They have got so much better since they have been here; they used to be so frightened.'

To this day, she protests her innocence, believing herself a victim not only of her husband Fred's sadism but also of a conspiracy by the Establishment to keep her behind bars. One rambling, deluded letter she wrote to Mr Potts read: 'There is so much more to this than meets the eye. Only once I had entered the prison system did I start to learn what it was motivating the authorities to act in such an appalling manner.

'When I started to receive the "paperwork" on which to build a "defence" and started to read certain pieces of "evidence", it started to become clear that for those in a position of great power and control, there was a lot of stuff that would never become public knowledge. Not only were they responsible for the most abominable inadequacy, neglect and incompetence that in my view would undermine the public's confidence in them, but they are also shown to be corrupt and even evil.

'It made clear to me just why after 20 years of asking for the authorities "help" with the terrible situation I found myself and my children in, not once did they "respond". We were being systematically used, abused and tortured, and they could only find it in their hearts to threaten us.'

A former inmate – 'Jenny' – who befriended her in Bronzefield, told the *Daily Mirror* in January 2008: 'Rose says she has been locked up for long enough for the crimes she actually committed. She knows she is a twisted and depraved child abuser, but thinks her time has been served.' She went on: 'Rose confided in me that she abused children. She said on several occasions Fred would call her upstairs and there would be a naked child held in their bedroom. She admitted going ahead with sickening, depraved acts, yet she made out she was going along with what Fred told her to do. Although she is a paedophile, she insists she never killed anyone.'

Jenny added: 'Rose opened up to me and told me things because we were neighbours and talked a lot. She sometimes opened up about Fred and her part in their crimes. Rose certainly knew her husband was a killer, or at the very least capable of murder. She said she lived in fear of her life when he would take her out in the car to a remote farm.

'Fred often lived out a warped fantasy of his, which involved tying Rose to a gate on a farm in the middle of nowhere, removing her clothes and having sex. Rose said she thought each time it happened he might kill her. It meant she knew he was a sick and evil man, and she was under no illusions about his character.'

Jenny said she knows that Rose, 54, will never apologise to the families of her victims and that she is not phased by publicity: 'Rose is always moaning about her press coverage. It's remarkable, as if she has pushed her crimes from her memory. But when there are stories in the newspapers Rose learns of, she says: "Well, at least they all still know who I am."'

It seems she believes she has been used as a scapegoat for the dreadful crimes unearthed at Cromwell Street and elsewhere, and that had Fred not killed himself, she might have walked free.

When Moors Murderer Myra Hindley died in November 2002, Rose West inherited the dubious distinction of being Britain's most notorious female killer. Her upbringing and sexual tastes certainly contributed to the ease with which she fell under the spell of Fred – an equally damaged personality. The combination of the two led to the torture and murder of women and girls whose total number will never be known for sure.

The fact remains that while Myra Hindley at least pretended to show remorse, Rose West has shown none.

34

'THE SUFFOLK STRANGLER'

'He said, "You've got nothing to be frightened about."
I didn't need to be frightened because he wasn't going to kill me;
I wasn't a prostitute.'

Wright's common-law wife, Pam

Name: Steve Wright
Crime: Serial killing
Date of Conviction: 21 February 2008
Age at Conviction: 49

At 10.30pm, on Monday, 30 October 2006, Tania Nicol, a 19-year-old prostitute who sold her body to buy crack cocaine, left home for work on the streets of Ipswich's red-light district. She failed to return home and was reported missing by her mother, Kerry, 48 hours later. Tania was never seen alive again.

Her mobile phone records showed regular incoming and outgoing activity leading up until just before midnight, then nothing. Police searched through CCTV footage but were unable to find anything concrete.

Two weeks later another prostitute, Gemma Adams – a crack addict like Tania – vanished from the streets of Ipswich. Her boyfriend raised the alarm on 15 November, when the 25-year-old didn't meet him, as planned. As with Tania, Gemma's phone records told a worrying story.

Police set up patrols to keep kerb crawlers off the streets as hopes of finding the two girls alive rapidly faded.

A further fortnight went by before the police and the girls' families' worst fears were realised. On Saturday, 2 December, Gemma's naked body was found in a stream at Thorpe's Hill, Hintlesham, about 15 minutes' drive south of Ipswich town centre. Five days later, police divers found Tania's body two miles away at Copdock Mill. Both girls had been submerged in water for some time, meaning forensic scientists had great difficulty collecting evidence.

On 10 December, a motorist phoned police to say he had seen what he thought was a mannequin in woodland near a private girls' school at Nacton, close to where Gemma and Tania were found. It turned out to be the naked body of 24-year-old Anneli Alderton. She had not been seen for a week, but had not been reported missing and so police were not looking for her.

Like the other girls, Anneli had turned to prostitution to fund her drug habit and had been working Ipswich's red-light area. She was last seen on CCTV, catching a train on 3 December, the day after Gemma's body was found. The mother-of-one, who was three months pregnant at the time, had been deliberately placed in the cruciform position. Unlike Tania and Gemma, however, Anneli's body had not been thrown in water, and so scientists started the urgent task of gathering forensic evidence that might nail her murderer.

Police knew they had a serial killer on their hands and urged all sex workers to stay off the streets. The newspapers had dubbed him the 'Suffolk Strangler' and Ipswich was paralysed by fear. The biggest investigation in the provincial Suffolk police force's history, it was stretched to the limit. More than 300 of its 1,300 officers were drafted in to the inquiry and 300 specialists brought in from other forces.

All cars going in and out of Ipswich town centre were logged using automatic number plate recognition. The atmosphere in the town was edgy and the red-light district's streets empty, save those who, despite the warnings, could not afford to stay home. Police urged all working girls to check on their friends to ensure they were OK.

Two prostitutes were missing. Annette Nicholls, 29, was last seen at 9.50pm on 5 December, working on Norwich Road in the red-light area. Paula Clennell, 24, had not been seen since just after midnight on Sunday, 10 December. Neither woman's mobile phone had been used from the moment they had vanished. It was a familiar story.

Just after 3pm on Tuesday, 12 December, a woman walking along Old Felixstowe Road, near Levington, spotted a body. As police began to seal off the area, they found the corpse of another naked female dumped nearby.

The bodies were identified as those of Annette and Paula. Like Anneli, Annette's corpse had been arranged in the shape of a crucifix. Again, like Anneli, neither victim had been dumped in water. Paula had been disposed of 100 yards away from Annette, at the foot of a tree, just a few metres from a road. This suggested that whoever left her there was either in a hurry, or was becoming more confident. Police were able to produce DNA profiles very quickly.

In the course of hundreds of police interviews since the killings started, one name repeatedly cropped up. Tom Stevens was an oddball loner, who knew most of the women who worked Ipswich's red-light district. He also liked to draw attention to himself and was only too pleased to offer himself up to the press as the man the police must want to question. Indeed, he was taken in for police questioning and it looked as if they had their man. All they needed was the DNA profile from the victims' bodies to match his.

On 17 December, detectives were told that the DNA recovered from Anneli, Paula and Annette could only belong to one person. It was not Tom Stevens. But they did have a full profile match on the national DNA database. The man they were after was called Steve Wright.

Forklift driver Wright, 48, was a twice-married father-of-two, who lived on London Road, in the heart of the red-light district. Police already had his DNA on record after a conviction for stealing £80 from a till while working as a barman in Felixstowe, in 2001. Wright's flat was just a few hundred yards away from where Tania Nichol was last seen. Police soon discovered he was well known to Ipswich's street prostitutes, many of whom regarded him as a friend as well as a client.

Despite the weight of scientific and circumstantial evidence against him, police did not arrest Wright straightaway. The fact that his DNA was found on three of the victims could be explained away. After all, it is not illegal to have sex with prostitutes.

At the Forensic Science Service in Birmingham, 250 of the centre's 275 scientists worked shifts around the clock, testing hundreds of samples from the bodies. They took minute fragments from Tania Nichol and Gemma Adams' hair and compared fibres with others taken from Wright's clothes, furniture and the carpet of his car. It was painstaking work, but it paid off.

One of the fibres recovered from Tania's hair was a direct match to the carpet in Wright's Mondeo. This crucial evidence proved Tania's head had been lying on the floor of the suspect's car and that she must have been dead at the time. Other tests found that traces of semen on the three girls, who were dumped on dry land, matched traces found on three pairs of Wright's gloves, which police believed he wore while carrying the bodies. Annette and Paula's blood was found on his reflective yellow jacket. Further tiny fibres discovered in his car and flat were identical to those found on all five bodies. In total, forensic scientists recovered 177 clothing or textile fibres from the victims that matched fibres from Wright's home, his car or his clothes.

Detectives still wanted to directly link Wright with the girls on the evenings they went missing. After trawling through many hours of CCTV footage, they did just that. A car matching Wright's Ford Mondeo Mark III was seen being driven in circuits around the red-light district on the night of 30 October, the night Tania Nichol disappeared. A camera with automatic number plate recognition photographed

Wright's Mondeo at 1.30am, driving out of town in the direction of the countryside, where Tania's body was later found. Judging by her mobile phone records, at this point she was already dead and police believed her body was in the car. Later that morning, at 7.31am, a Mondeo driven by a man wearing a distinctive fluorescent yellow jacket was photographed on London Road. Again, the plate was registered to Wright. A yellow jacket matching the one worn by the Mondeo driver was found at Wright's flat.

On 3 December, the night Anneli Alderton went missing, a CCTV camera captured a car matching Wright's driving round the red-light area at 11.18pm. More than two hours later, at 1.41am, the Mondeo was filmed driving out of town in the direction of the A14, the road leading to where Anneli's body was found.

Police knew they had their man and on 19 December, 17 days after the first body was found, Steve Wright was arrested. He denied all charges and his trial, which lasted six weeks, began at Ipswich Crown Court on 14 January 2008. The court was located less than half a mile from the defendant's home.

Prosecutor Peter Wright, QC, slowly and deliberately went through each piece of damning evidence against the accused. He told the jury that Wright, 'systematically selected and murdered' the five vice girls, while his partner worked the night shift at a call centre. The barrister said each girl was addicted to hard drugs and sold sex to fund their habits, which 'ultimately proved fatal.'

He added: 'He was a user of prostitutes, a local resident and a man with transport. He had the wherewithal not only to pick up prostitutes in the red-light area of Ipswich, but also to transport and dispose of their bodies after killing them. A man who had the opportunity to commit these offences at a time when his partner was at work and accordingly out of the house; a man who was not a stranger to the prostitutes of Ipswich. Women who would therefore be at ease in his company, unsuspecting of him or his motives in picking them up, particularly at a time of heightened awareness as the bodies began to turn up. He simply could not restrain himself. Having sex with them was not sufficient a thrill; he needed more, and achieved it at their expense.'

On day 25 of the trial, Steve Wright took to the witness box, where he was cross-examined by the prosecution. In an exchange that few in court that day will ever forget, the accused claimed he was a 'victim of circumstances.' Wright said it was by chance that he happened to have sex with four girls just before they were murdered, and by chance that a fifth girl had recently been in his car before she, too, met her death.

The prosecutor suggested to him: 'It would seem in terms of picking up prostitutes in Ipswich, you have been singularly unfortunate.' Wright answered: 'It would seem so, yes.'

In the course of a woeful witness-box performance, the defendant robotically gave the same answer of, 'It would seem so, yes' a total of 53 times. Below is an extract from that exchange:

QC: There are a number of coincidences in this case, aren't there, Mr Wright?

Wright: If you say so, yes.

QC: You selected five women from the streets of Ipswich amongst others and each of them died. Is that a coincidence?

Wright: It would seem so, yes.

QC: On your own account they all died very shortly after they left your company. Is that a coincidence?

Wright: It would seem so, yes.

QC: You selected five women from the streets of Ipswich in the order in which they died. Is that coincidence?

Wright: It would seem so, yes.

QC: There are further coincidences, are there not? Shall we start with your DNA? That's another coincidence, isn't it?

Wright: It would seem so, yes.

278

QC: It would seem your full profile is on the bodies of the three women who were recovered from dry land. Is that a coincidence?

Wright: It would seem so, yes.

QC: It would seem that there are fibres connected to you and your home environment in respect of these women when their bodies were found. Is that another coincidence?

Wright: It would seem so, yes.

For the defence, Timothy Langdale, QC, did his best for his client against all odds. In his closing speech, he told the court: 'In this remarkable and unusual case the prosecution have put before you a mass of evidence. They suggest that it presents an overwhelming case against this defendant. But we ask, an overwhelming case of what? All that evidence adduced by the prosecution demonstrates, you may think, quite clearly there is a close association between Steve Wright and the five young women who died – and a close association between them and him not many hours before they died. That is not in dispute. What all the evidence does not do, we suggest, is demonstrate beyond a reasonable doubt, to use an old-fashioned expression, that Steve Wright is responsible for their deaths.'

After less than six hours' deliberation, the jury of nine men and three women found Wright guilty of all five murders and the Suffolk Strangler was told he would die behind bars.

Judge Mr Justice Gross said: 'Drugs and prostitution exposed these women to risk, but neither drugs nor prostitution killed them. You did; you were responsible for their deaths.'

With his arms folded, Wright stared ahead as the judge said that he had carried out 'a targeted campaign of murder,' which involved 'a substantial degree of premeditation and planning.' Mr Justice Gross added: 'The stark evidence of the case speaks for itself and points to a whole life order. You selected your victims; sexual activity followed.

They were unable to resist and you killed them, stripped them and abandoned their bodies. The women were vulnerable in that they were exposed to the inherent risks of their occupation.' Looking down at the floor, Wright made no eye contact with anyone else in court as he was led away to spend the rest of his days in jail.

Outside court, the family of Tania Nicol called for the death penalty for the serial killer. In a statement, they said: 'While five young lives have been cruelly ended, the person responsible will be kept warm, nourished and protected. In no way has justice been done. These crimes deserve the ultimate punishment.'

Wright's six-week murder spree was an unprecedented rate of killing unmatched by even Harold Shipman, whose murderous reign lasted 23 years, Fred West, who killed 12 women and girls over 20 years, or Yorkshire Ripper Peter Sutcliffe, who was convicted of killing 13 women over six years. Experts believe Wright could have killed more. Criminologist Colin Wilson said: 'There are probably other women Wright has killed in the past. Most serial killers leave a long gap between the first and second murders, sometimes years, so to kill five women in just six weeks suggests the end of a cycle, not the beginning.'

Indeed, Wright has been linked with several unsolved cases, most notably the disappearance of estate agent Suzy Lamplugh. In the early 1980s he worked as a steward on the QE2, the same time as Suzy worked on the luxury liner as a beautician. The pair became friends and stayed in touch before she vanished on 28 July 1986.

Wright's ex-wife Diane Cole – who suffered domestic violence at his hands – revealed he had shore leave around the time Suzy went missing. Diane, who also worked on the QE2, said: 'I knew Suzy Lamplugh by sight. I saw him talking with her in the corridor. I was too downtrodden to challenge him about it then because he was such a Jekyll-and-Hyde character and you never knew when he would flip, but when I look back I can see how he was probably flirting with her.'

She added: 'I really want him to tell us if he killed her for my peace of mind – for her family's sake.'

Suzy Lamplugh vanished after going to meet a client, whose name she had noted in her work diary as 'Mr Kipper', in Fulham, West London. Police never traced the 'client' and Suzy, whose body has never been found, was declared dead in 1994. Diane said: 'I'm sure Steve used the word "kipper" as slang for face. He used to say, "What's up with your kipper?"'

The person closest to Wright during his killing spree was his common-law wife Pam, whose maiden name is also Wright. She shared a bed with him throughout those six murderous weeks, and once her husband was jailed, she gave a chilling insight into his warped mind. She recalled an evening when, at the height of the murders, they were sat in front of the TV, eating her homemade lasagne, Wright's favourite meal. As they watched coverage of the murders on the news, she asked him 'what sort of monster' might have committed such crimes.

Pam said Wright merely shrugged and 'then carried on watching *EastEnders*.' She added: 'He just didn't seem to want to talk about it like everyone else in the town. But that's not surprising now, is it? The Suffolk Strangler was my Steve. I was living with a serial killer and I know people will think I'm totally stupid, but I simply didn't have a clue.

'I told him that night that I was terrified but he said, "You've got nothing to be frightened about." I didn't need to be frightened because he wasn't going to kill me; I wasn't a prostitute. I was the woman who shared his bed and cooked and cleaned for him, and hoped to marry him.'

35

'AN UNCONTROLLABLE FREAK'

'Be quiet or I'll kill you.'

Wilson to elderly victim.

Name: Simon Wilson
Crime: Rape and murder
Date of conviction: 5 September 2008
Age at conviction: 51

'Everyone thought he was a weirdo', recalled Dave Garforth, a former drinker at the London pub where sex killer Simon Wilson rented a room. 'He was friendly but there was a creepiness to him. When he was drunk he was over-friendly, especially with women. He'd look them up and down without any attempt to hide it. And if he was caught doing it, he'd chuckle to himself and mutter stuff under his breath.

'But I never thought for a minute he was capable of the crimes he's committed. When I read in the papers about the things he's done, I felt sick. To think I've sat next to him at the bar.'

Calling himself Dave Flynn, Wilson rented a £35-a-night room above the Central pub near West Ham's football ground. His desire to keep his real name secret from the staff and the clientele was understandable – he did not want anyone to find out that he had recently been deported from Australia for killing and sexually assaulting elderly women

Born in Northamptonshire in 1958, Wilson was just a toddler when his family emigrated to the Australian capital of Canberra. He was still at school when he was arrested for his first known sex offence – the indecent assault of a girl aged under 16. It was the first of a string of 77 crimes including six rapes and a brutal murder. For a decade Wilson drifted in and out of work, rarely holding down a job for more than a few months. He was a borderline alcoholic and spent every night drinking. When he secured a six-month contract as a night security guard for a cold storage firm, he was unable to change his drinking habits. He lasted a week before being found asleep and drunk in front of the CCTV monitors he was supposed to be watching.

He became a drifter and in 1985, the balding 27-year-old made his first known sex attack on a pensioner. He followed the 67-year-old along a Melbourne street at night and pounced on her from behind. He dragged her into bushes, put a knife to her face and threatened to kill her if she screamed. The snarling pervert then ripped out her dentures and raped her twice. When the sexual assault was over, he battered his trembling, half-naked victim around the face and left her for dead.

Wilson was jailed for 10 years for the attack but he was released early after serving two-thirds of his sentence. Within months of being a free man, he progressed from brutal rapist to killer. On July 12, 1992, he spotted Joan Randall, 55, as she took an early morning stroll through a park in Mackay, Queensland. He stripped her naked, smashed her face in with a lump of concrete and kicked and punched her all over her body. Detective Sergeant Dennis Hansen, who led the subsequent murder hunt, said: 'Her cheekbones were broken, her jaw was fractured, she had broken chest bones and rib fractures and bruised lungs. Her injuries were consistent with being kicked and jumped on.' Wilson broke his hand punching her.

The murderer was sentenced to life in prison after psychiatrists and police told the court that he would always be an extreme danger to women. But he was released in January 2008 after serving 16 years and the Australians, under their tough rules for foreigners who abuse their residency, deported Wilson back to his native UK.

Within days of touching down on British soil, Wilson successfully applied for £70.85 a week in housing benefit and found himself lodgings at the Central pub. He admitted to staff that he had been in prison in Australia for murder but said he was provoked into a pub fight. The authorities could not force him to sign the sex offenders register because while the Sexual Offences Act 2003 dictates that those convicted of sex crimes abroad must sign the register, it says a criminal convicted of such an offence before 1997, like Wilson, does not have to. When asked to sign the register, Wilson refused. He was obliged to tell the police where he was staying and he did so. But they did not have the resources to put him under 24-hour surveillance and so a police liaison officer was tasked with keeping tabs on him, usually by telephone.

On April 13, three months after his arrival, Wilson attacked a 71-year-old woman on her doorstep in Camden, central London, slashing her across the face and body as he tried to rape her. She spent five days in hospital and doctors fear she may lose the use of one of her arms. His petrified victim later described her ordeal to the *Daily Mail*. The frail, 5ft tall grandmother told the paper: 'I was walking home to my flat and had my key in the door when he grabbed me from behind. He had a knife and he said, "Be quiet or I'll kill you".

'I lied, telling him my children were in the house and they would hear, but he said, "Shut up or you'll never see your children again". He hit me all over and he called me a bloody bitch. I was terrified. He was holding the knife by my chest. I grabbed it around the blade with my left hand. It cut into my tendons and there was blood all over the floor. But he pulled the knife out and used it to cut open my T-shirt down the front. He also cut my skirt the same way.'

Wilson tried to rape his elderly victim but he fled when disturbed by a couple leaving a nearby bar. He was caught when his image, recorded on a police database when he arrived from Australia, was matched to CCTV footage of him stalking his victim. Nine days after the attack, Wilson was arrested as he entered the Central.

On September 5, 2008, he appeared at London's Blackfriars Crown Court where he admitted attempted rape, wounding his victim with intent to cause her grievous bodily harm and causing her to engage in sexual activity without consent. The balding 6ft 2in deportee stared at the ground as he mumbled his guilty pleas in a thick Australian accent. Sporting a bushy moustache and wearing a light blue open-necked shirt under a grubby pink pullover, he remained impassive as prosecutor Constance Briscoe told the court: 'The victim was severely injured. She was slashed across the face and we understand she may lose the use of an arm as a result of the injury that was inflicted. The victim said she was so scared that being scared made her voice disappear.' The lawyer added: 'We will certainly be making submissions at sentence that this defendant is highly dangerous and ought not to be released in the future.'

Five weeks later, after pre-sentence reports, judge Aidan Marron QC jailed 51-year-old Wilson for the rest of his life, telling him: 'You are an exceptionally dangerous man.' After Wilson was sentenced, DS Dennis Hanson said from Australia: 'This freak needs supervision at all times. Details of what he's done in Australia would obviously have gone with him to the UK when he was sent over there. I am appalled that he was let loose into the community after a judge had sent him to prison for life. I don't think he should ever have been allowed to return to society.' A colleague who worked with him on the Joan Randall case said Wilson was 'an uncontrollable freak who should never have been released.'

The Wilson case reopened the long-running debate over the UK's policy on dealing with people from abroad who commit crimes on our shores. Tory MP Philip Davies said: 'Our policies in this country should be more in tune with the way the Australians do it. They have a zero-tolerance approach while we pussyfoot around. We are far too bothered about the human rights of criminals rather than the rights of citizens.' He added: 'In an ideal world we wouldn't want this man back in the country, but it goes to show that we have a lamentable approach to deporting foreign criminals in this country compared with other countries.'

Wilson's return to the UK is one of a string of recent cases where Australia has sent back British criminals. In 2005, 66-year-old Robert Excell hit the headlines when he returned after spending 37 years in jail in Australia for child sex offences. Then in March 2008 the Australians deported 61-year-old paedophile Raymond Horne after he had lived there for more than 50 years.

BIBLIOGRAPHY

1. 'The Little Doctor' (Andrezej Kunowski)

Daily Mail

- Weeping man tells jury how he stumbled on daughter's murder – 17/03/2004, p.29
- Psychopath was given heart bypass on the NHS – 01/04/2004, pp.6, 7, 8

Sun

- Beast raped 70 women and kids…yet he still came to UK as illegal migrant and killed a child – 01/04/2004

The Times

- Girl's killer was illegal immigrant – 01/04/2004, p.5

Evening Standard

- I was face-to-face with man who had killed my daughter – 16/03/2004, p.5
- Killer and his trail of sex crimes in Britain and Poland – 31/03/2004, p.15
- Scandal – 31/03/2004, p. 1

Sunday Express

- Anguish of mum whose daughter was taken from her by serial rapist – 04/04/2004, p.43

News of the World

- I heard fiend kill our little girl, but my wife was sure I did it – 04/04/2004
CourtNewsUK.co.uk
- Andrezej Kunowski: The Polish Child Choker, by Peter Stubley

2. 'Captain Cash' (William Horncy and Kenneth Regan)
The Times
- Family slaughtered to seize £5m firm as front for drug deals – 09/11/2004
- Three generations slaughtered over drug plot – 02/07/2005
- Killers made victim tell his wife that he was ok, court told – 10/11/2004
Guardian
- Father of murdered family 'forced' to sign away firm – 10/11/2004
- Life terms for gang that killed a family – 06/07/2005
Sun
- Family 'murdered out of pure greed' – 09/11/2004
Daily Express
- Greed drove gang to execute family – 09/11/2004
- The clue in the sock – 11/11/2004
Daily Mail
- The gangsters who wiped out a family – 06/07/2005

3. 'Mistaken Identity' (Paul Glen)
Peterborough Evening Telegraph
- CSI Peterborough: The vital clues which led to a murderer – 06/01/2006
- Still shocked after 30 years of killings – 15/02/2007
- Bogle hitman appeal – 24/09/2005
- Bogle: Builder jailed – 31/08/2005
- Evil plotters' deceit unravelled in court – 30/07/2005
- Family's tribute to murdered son – 30/07/2005
- Drug dealer stabbed Bogle – 15/07/2005
- Bogle killing 'similar to 1989 murder' – 14/07/2005
- Alleged killer's boots matched prints – 30/06/2005

- Teenage girls tell of seeing stab victim – 29/06/2005

Blackpool Gazette

- Hitman marries in jail – 03/02/2007

4. 'Paperboy Predator' (Victor Miller)

Wolverhampton Express and Star

- Sex killer's prowl for victims of lust – 04/11/1988, p.14
- Mum's tragic prediction was fulfilled – 04/11/1988, p.15
- I blame myself – killer's gay lover – 04/11/1988, p.1

Birmingham Post

- Newsboy's murderer starts life sentence – 04/11/1988, pp.1, 2

The Times

- Man confesses to murdering newspaper boy – 12/02/1988
- Vicar asks parents to be ready to forgive – 10/02/1988
- Sadistic child killer will spend rest of his life in jail – 14/11/1988

Guardian

- Newsboy's murderer exposed by hypnosis – 04/11/1988

5. 'The Bus Stop Killer' (Levi Bellfield)

BBC news website

- Bellfield given whole life term – 26/02/2008
- Profiles of Bellfield's victims – 25/02/2008
- Race against time to catch a killer – 25/02/2008

Hillingdon Times

- My dad: 'nasty and evil' – 06/03/2008

Mail on Sunday

- I feel such guilt for having given my son a murderer for a father – 02/03/2008, p.22

News of the World

- Bellfield strangled, tortured and raped me – 02/03/2008

Daily Mail

- Bellfield's final act of defiance; killer refuses to appear in dock for sentence – 27/02/2008
- The killer with a hatred for blondes – 26/02/2008

Daily Mirror

- Did he kill at age 12? – 27/02/2008

Sun

- He raped wife and bragged to her of 100 more – 27/02/2008
- He killed Milly too – 26/02/2008
- The bisexual blonde-hater with 11 kids – 26/02/2008

6. 'Death in the Drains' (Dennis Nilsen)

- Killing for Company: Case Dennis Nilsen by Brian Masters (published by Arrow Books)

Daily Mail

- My first victim was a boy of 14, says Nilsen – 10/11/2006, p.44
- No ordinary monster – 11/01/2006, p.18

Daily Mirror

- Dennis Nilsen: My prison life of drink and drugs – 27/08/05, p.28

BBC news website

- 1983: Nilsen 'strangled and mutilated' victims – 24/10/2006

7. 'Rot In Hell' (John McGrady)

The Times

- Rapist admits killing girl after phone box kidnap – 13/04/2006, p.3

www.icsouthlondon.co.uk

- Rapist chopped victims into pieces – 14/04/2006
- Fears for safety on the 'bin bag' estate – 18/04/2006

Evening Standard

- Rapist who chopped up schoolgirl victim facing life behind bars – 15/03/2006, p.21
- Rapist who killed Rochelle will die in jail – 16/05/2006, p.5

Daily Mirror

- Ulster fiend cut up teenager – 16/05/2006, p.7
- You will die in jail – 17/05/2006, p.4
- Thank God we never saw what he did to our baby – 02/10/2006, p.32

Daily Mail **(online)**

- Life for convicted rapist who murdered girl, 15 – 16/05/2006

Daily Mail

- Why was the rapist who butchered our beautiful daughter allowed to walk the streets unsupervised? – 17/05/2006, p.17

Metropolitan Police website

- Murderer of Rochelle Holness jailed for life – 18/05/2006

8. 'The Fox' (Arthur Hutchinson)

Northern Echo

- Hotel visitor who signed Mr A Fox – 08/09/1984, p.14
- How police lost quick-silver killer – 15/09/1984
- Guilty of murder. Guilty of rape – 15/09/1984, p.1
- Jury sees grim video – 07/09/1984, pp.1, 5
- Killer on run kept tape recording – 07/09/1984, p.5
- I won't give in…even when they shoot me – 08/09/1984, p.1
- Teeth marks in the cheese – 08/09/1984, p.8
- I've been lying, says Hutchinson – 06/09/1984

Guardian

- I did not invite intruder, murder trial told – 06/09/1984
- Murder jury hears tape made by Hutchinson – 08/09/1984
- Jury sees unedited version of killings – 11/09/1984
- Triple killer gaoled for life – 15/09/1984
- Arrogant killer with a tangled background – 15/09/1984

9. 'The Gay Slayer' (Colin Ireland)

Daily Mail

- Man is quizzed on gay serial killings – 21/07/1993, pp.1, 2

- This man must never be freed – 21/12/1993, p.18

Guardian

- Gay stalker 'on roller coaster' – 21/12/1993, p.3

Evening Standard

- Can the police ever root out their bigots? – 20/12/1993, p.9
- Enigmatic loner was driven to murder five times – 20/12/1993, p.7
- Serial fantasy of London gay killer – 20/12/1993, p.6

The Times

- Mass murderer who craved fame preyed on gay masochists – 21/12/1993

Independent

- Serial killer locked up for life – 21/12/1993, p.1
- Calculated murderer who preyed on gays – 21/12/1993, p.6

10. 'The Shopping Spree' (Michael Smith)
Stoke Sentinel

- Family anger over father's 'evil' killer, 17/05/2007, p.3
- How murderer had struck before – 15/05/2007, p.3
- Man admits murdering drug addict – 23/01/2007, p.7
- Police appeal for help tracing Peter's killers – 06/09/2006, p.7
- Life for killer who beat pal to death – 18/05/2007, p.27

11. 'The Highly-Intelligent Psychopath' (John Childs)
Guardian

- Murder that never happened – 29/10/2003, p.11
- Inside story: The ordeal of Terry Pinfold – 14/07/2003, p.14
- £1m claim by two men jailed for 23 years on word of pathological liar – 16/12/2003, p.7
- Murder case pair convicted on word of a liar are to be cleared – 31/10/2003

Daily Telegraph

- Man convicted of four killings set to be cleared after 23 years – 31/10/2003

BIBLIOGRAPHY

Daily Mirror

- The only way to make Childs laugh is start talking about killing people – 17/11/1998, p.4
- Confessions of a killer – 17/11/1998, p.4

The Times

- Bodies of six murder victims were dismembered and burnt in grate, prosecution alleges – 08/10/1980
- Uproar at Central Criminal Court as 'Big H' is given life sentence for four murders – 29/11/1980
- Prisoner tells of 'admission' by witness – 07/11/1980
- Murder case witness says he fears for his life – 14/10/1980
- Man was shot for his wife and house, murder trial jury told – 10/10/1980
- Man accused of six killings says he is a life saver – 04/11/1980
- Murder case accusation – 05/11/1980
- New sentence on 'contract killer' – 21/12/1979
- Man jailed for life for six 'horrific' murders – 05/12/1979

12. 'I Was Mad' (Stephen Ayre)

Daily Express

- Report on killer freed to rape a boy is kept secret…to protect HIS rights – 08/06/2007, p.15
- Brutal, vile and sadistic – 27/04/2006, p.13

The Times

- Rapist and murderer will never be freed – 27/04/2006, p.9
- Paedophile rape report suppressed to protect a killer's right to privacy – 08/06/2007, p.3

Guardian

- Murderer raped boy, 10, while freed on licence – 27/04/2006, p.13

Yorkshire Post

- Violent past of murder rage rapist – 07/06/2007
- Inquiry after freed killer abducts and rapes boy, 10 – 02/03/2006

13. 'Tonight's The Night' (Jeremy Bamber)

BBC news website

- Blood Relations: Jeremy Bamber and the White House Farm Murders, by Roger Wilkes (published by Robinson)

Sun

- You'll die in jail – 17/05/2008

Daily Mail

- The lost clues that could clear the Bambi killer – 12/01/2008, p.8
- Is Bambi's brother innocent after all? – 12/10/2002, p.44
- Bamber took the rifle from the wall and slipped silently into the farmhouse – 30/07/1994, p.30

Essex Chronicle

- Retrial call as Bamber passes lie detector test – 24/05/2007, p.3

Daily Express

- We know Bamber is a liar and a killer – 28/04/2007, p.22
- Could Bambi's killer go free this time? – 08/10/2005, p.33

Guardian

- The trail that led to Bamber – 29/10/1986

14. 'Hannibal the Cannibal' (Robert Maudsley)

- *Hideous Crimes* documentary, first aired on Channel 5 in May 2003

Independent

- Special new unit for Britain's three most dangerous prisoners – 25/08/1999, p.7

Daily Express

- Mercy plea for the killer who ate his victim's brain – 22/06/2003, p.19

The Times

- Give me a budgie or a cyanide pill, pleads serial killer – 23/03/2000
- I feel I've been buried alive – 24/02/2003

Observer

The caged misery of Britain's real Hannibal the Cannibal – 27/04/2003, p.8

Liverpool Daily Echo

- Crimes that keep Maudsley locked up – 07/05/2003, p.7

Daily Mail

- Britain's Hannibal – 19/06/2004, p.44

Master Detective magazine – September 2003

- The caged misery of Britain's real Hannibal The Cannibal, by Tony Thompson, pp.3–5

15. 'The Tollpath Stalker' (Anthony Entwistle)

Daily Mail

- 25 years for friend who throttled shy Michelle – 10/03/1998

Lancashire Evening Telegraph

- The face of an evil monster – 10/03/1988, p.1
- Strangler's 'nightmare' – 08/03/1988, pp.1, 3
- Killed for her cries – 09/03/1988, p.1
- Sex beast strikes – 14/04/1987, p.5

Lancashire Evening Post

- Murder charge man had been jailed for rape – 10/03/1988, p.4
- A family's private sorrow – 10/03/1988, p.5
- Twice he left jail to attack yet again – 10/03/1988, p.5
- A mother's grief – 16/04/1987, p.1
- Murdered girl's row over boyfriend – 15/04/1987, p.1
- Sex beast murders girl, 16 – 14/04/1987, p.1

16. 'The Moors Murderer' (Ian Brady)

- *Beyond Belief: The Moors Murders: The Story of Ian Brady & Myra Hindley*, by Emlyn Williams (published by Pan Books)
- *The Moors Murders: The trial of Myra Hindley & Ian Brady*, by Jonathan Goodman (published by Paragon Plus)

Daily Mail

- Bloated, jaundiced, Ian Brady has hardly left his cell for 15 years – 23/11/2002

BBC News website

- Ian Brady only wants to die – 04/03/2003
- Ian Brady: A fight to die – 10/03/2000

Crime & Investigation Network website

- Famous Criminals: Ian Brady

17. 'The Man in Black' (Peter Moore)

Independent

- Serial killer to sue police over 'wrecked' house – 15/05/200, p.5
- Killer wins payout for theft of his garden gnomes – 28/04/2000, p.13
- Man in black is jailed for life over gay serial murders – 30/11/1996, p.9

The Times

- Gay serial killer should never be let out of jail, says judge – 30/11/1996
- Mother's death gave free rein to sadistic fantasies of 'miracle son' – 30/11/1996
- Cinema owner 'dressed to terrify and murdered for fun' – 12/11/1996

Guardian

'Gay sadist stabbed four men to death for fun' – 12/11/1996, p.3

Alleged gay killer blames friend – 26/11/1996, p.4

Master Detective **magazine**

- Cinema owner murdered four men for fun – March 1997 issue, pp. 2–8

18. 'We Had A Little Argument' (Glyn Dix)

Birmingham Evening Mail

- Probe on release of killer – 07/09/2004, p.7

Sunday Mercury

- Monster cut our mum into 16 pieces and said: We had a little argument – 12/09/2004, p.4

News of the World

- Beast free from prison psycho ward chopped my mum in 16 little pieces – 12/12/2004

Gloucester Citizen

- You will die in jail, double killer is told – 19/12/2005, p.19

- First victim was shot – 19/12/2005, p.19

Birmingham Post

- Life for killer who cut up wife's body – 17/12/2005, p.5

19. 'Viagra Man' (Paul Culshaw)

Wigan Evening Post

- Sex beast killer to serve life – 11/02/2005
- Sex-crazed strangler – 11/02/2005, pp.1, 2

BBC news website

- 'Shoelace killer' faces life term – 10/02/2005

Lancashire Evening Post

- The vicious past of a sexual predator – 11/02/2005, p.2
- Murder case man tried to kill before – 08/02/2005, p.6

20. 'A Loving and Caring Father' (Rahan Arshad)

- BBC documentary: *Honour Killings*. First aired BBC 3 23/10/2007 9pm.

BBC news website

- Killer father must explain why – 13/03/2007
- Man convicted of murdering family – 13/03/2007
- Jury out in 'family killing' case – 13/03/2007
- Man 'cannot recall' killing wife – 08/03/2007

Manchester Evening News

- Inside the hunt for a killer – 22/10/2007, p.18
- Untitled article – 14/03/2007, p.5

21. 'I Want To Hurt Somebody' (Mark Martin)

Derby Evening Telegraph

- Victim of a 'serial killing' – 16/01/2005, p.1
- 'Grisly game' of murder acused – 17/01/2006, p.1
- 'Killer boasted of smashing Zoe's legs like biscuits' – 18/01/2006, p.4
- Sickening boasts of man who wanted to be city's first serial murderer – 24/02/2006, p.2

Birmingham Post

- Drifter 'killed to be first serial murderer in city' – 17/01/2006 – p.8

Nottingham Evening Post
- Lured to her death – claim – 18/01/2006, p.4
- A journey into the city's underworld – 18/01/2006, p.4
- Boasts of a killer – 25/02/2006, p.2
- Guilty – men who brought terror to the city – 25/02/2006, p.2

22. 'The Beast of the Night' (Trevor Hardy)

- *Cause of Death: Memoirs of a Home Office Pathologist*, by Dr Geoffrey Garrett and Andrew Nott (published by Robinson)

Manchester Evening News
- Warped mind of triple killer Trevor Hardy – 03/05/1977
- Hardy 'confession' – 27/04/1977
- Girls in fear of Sharon's killer – 10/03/1976
- Hardy takes over his own defence – 25/04/1977
- A woman hater who could kill again – 29/04/1977
- In trouble at 8…and ever since – 03/05/1977
- Hardy guilty of three murders – 02/03/1977

Daily Express
- Freed…to slay girls – 03/05/1977

23. 'Local Hard Man' (Gary Vinter)

Northern Echo
- Rail worker accused of killing colleague – 15/05/1996, p.7
- Court told of rail death stabbing – 16/05/1996, p.4
- Rail murder signalman jailed for life – 21/05/1996, p.4
- Fury at 12 year murder sentence – 24/09/1996, p.4
- Sentenced to life – freed to kill again – 22/04/2008, p.1

Middlesbrough Evening Gazette
- Three jailed after melee – 07/07/2007, p.7
- Mum found dead – 11/02/2008, p.1
- We have life sentence – 22/04/2008, p.3

- He met the gaze of his victim's family, sneered and uttered guilty – 22/04/2008, p.2
- Why was he freed to kill again? – 22/04/2008, p.1

24. 'An Extremely Dangerous Man' (Phillip Heggarty)
South Wales Echo
- Greed ended in murder – 15/01/2004, p.2
- Accused man's flat 'spattered with blood' – 30/06/2004, p.3
- 'I lied to police in blind panic' – 10/07/2004, p.4
- 'Skull was shattered into 23 pieces' – 17/06/2004, p.12
Liverpool Daily Post
- Life for murdering best friend – 24/07/2004, p.2
Western Mail
- Car fire body had hammer marks – 17/06/2007, p.6
- Burnt body trial told accused was 'flush' – 26/03/2004, p.5
- Accused repeats denial of murder – 16/07/2004, p.6
- Jury told of man's grisly end – 26/06/2004, p.7

25. 'The Enforcer' (Victor Castigador)
www.hmcourts-service.gov.uk
- The decision in the case of Paul Stephen Clinton
Guardian
- Soho arcade 'assassin' jailed for life after human torch murders – 01/03/1990
- Arcade guard begged to be shot – 22/02/1990
- Arcade guards herded in cage and set on fire – 20/02/1990
Independent
- Blaze agony of arcade manager – 21/02/1990

26. 'The Frankenstein Killer' (Viktors Dembovskis)
Independent
- Police make arrest in Latvia over rape and murder – 04/06/2005, p.8
Sun

- 'My son could do bad things... but not kill' – 04/06/2005
- Agony of Jeshma Murder Suspect's Mum – 04/06/2005

Guardian

- Images show Jeshma an hour from death – 02/06/2005, p.17

Daily Telegraph

- Dark secret of the migrant who killed Jeshma – 30/03/2006, p.6

Daily Mail

- A monster let into Britain; no checks on Latvian who killed teenager – 30/03/2006, p.18
- This Latvian came to Britain after raping two women – 14/03/2006, p.9

Daily Mirror

- How did serial rapist get into UK to kill our girl? Mum's fury as Latvian beast is jailed for life – 30/03/2006, p.9

BBC News website

- Missing teenager stabbed to death – 26/05/2005
- Life sentence for Jeshma killer – 29/03/2006

27. 'A Madman On The Loose' (Anthony Arkwright)

Doncaster Star

- Murder victim's father kills himself – 20/06/2002

Yorkshire Post

- The sick killer who lived up to his Ripper boasts – 20/06/2002

Guardian

- Triple killer jailed for life – 13/07/1989

True Detective **magazine**

- The shocking crimes of Anthony Arkwright, by Brian Marriner – February 2008

28. 'The Body-in-the-bags Killer' (Malcolm Green)

South Wales Echo

- Evidence is overwhelming – 29/10/1991
- Cold, sadistic...a very dangerous man – 04/11/1991

BIBLIOGRAPHY

- Victim 'hit with blunt object then cut up' – 24/10/1991
- Accused 'best friend of victim' – 25/10/1991

Independent

- 'Body-in-bags' killer gets life – 31/10/1991

29. 'The Railway Rapist' (John Duffy)

Daily Telegraph

- They were like two bodies with one brain, raping and killing for kicks – 03/02/2001, p.10
- 'Murder spree' of the men who did everything together – 04/10/2000, p.10
- We hunted for girls to rape. It was a game with the police – 04/11/2000, p.4
- How justice caught up with swaggering killer – 03/02/2001, p.8
- Forged in the playground, a bond that led to unspeakable acts of cruelty – 03/02/2001, p.6

Sun

- How we killed these three women – 07/11/2000
- We played together as kids, we raped together as men – 04/11/2000
- Thriller Killers – 03/02/2001

Daily Mirror

- The Thriller Killers: 15 crimes of desolating wickedness – 03/02/2001

30. 'My China Doll' (Mark Hobson)

Yorkshire Post

- Four-times killer caged until he dies – 28/05/2005
- Consequences of poor judgment – 23/04/2005
- Downward spiral into violence and murder – 19/04/2005
- Tragic pair shared life and death – 19/04/2005
- Secret hit-list of four-time murderer – 19/04/2005
- 'I killed twin sisters and elderly couple' – 01/03/2005

Daily Mail

- We've got him − 26/07/2004, p15
- A terrifying hunger for violence − 19/04/2005, p.10

News of the World

- Evil urges forced me to slay 4 innocents − 08/01/2006

Sun

- We've got him − 26/07/2004

Sunday Mirror

- I was lured to house of horror by psycho…to be victim No5 − 24/04/2005

31. Donald Neilson (The Black Panther)

- *Real Crime: Four Crimes Which Shocked a Nation*, by Shari-Jayne Boda (published by Granada Media)

Sunday Mirror

- Months to live…the Black Panther − 29/06/2008, p.25

BBC News Website

- Profile: Donald Neilson − 12/06/2008
- On this day: Heiress Lesley Whittle kidnapped
- On this day: Kidnapped heiress found kidnapped

32. 'Gotcha' (David Tiley)

The Times

- Sex offender killed fiancée and her carer who visited eight days later − 16/06/2007

www.thisishampshire.net

- Life should mean life for my brother − 16/06/2007

www.bbc.co.uk/news

- Man killed fiancée and her carer − 14/06/2007

Daily Mail **(online)**

- Rapist freed early from jail murdered his fiancée and her carer in stabbing frenzy − 14/06/2007

***Hampshire Chronicle* (online)**

- Judge's statement to convicted double murderer – 14/06/2007

33. 'The House Of Horrors' (Rose West)

Daily Mirror

- The lifer of luxury; Rose West in her cell – 23/01/2008, pp.1, 5

Gloucester Constabulary website

- The Cromwell Street Enquiry Media Information Pack

***Daily Mail* (online)**

- Rose West distraught after inmates murder her pet guinea pigs – 12/02/2007

Daily Mail

- Fantasy world of Rose West – 24/01/2008, p.46

News of the World

- Even a girl in my position needs a man with a little more prospects – 28/09/2008

34. 'The Suffolk Strangler' (Steve Wright)

Sun

- DNA that trapped a monster – 22/02/2008
- Five women systematically selected then murdered – 17/01/2008

Daily Mail

- Did he murder Suzy Lamplugh? – 22/02/2008, p1
- Suffolk Strangler's partner gives intimate portrait – 24/02/2008, p.10
- I'm just a victim of coincidences, says Strangler suspect – 09/02/2008

Mail on Sunday

- I didn't have a clue…Pam wants Wright to confess – 24/02/2008, p.10

BBC News website

- Wright guilty of Suffolk murders – 21/02/2008
- Killer steeped in vice – 21/02/2008
- Suffolk killer will die in prison – 22/02/2008
- Timeline: Suffolk killings – 14/01/2008

- Profiles: The murdered women – 21/02/2008

35. 'An Uncontrollable Freak' (Simon Wilson)
Daily Mail
- A freak who should never have gone free – 06/09/2008, p.13
- Australia sent this murdering rapist back to Britain. Just three months later he struck again – 06/09/2008, p.13

Sun
- Evil returns – 06/09/2008
- Deported fiend will die in jail – 11/10/2008

Sunday Herald Sun (Australia)
- Serial rapist jailed for life – 12/10/2008, p.34
- Life jail tip for rapist – 07/09/2008, p.36

Sunday Mail (Australia)
- Behind bars again – Qld crim in savage UK attack – 07/09/2008, p.22

Sunday Telegraph (Australia)
- UK fury at exiled killer – 07/09/2008, p.17